IMAGES
of America

EAST and WEST SOUTHERN PINES

IMAGES
of America

EAST *and* WEST SOUTHERN PINES

Sara Lindau and Pamela M. Blue

ARCADIA
PUBLISHING

ISBN 978-0-7385-1666-0

Published by Arcadia Publishing
Charleston, South Carolina

Printed in the United States of America

Library of Congress Catalog Card Number: 2004104883

For all general information contact Arcadia Publishing at:
Telephone 843-853-2070
Fax 843-853-0044
E-mail sales@arcadiapublishing.com
For customer service and orders:
Toll-Free 1-888-313-2665

Visit us on the Internet at www.arcadiapublishing.com

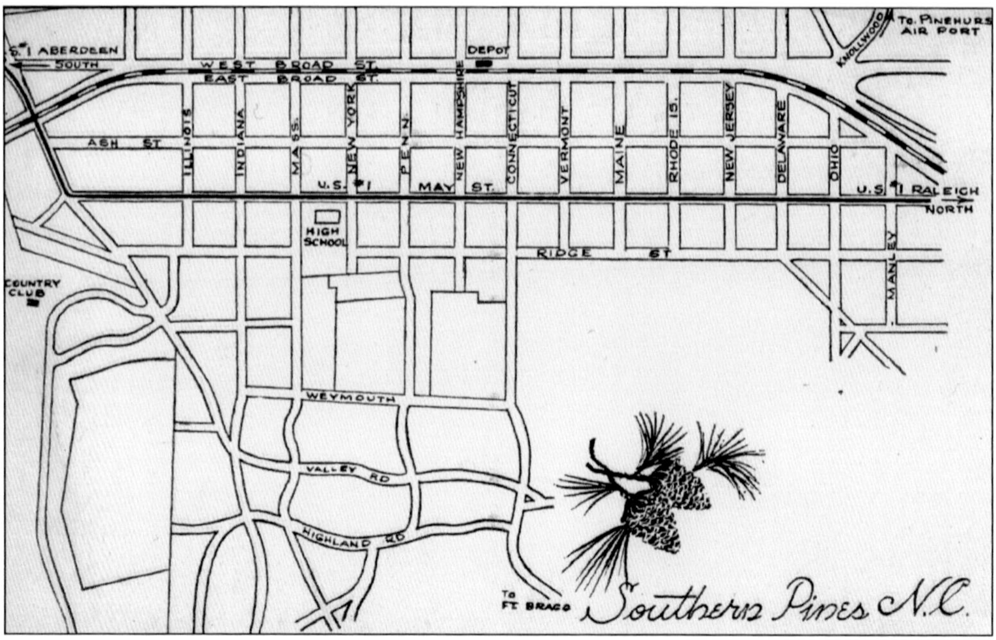

This street map of Old Southern Pines is shown on a postcard, probably in the late 1920s before the town extended its residential area north to Knollwood. The primary residential area is Weymouth Heights. The core downtown May Street, U.S. 1, going north to Raleigh and south to Aberdeen are the main routes. (Courtesy of Lawrence Koster.)

Contents

ACKNOWLEDGMENTS

The authors gratefully acknowledge the support and encouragement of A.E. (Tony) Parker, Moore County Library, Carthage, NC, Edward and Jane Blue, Maria Luisa Dominguez, Oliver and Hattie Goode, Dr. James R. Gaddy, James E. Pugh, Sue Hudson, Rick Blue, and David L. Meta and his staff of Susan and Lakita.

Special thanks go to Melissa Breedlove, who volunteered many hours and much encouragement in scanning more than 200 historical photos and postcards, and also to David Woronoff, the Moore County Historical Association, Lawrence Koster, Ellenore Eddy Smith, Ansol E. Graham, Gertrude Alexander, Archie Phillips, Helen and Myrtle Lewis, St. Anthony of Padua Catholic Church, Holly Spofford Bell and Pine Needles Lodge & Golf Club, Felton Capel, Millie Waddell Wells, Sondra and Barbara Nelson, Rochell Small, Ann McDonald, Dorothy Headen Lutz, and Bea Swanson. We also want to thank Southern Pines police chief Gerald Galloway, Norris Hodgkins, and Deirdre Newton. We found valuable information from the following: *Young Southern Pines* by Helen Huttenhauer, a book published by Gouger, O'Neal, and Saunders; *Southern Pines: The First 100 Years* by Betsy Lindau, a book published by the Town of Southern Pines; *Treading New Ground: A History of the Moore Country Schools* by Pauline F. Myrick, a book published by the Moore Country Schools; *Sandhills Classics: The Stories of Mid Pines and Pine Needles* by Lee Pace, a book published by Pines Needles County Club Inc. & Mid Pines Development Group LLC; *Oral History of West Southern Pines North Carolina* by Nancy Mason, a book published by the Town of Southern Pines; the local historians' Bible, *Miscellaneous Ancient Records of Moore County, NC*, a book by Rassie Wicker; and "Sand and Pines," a brochure published by the Sandhills Area Chamber of Commerce. Other valuable materials were found in newspaper and library archive files of *The Pilot*, *The Sandhill Citizen*, the North Carolina Institute of Government, Wilson Library, Academic Affairs Library, The University of North Carolina at Chapel Hill.

INTRODUCTION
East Southern Pines

By Sara Lindau

In 1884, John T. Patrick, the state commissioner of immigration, advertised an area in North Carolina as an ideal destination for invalids seeking clean air, a mild climate, and pine-scented breezes. This announcement encouraged railway passenger service to the region from many cities on the East Coast. To accommodate the influx of visitors, Patrick struck a deal with a local family, the Shaws of Shaw's Ridge (whose log cabin, built in the 1830s, still stands at the Morganton Road and Bennett Street crossroads.) From the family, Patrick purchased a sizeable tract of cutover timberland at $2.50 an acre, which he established as the town site. Patrick's new town, at first called Vineland, came to be known as Southern Pines.

The steady flow of visitors from the North inspired some residents to settle in Southern Pines permanently to earn a living off of the demands of tourists, which included food, lodging, medical care, and many other services. This settlement, probably the first by Northerners in the mid-South after the Civil War, quickly grew from a population of about 100 to today's count of just over 11,000 residents. As the community prospered, affluent Northerners influenced not only its commerce but also its architecture and transportation: for example, James Boyd, a Pennsylvania coal merchant, purchased thousands of acres on the east side of town and built an estate that is preserved today as Weymouth Center for the Arts and Humanities. Boyd's Chicago and New York architect friends designed many important buildings that still stand in the area today. Boyd and his descendants also helped to provide the funds to surface a stretch of the first divided highway in North Carolina, today called Midland Road or N.C. 2, and his daughter, Helen Boyd Dull, established precursors to the garden club, the public library, and the civic club.

The original layout and streets named for Northern states still exist in Southern Pines's historic district, forming a downtown core just as vibrant as it was in the beginning. However, there are a few noticeable changes: the Jefferson Inn still exists, but the nine other inns and hotels that once stood downtown have been replaced by two golf resorts, Pine Needles and Mid Pines, which host major tournaments and continue to draw visitors to the town.

From the beginning, African Americans came for jobs. They settled on the west edge of Southern Pines. The residents of the predominantly white population on the east side referred to this new community as "Jimtown," a term which would be considered politically incorrect today. It was this racial divide that brought about the distinction between East and West Southern Pines.

East Southern Pines continues to be a resort destination of the rich and famous, as well as some not-so-famous, as it serves as an equestrian center for thoroughbred training and boarding and as a golf mecca for international sports greats, such as Jack Nicklaus and Michael Jordan.

INTRODUCTION
West Southern Pines

By Pamela M. Blue

This historical volume on Southern Pines, both the east and the west sections, includes many photos not previously published. The book gives a rare glimpse into everyday life in West Southern Pines, which was one of the first African-American incorporated towns in North Carolina. It looks at the town's history in a new and unbiased way and places it in context of the nation's history from 1923 to 1931.

It is unclear why or when the small African-American community decided to incorporate and become separate from East Southern Pines, but a man known as "Lieut." Oxley from Raleigh is believed to have encouraged it. On the night of Friday, March 16, 1923, the first town meeting was held in the school auditorium with a large majority of citizens present. The "Minutes of the Organization Meeting of the Town of West Southern Pines" states that the objectives of the meeting were ". . . the proper installation of the newly appointed officers, and perfecting the organization and the enactment of certain initial ordinances for the proper government and welfare of the town." J. Talbot Johnson was retained as legal counsel. He explained the advantages of incorporating as a town, as well as the methods and procedures necessary in municipal government. He read the town charter and explained each of the sections to the audience. Based on these minutes and the minutes of other meetings, one can argue that West Southern Pines was certainly capable of governing itself.

Between the end of World War I in 1918 and the Great Depression, West Southern Pines became a newly-incorporated town. North Carolina and the rest of the country were economically affected. A bank in nearby Vass had to close for a few days, as many banks had to do across the nation. A new municipality would naturally have financial concerns, especially during this time of financial hardship. Several years later, though, the charter granting West Southern Pines its independence was abruptly revoked, with finances being one of the reasons given.

The second portion of the book is dedicated to my grandparents, Vera and Claude Blue, who lived in West Southern Pines, to my parents Edward and Jane Blue, and to those citizens who are no longer with us. It is because of these people that I became interested in the history of West Southern Pines. Because of them, I sought the truth behind the many stories that have circulated about the conditions of the town and about the revoking of West Southern Pines's charter. Many stories have presented the town in an unfavorable light. This part of the book will correct what I believe to be misconceptions about the town being a haven for criminals and its supposed inability to govern itself. Through my research of court documents, town minutes, the U.S. Census, newspapers, and letters, I found what I believe to be a more plausible explanation for the charter's revocation.

One

East Southern Pines

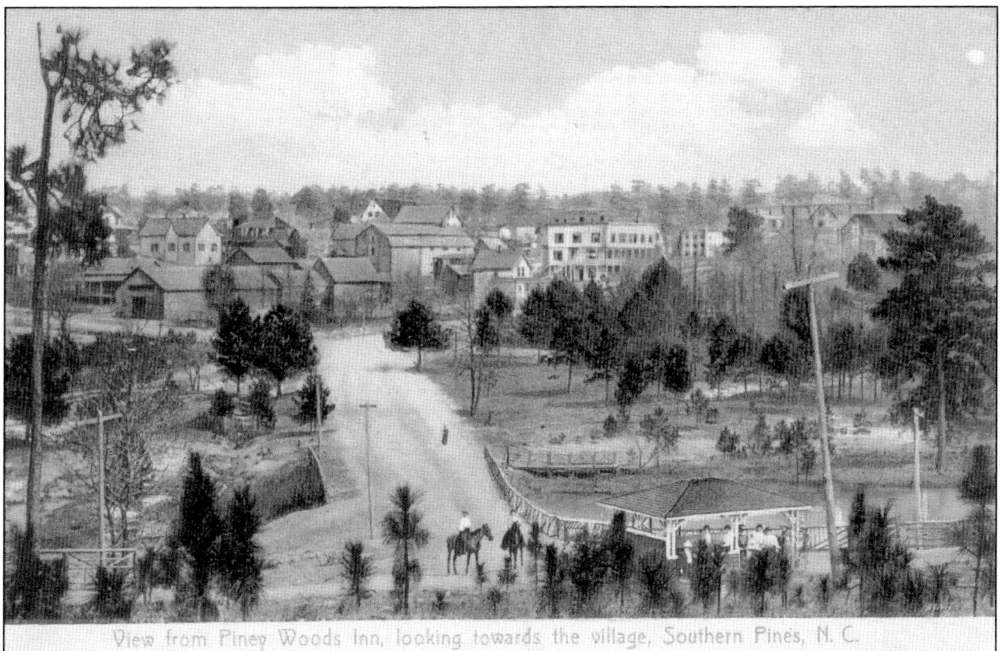

This postcard view shows the "village" of East Southern Pines from the Piney Woods Inn, which stood on a hill in what is now West Southern Pines. The inn was one of 10 that sprang up around the turn of the 20th century.

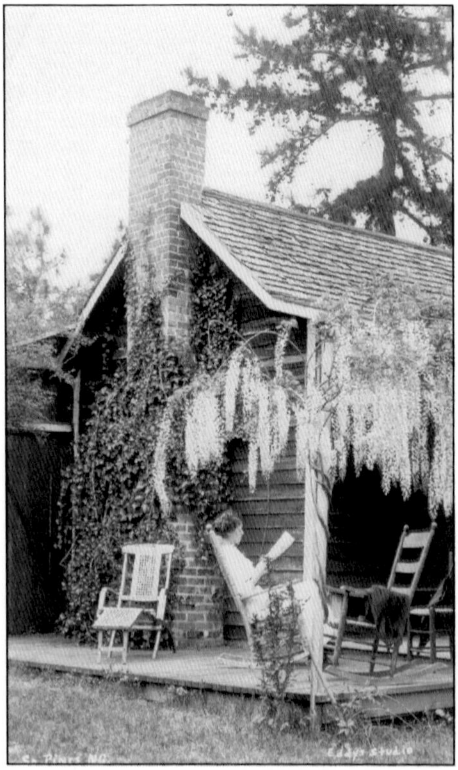

An early Southern Pines lady relaxes on the wisteria-covered porch of her cottage. She could be Ellenore Eddy Smith's mother. Smith's father, E.C. Eddy, a photographer, opened a studio in Southern Pines. His postcards record the history of the town around the turn of the century. Smith still resides in Southern Pines today.

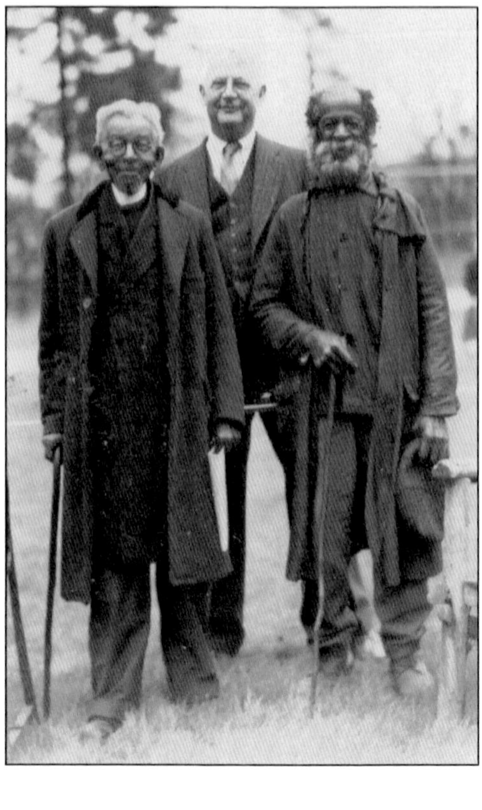

Southern Pines postmaster Frank Buchan poses with two former slaves in what was probably the first Old Slave Day held in Southern Pines in 1934. The two men with him, were both over 100 years old. One is the Rev. T.B. McCain. The other is unidentified. On this day, members of antebellum families who owned the slaves provided a festive picnic while the former slaves traded stories of old times.

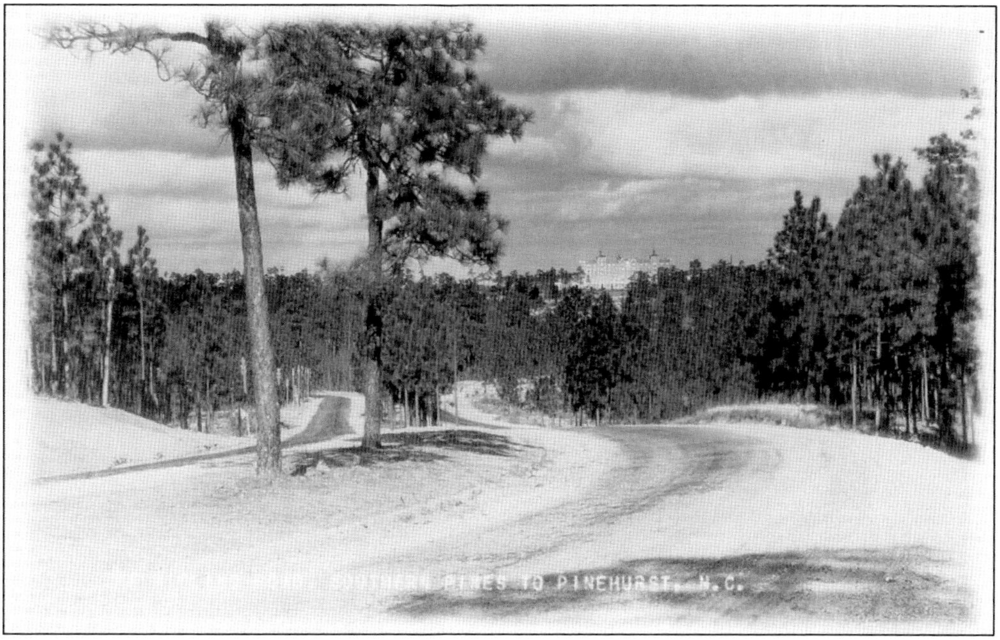

Midland Road is one of Southern Pines's historic landmarks. It was the first divided highway in North Carolina. The roadbed was the path for Native Americans and animal migration from the Yadkin Valley in the west to the coast on the east. Visitors to Pinehurst and Southern Pines often praise and write articles for golf magazines about the road's long-leaf pine–lined median and unique views.

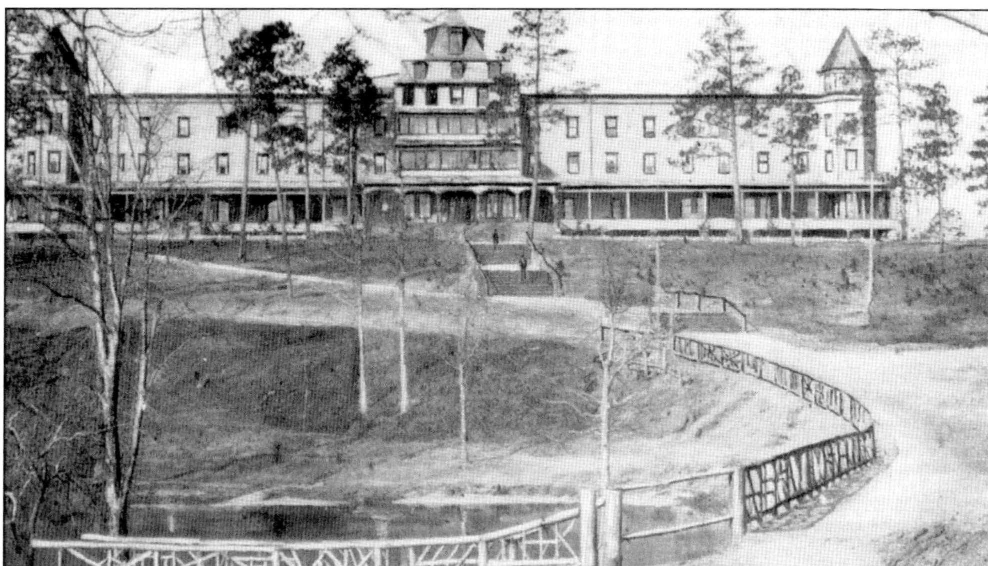

The sprawling Piney Woods Inn opened in 1895 on a hill that now overlooks Calvary Christian School on South Bennett Street in the original East Southern Pines. The inn quickly became the leader in refined entertainment for visitors and the community. One of 10 hotels during the turn of the century, its heyday was over in 1910 when it burned.

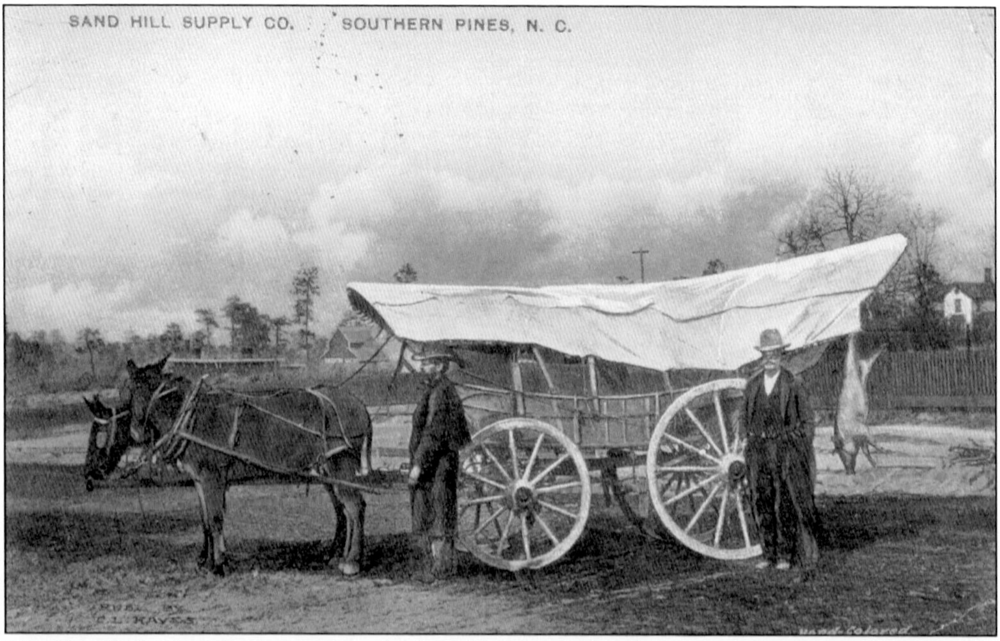

The Sandhills Supply Company, which sold meat and other items, owned this "schooner" pulled by trustworthy mules. Notice the butchered hog hanging from the back of the wagon. From the time Southern Pines was founded in the 1880s, until at least 1926, such wagons could be seen on the sandy streets. Even after the horseless carriage made its debut, the beaten paths were better traveled by mule, horse, or even oxen.

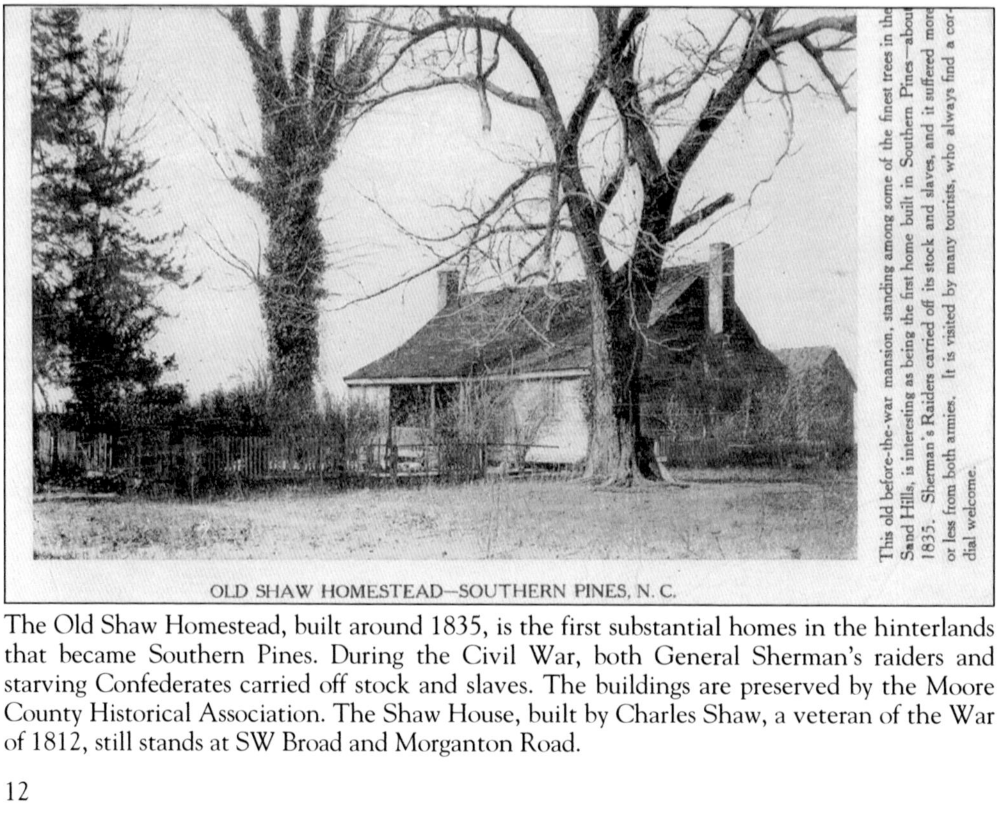

The Old Shaw Homestead, built around 1835, is the first substantial homes in the hinterlands that became Southern Pines. During the Civil War, both General Sherman's raiders and starving Confederates carried off stock and slaves. The buildings are preserved by the Moore County Historical Association. The Shaw House, built by Charles Shaw, a veteran of the War of 1812, still stands at SW Broad and Morganton Road.

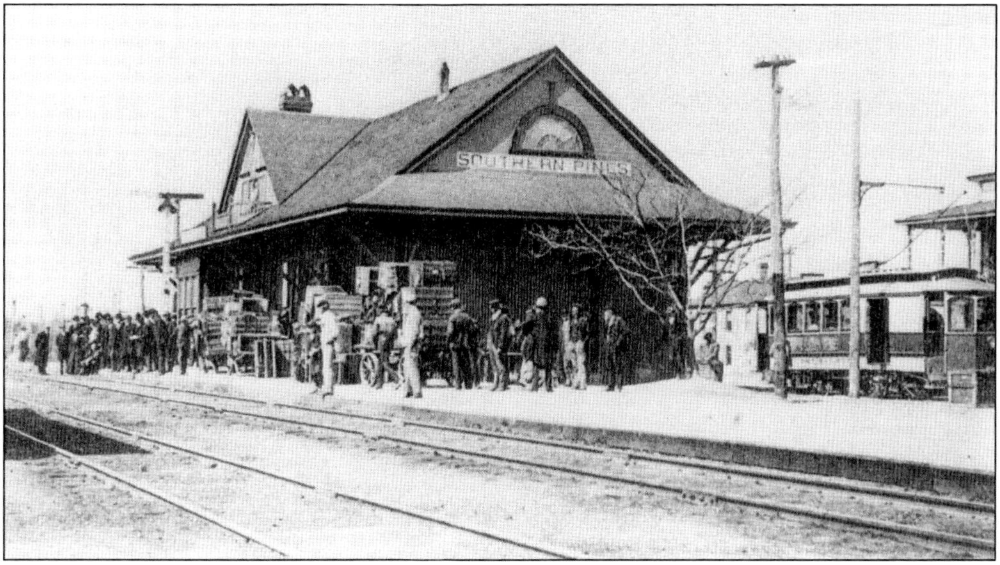

The passenger railway station that still operates in downtown Southern Pines brought visitors from the North and started the town's still-thriving tourist business. State Commissioner of Immigration John Patrick bought 675 acres at $2.50 an acre from the Shaw family in 1884 during the hard times following Reconstruction. The railroad serving the station was originally the Raleigh and Augusta Railroad and is now Amtrak. The passenger depot has been rebuilt.

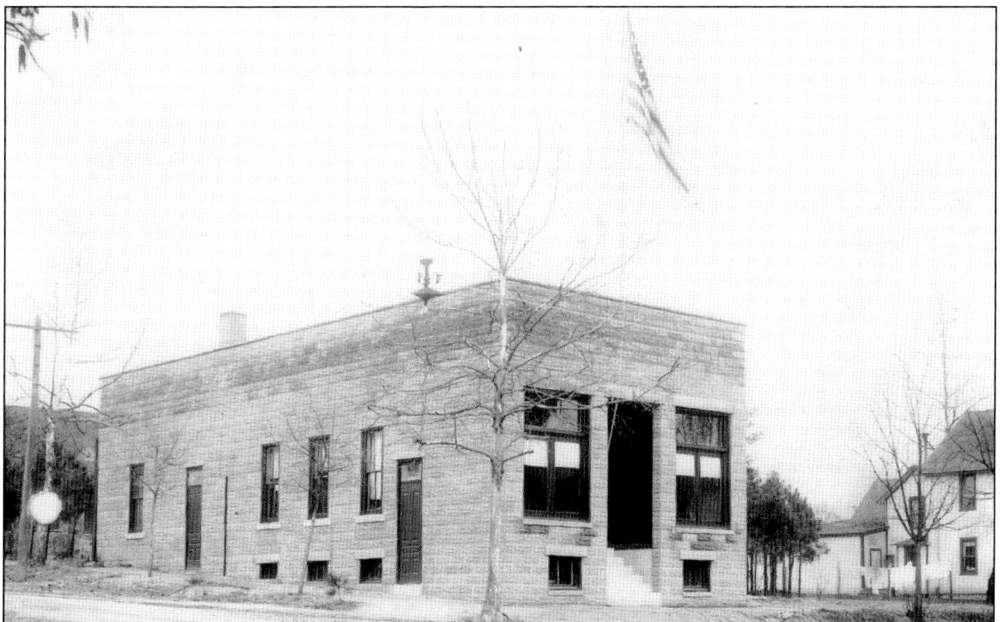

Starting c. 1911, this building at the corner of West Pennsylvania and North Bennett Street housed the weekly newspapers that served the community. The *Tourist Weekly*, founded in 1903, was produced here. It was succeeded by *The Sandhill Citizen* from 1915 until 1935 or 1936. Since then, the building that still stands has been rented to other businesses. It is owned by *The Pilot*, Moore County's local tri-weekly newspaper still published in Southern Pines.

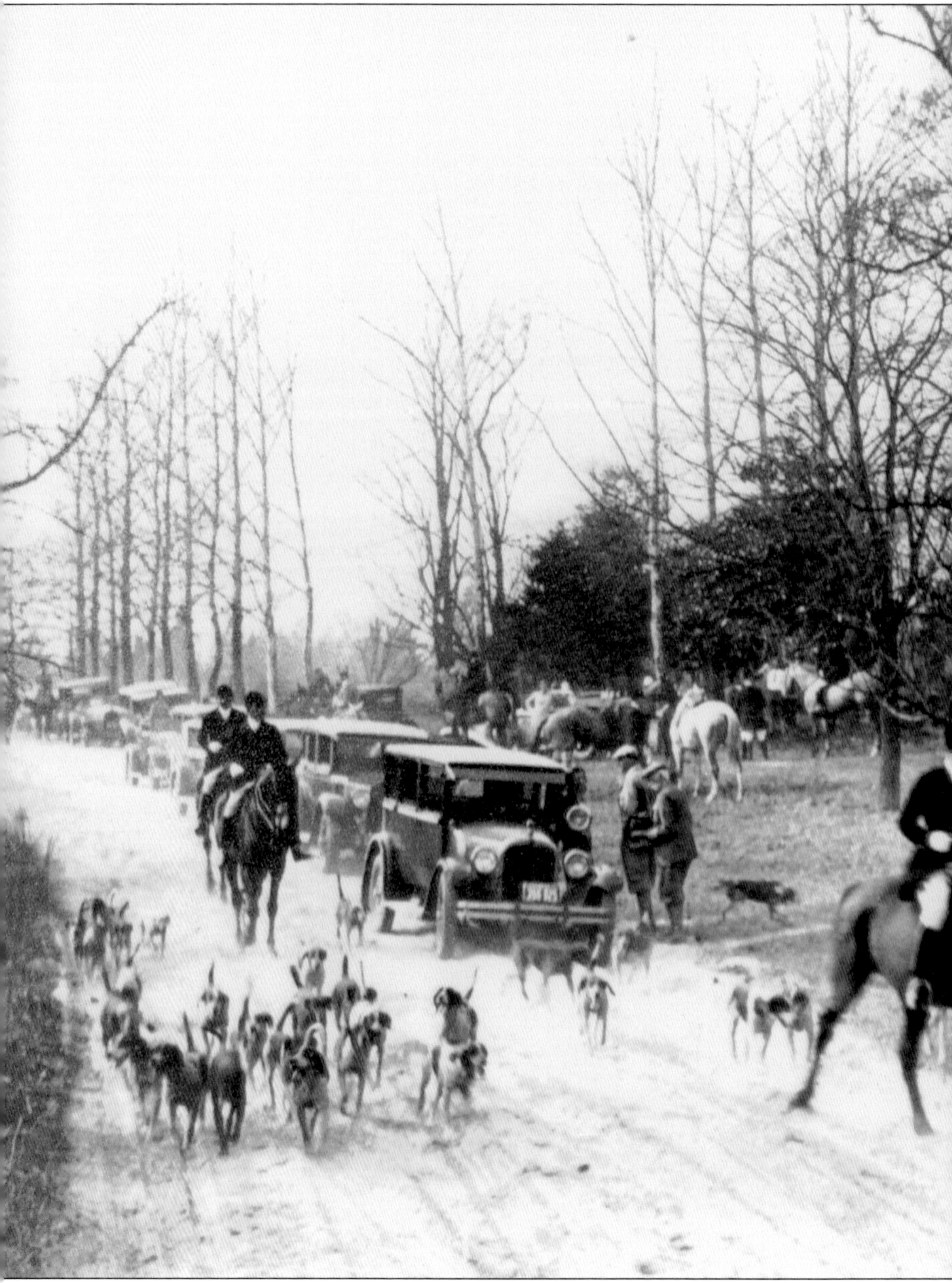

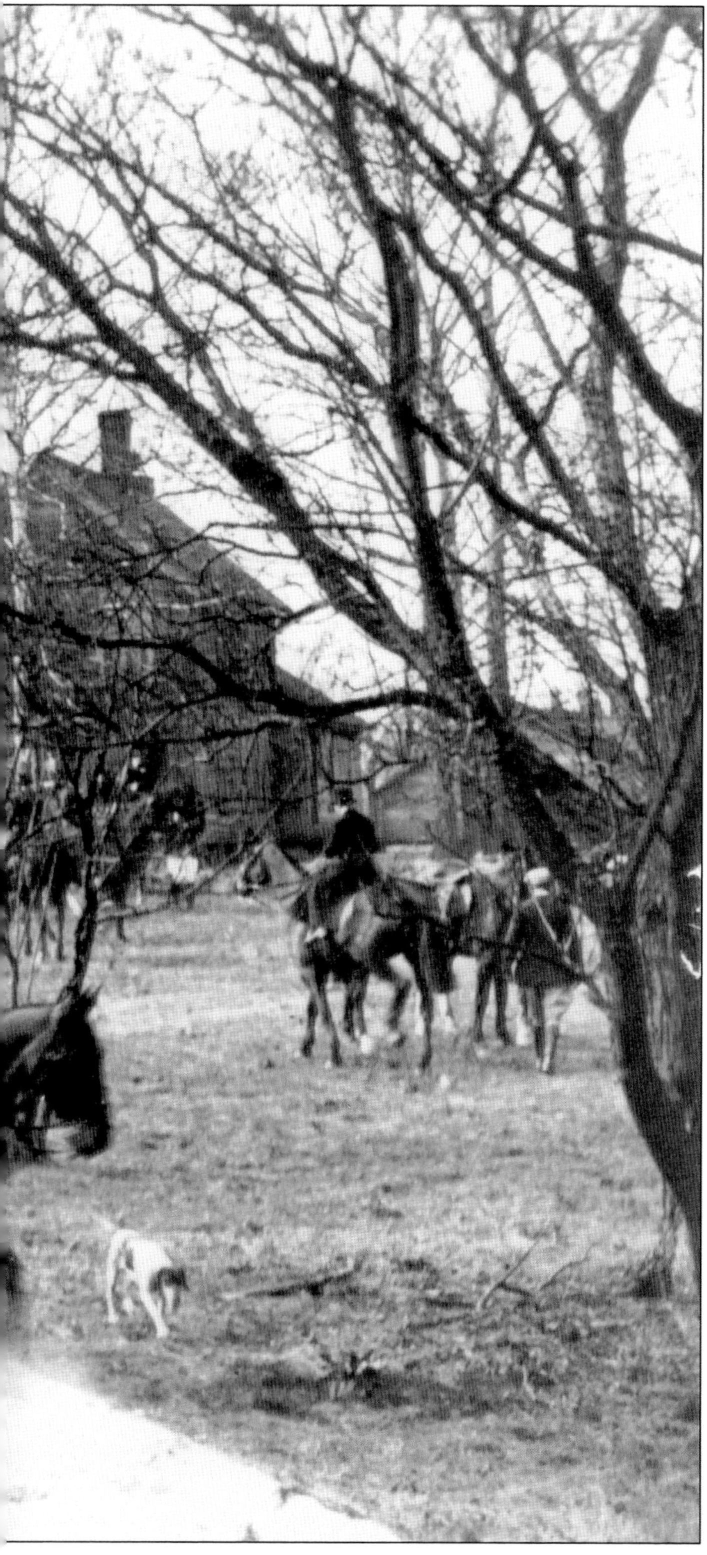

Young's Road was named for an old farm and remains the home of big horse farms that train thoroughbreds for racing and other national and international equestrian events, including the Olympics. The Moore County Hunt founders, Jim and Jack Boyd, and Katharine Boyd, Jim's wife, lead a foxhunt along the then-unpaved Young's Road at Young's Farm *c.* 1920. The Boyd brothers founded the hunt in 1914, after the death of their grandfather, James Boyd. A Pennsylvania coal merchant, the first James Boyd brought his wealthy family to Southern Pines at the turn of the century and purchased thousands of acres on the east side of Southern Pines. Boyd named his huge estate Weymouth Heights and Weymouth Woods. He and his descendants became civic leaders. He funded improvements to Midland Road that links Southern Pines to Pinehurst, while his daughter initiated a movement that resulted in a town library, garden club, and civic club.

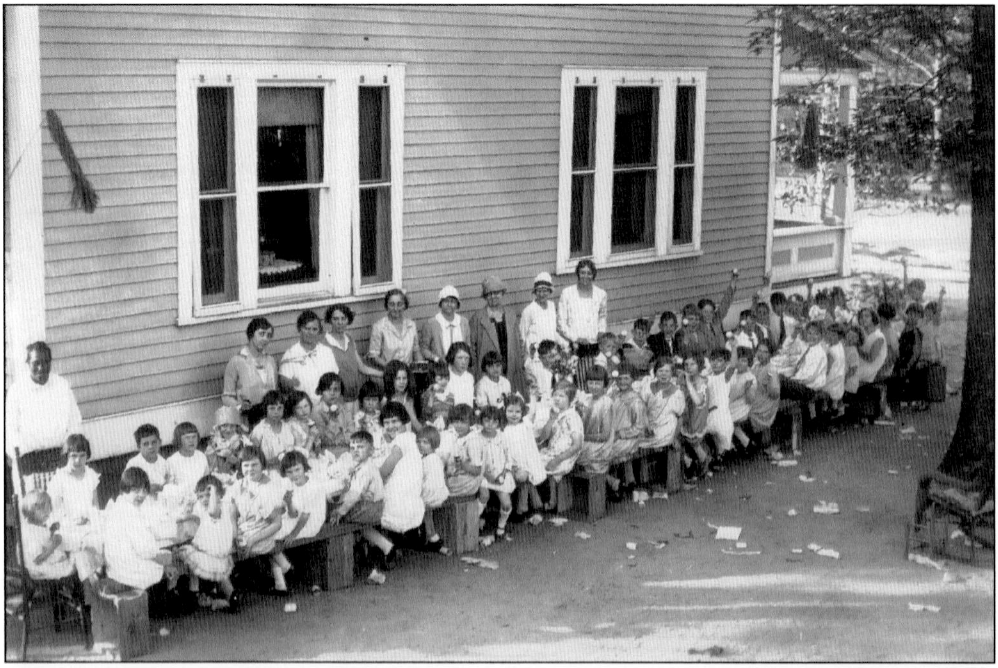

These children are Ellenore Eddy Smith's guests at her May party, one of the simple pleasures of the 1920s and 1930s in East Southern Pines. During the party, the elders of the community liked to listen to the radio, make social visits, and sit on front porches to watch the passing parade.

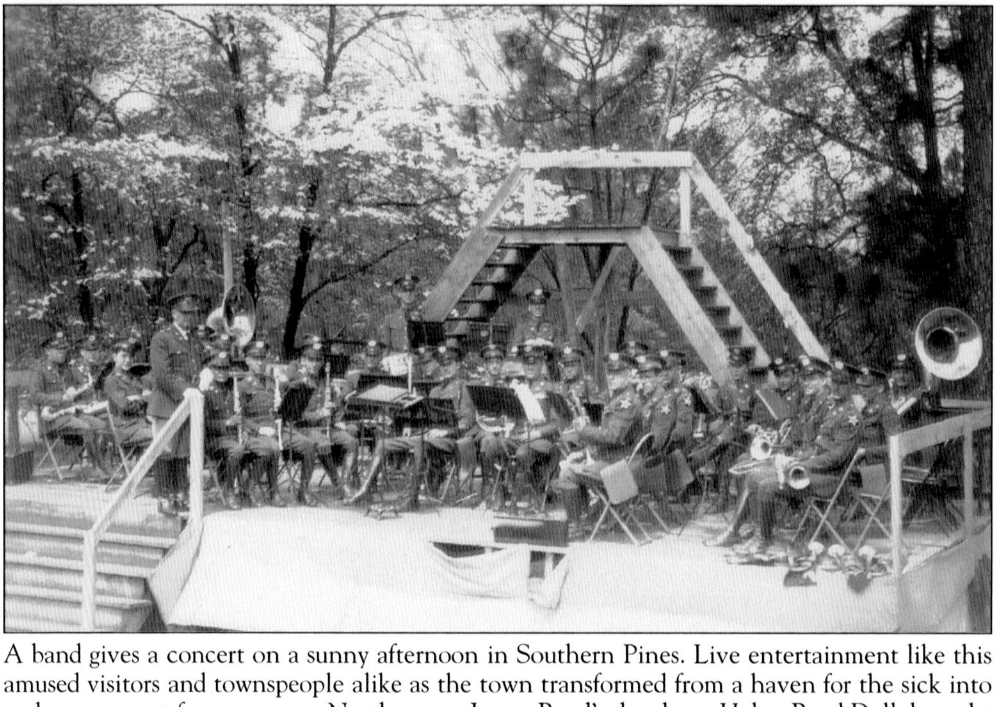

A band gives a concert on a sunny afternoon in Southern Pines. Live entertainment like this amused visitors and townspeople alike as the town transformed from a haven for the sick into a pleasure resort for prosperous Northerners. James Boyd's daughter, Helen Boyd Dull, brought sophisticated and professional entertainment to East Southern Pines in the early 1900s.

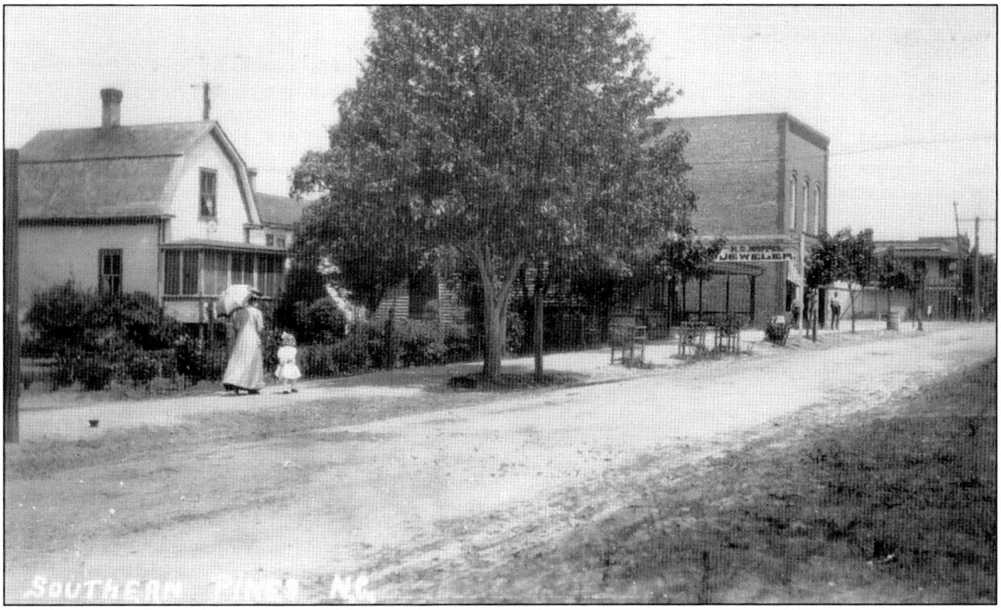

Early Southern Pines had an unpaved, frontier look. This lady and her daughter sometimes shared the roads with wandering livestock. An Aberdeen freight agent realized that a sand-clay mixture provided a smooth surface for travel, and the discovery was put into action by Pinehurst founder James W. Tufts. He used this mixture on Midland Road, the divided highway between Pinehurst and Southern Pines. The road was eventually paved in the late 1920s.

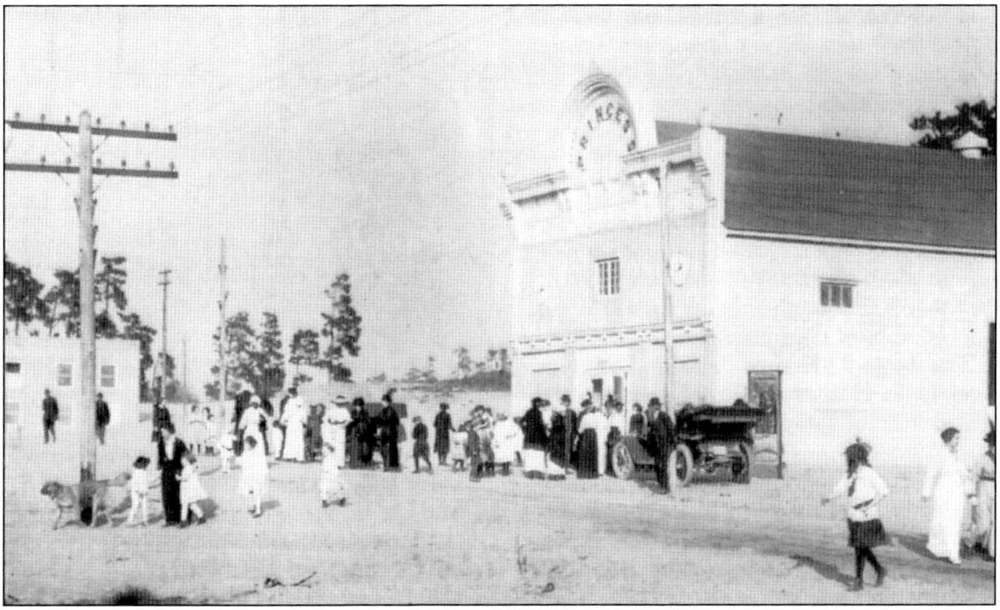

The Princess Theater attracts moving picture fans along the east side of Broad Street. Charles Picquet built the theater in 1914, and it remained in operation, showing the more sophisticated films through the post–World War II years, until newer, bigger, chain-owned theaters came to the outskirts of town in 1970. The theater building still stands and is used as a boutique shop and an antique furniture store. The Sunrise Theater, built later across the tracks, is preserved by a theater group.

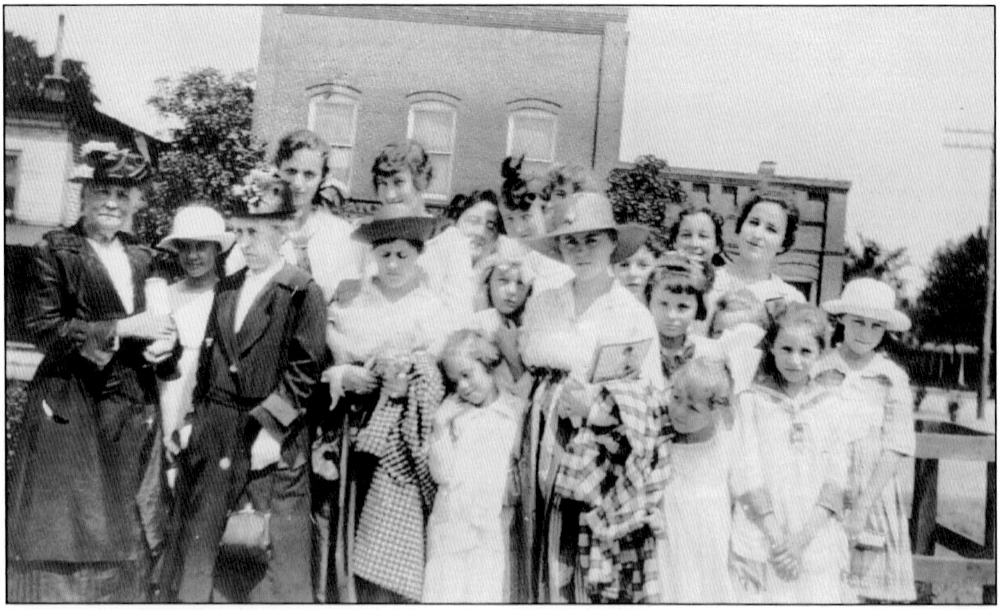

Downtown shoppers came in groups like this one to look at the goods in Southern Pines. Customers could buy vegetables, fruit, and meats out of carts brought in by nearby farmers, but they also could shop for clothing and other items in shops. Broad Street ran through downtown. Lodging, which catered to travelers arriving by train, was located within a few blocks of Broad on both sides of the tracks.

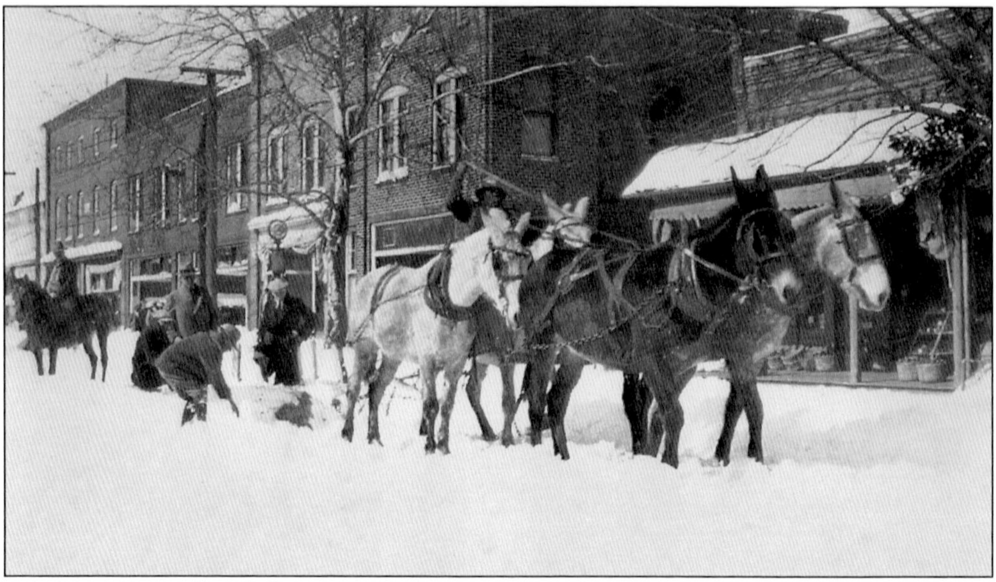

Reliable mules pull a sledge, scraping downtown Southern Pines streets during a memorable snow of 30 inches on March 1 and 2, 1927. The bizarrely heavy snowfall caught the town by surprise, as occasional heavier-than-an-inch-or-two snowfalls have ever since. Unfortunately, no mules were available for transportation during the 24-inch snowstorm of 2000!

Road hazards like this for the horseless carriage existed all over the sandy Sandhills well into the 1930s on some less-traveled byways. Main roads around the resorts of Southern Pines and Pinehurst were the first to be improved for tourists coming in by car, which gradually replaced the train in popularity. Still, deep sand and hastily hacked-out roads were more accessible by horsepower and cart than car for a long time.

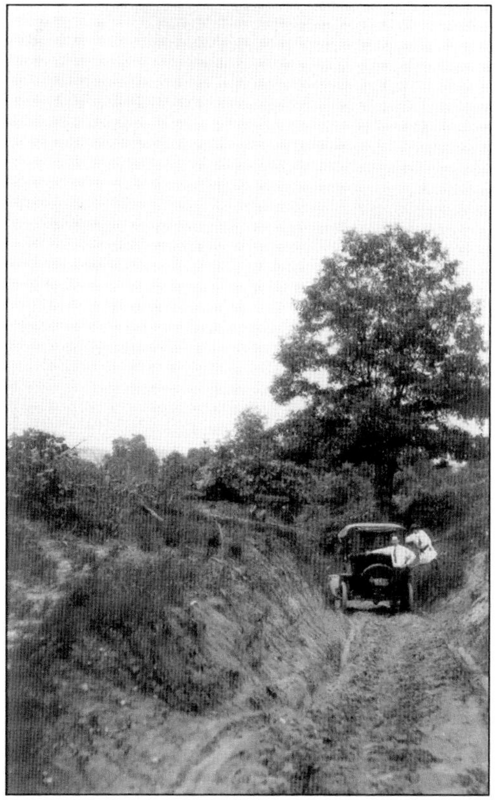

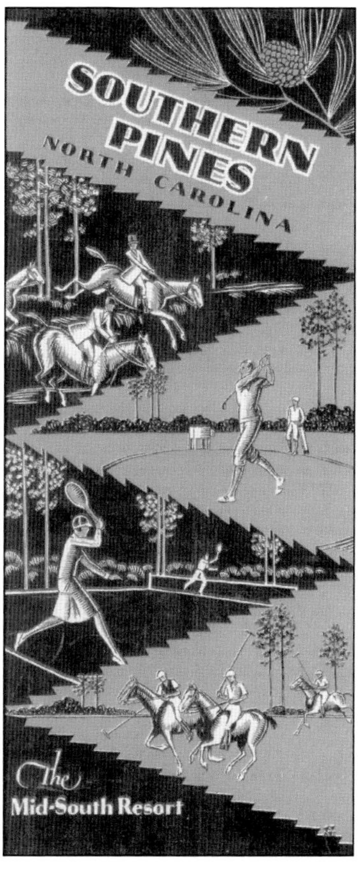

The advertisement of Southern Pines as "the Mid-South Resort" was created in the 1930s to attract well-heeled visitors for year-round outdoor recreation like golf, tennis, polo, and foxhunting. This brochure was originally printed in green and black. Maps inside the folded brochure tout major federal highway access along U.S. 1 to Southern Pines, emphasizing its central location: 350 miles south of Washington, D.C., and 450 miles north of Jacksonville, Florida.

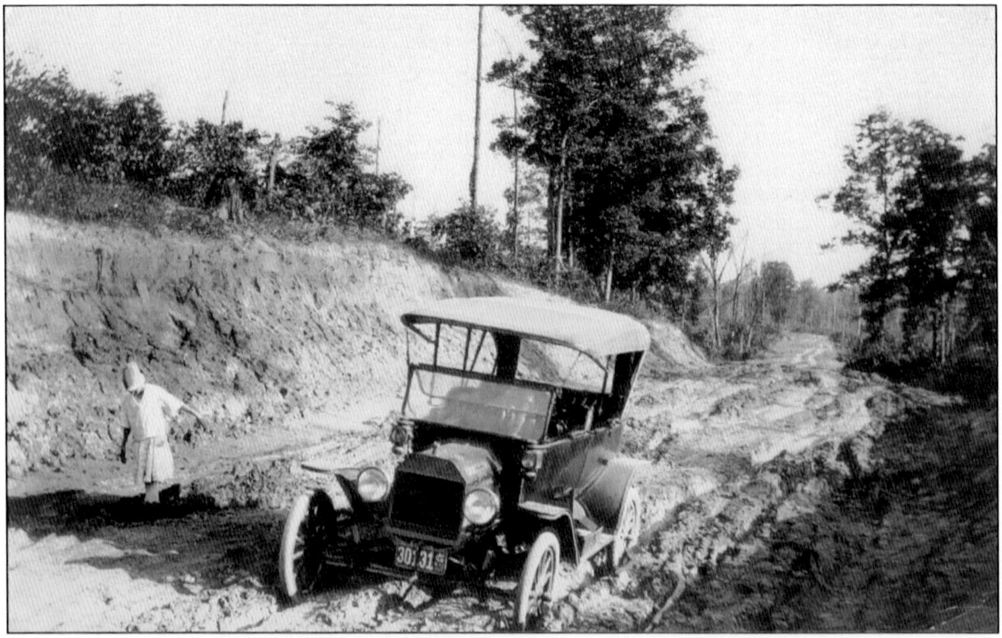

Despite the major federal and state highway system that was quickly adapting the area to automobile tourism, some sandy roads still existed in Southern Pines. This Model T bogged down in deep sand is about as useful as a boat in this rural area.

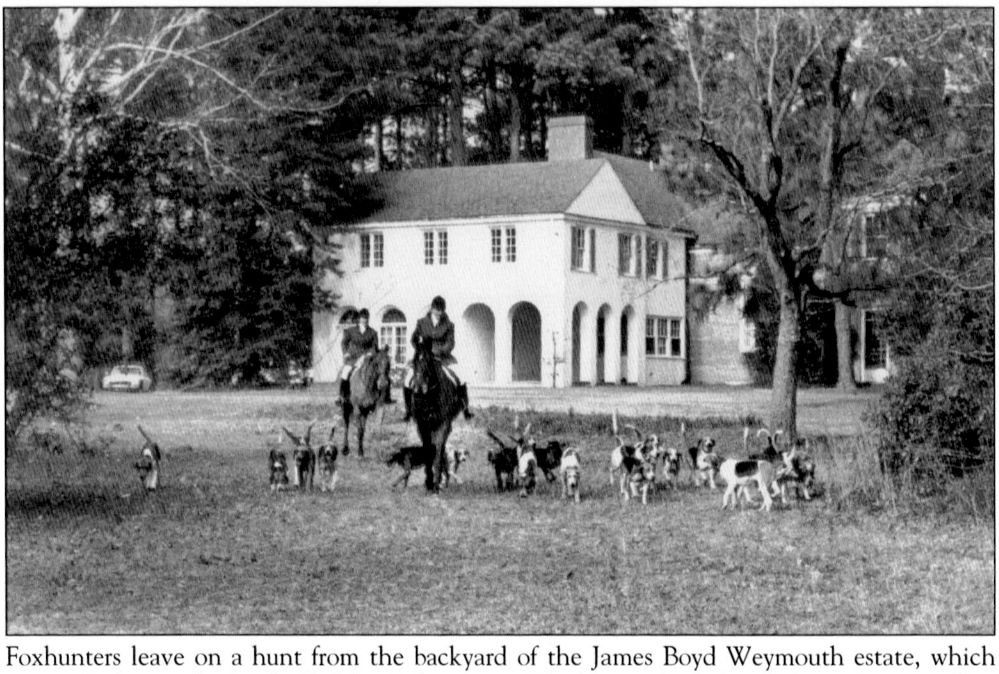

Foxhunters leave on a hunt from the backyard of the James Boyd Weymouth estate, which occurred often in the first half of the 20th century. The home of novelist and poet James and his wife Katharine is preserved today by a non-profit volunteer foundation. It is rented for weddings and other events, and it hosts a writer's retreat program. Interestingly, Boyd himself once said he would rather ride than write.

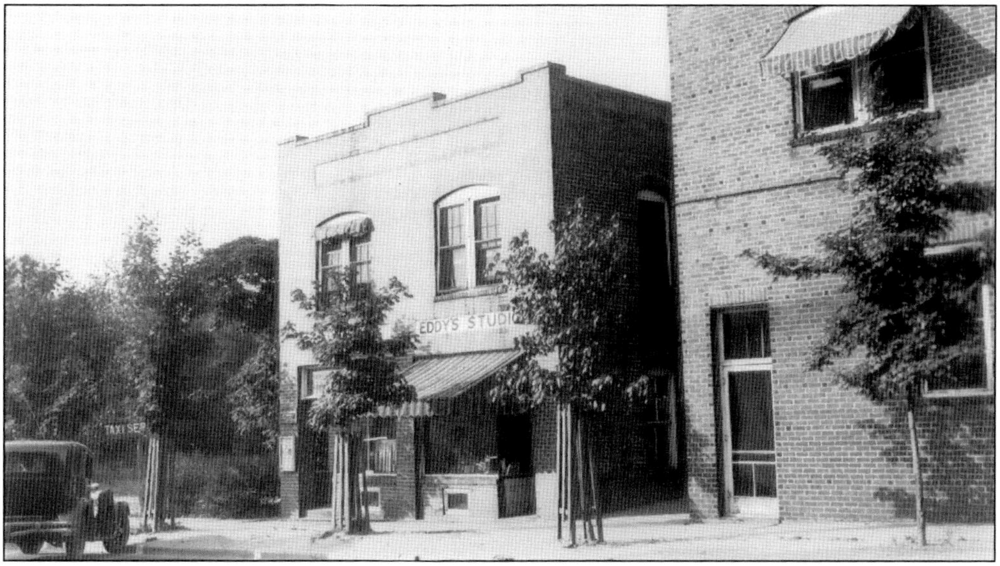

Eddy's Studio occupied a prominent storefront on Broad Street in Southern Pines during the early years. A New England native, E.C. Eddy came to the area in 1907 and moved to Southern Pines in 1911. He was a prolific postcard photographer of many scenes and landmarks that are preserved by no one else. He died in 1945. His only surviving daughter, Ellenore Eddy Smith, still lives in Southern Pines.

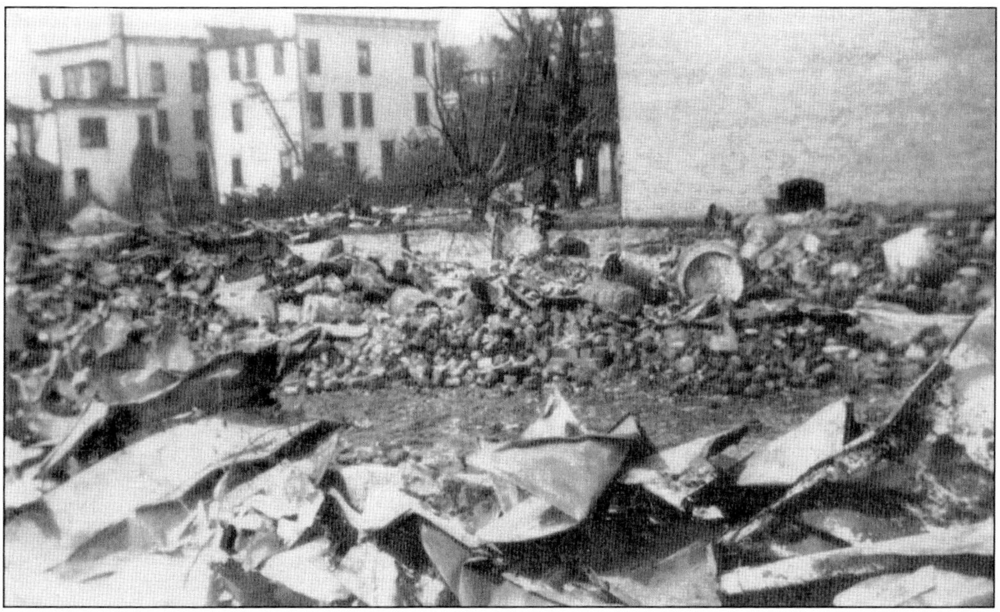

The fire on April 13, 1921, was a catastrophic event for Southern Pines. It destroyed most of the structures downtown, despite the efforts of a host of volunteer firefighters. Most brick buildings survived the fire, and many of them are still operating as viable businesses today. The Jefferson, one of the original 10 inns, still stands.

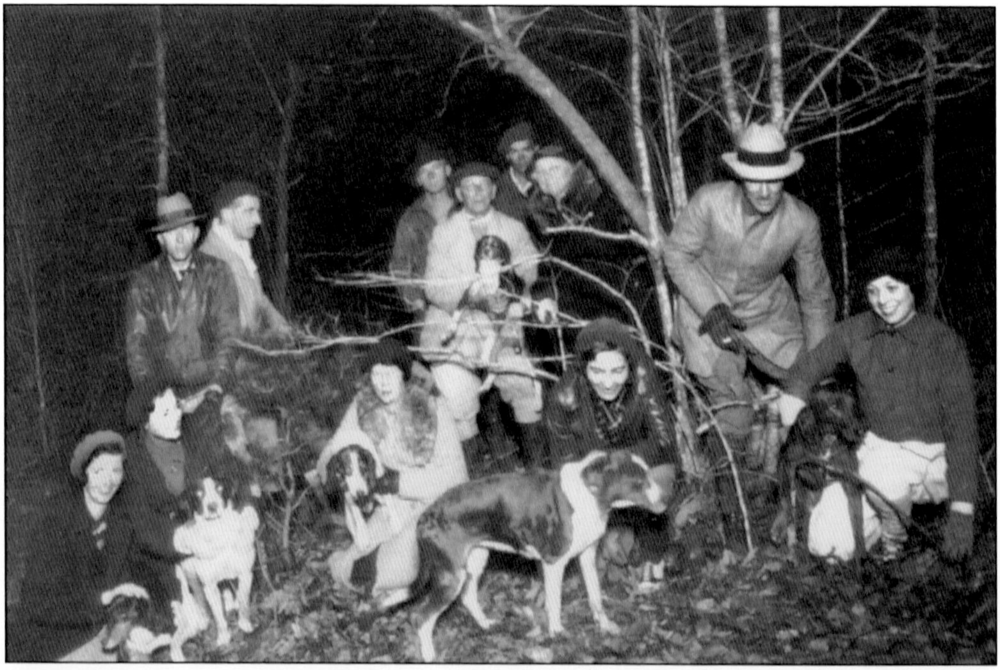

Possum hunting was an old Southern pastime. Although possum meat was often used in stews in early times, the hunt itself was more for the diversion and novelty of it than to put food on the table.

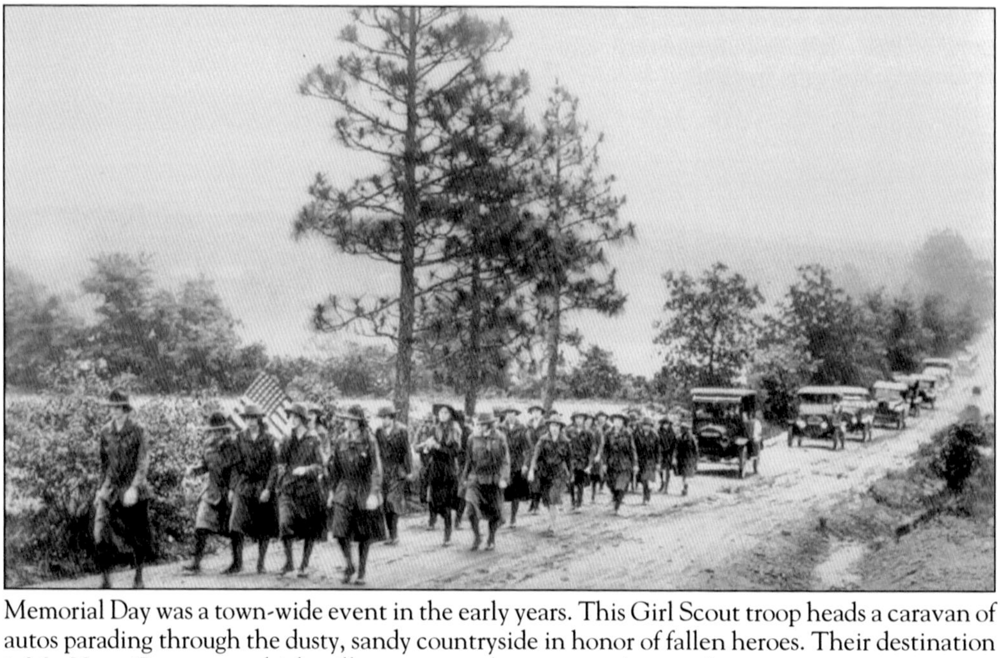

Memorial Day was a town-wide event in the early years. This Girl Scout troop heads a caravan of autos parading through the dusty, sandy countryside in honor of fallen heroes. Their destination is Mt. Hope Cemetery, which still operates under municipal ownership.

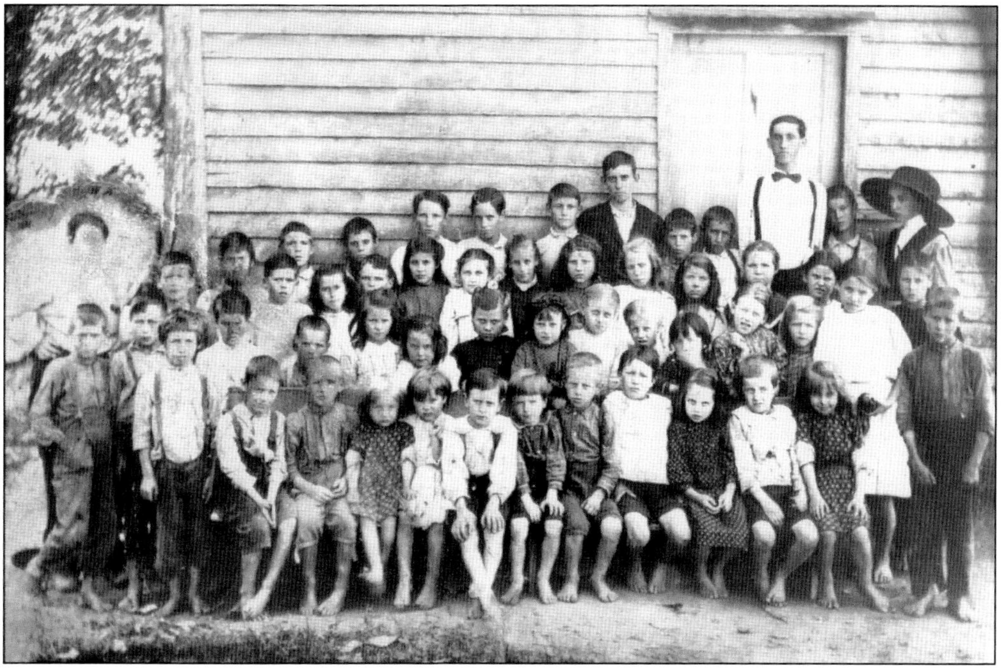

A Southern Pines school for white children opened as early as 1886, but there was not much of a public school system as such in those days. These barefooted boys and girls are probably students at the very first school building, which was located next to Fisher's Flattop, a downtown boarding house on Broad Street near the railway depot.

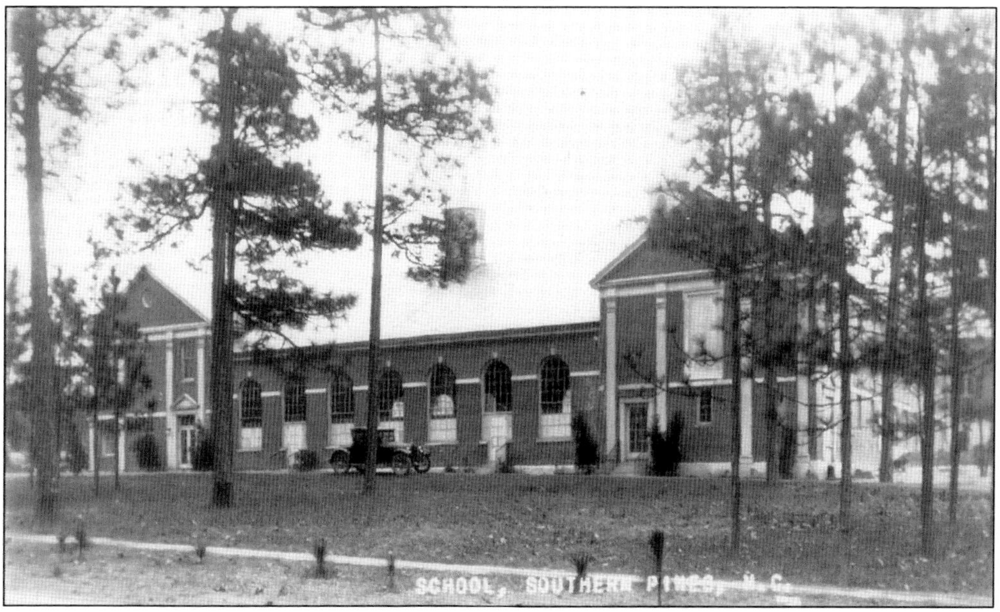

This accredited high school for white students, *c.* 1920s, is located at East Massachusetts Avenue and North May Street; this was the site of the town's first comprehensive school for all grades, built in 1908. The brick building has had several facelifts, has undergone school consolidation and integration, and now houses classes for third through fifth grades. The segregated (East) Southern Pines City School system is long gone.

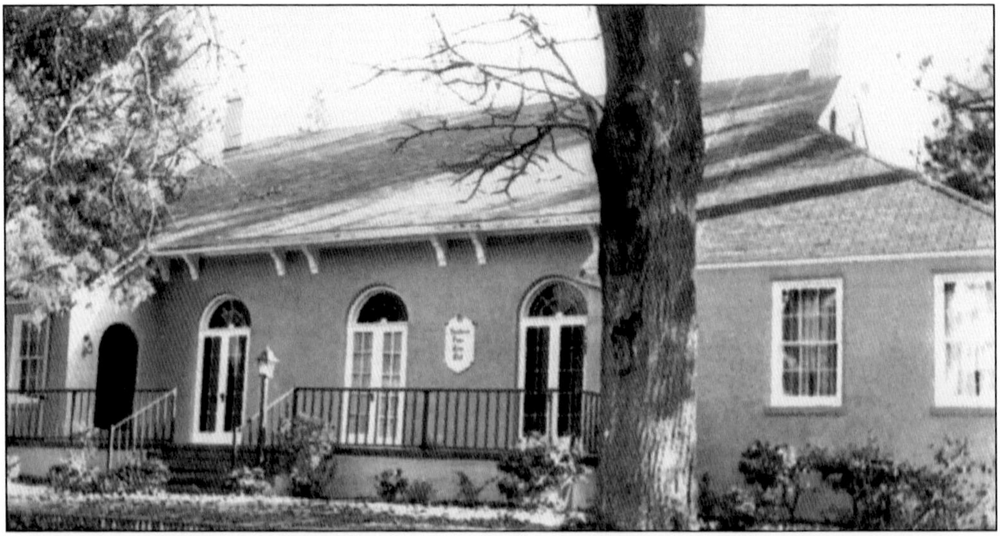

The Southern Pines Civic Club, at the corner of Ashe Street and Pennsylvania Avenue, was constructed in 1925, after the death of the club's founder Helen Boyd Dull, the daughter of the first James Boyd of Weymouth. The club was formed in 1907 with the aim of improving civic and cultural life in the town. The purposes have changed over the years, but the club and its building still serve Southern Pines.

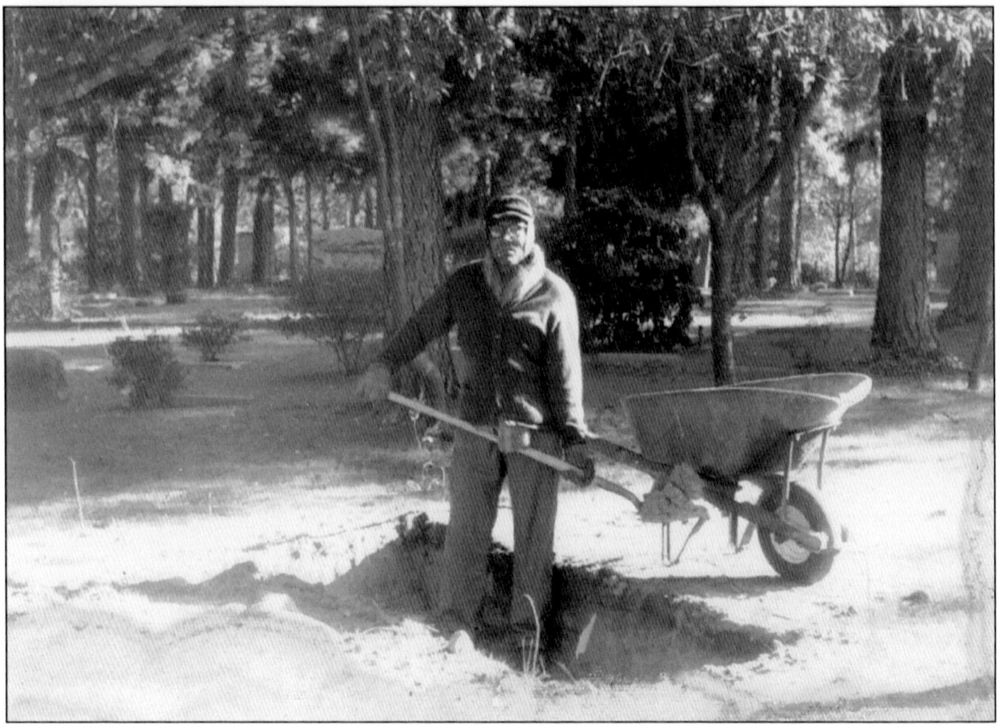

Gravedigging in Southern Pines was done manually, as town employee James McZorn demonstrates, c. 1950s. The town used the wheelbarrow-and-shovel method of digging graves at Mt. Hope Cemetery until very recent times when heavy equipment took over the task of moving earth.

Southern Pines promotional material, c. 1930s, features a small map with the town's attractions in a nutshell on the front page of a 16-page brochure. The arrow points to the town's exact location.

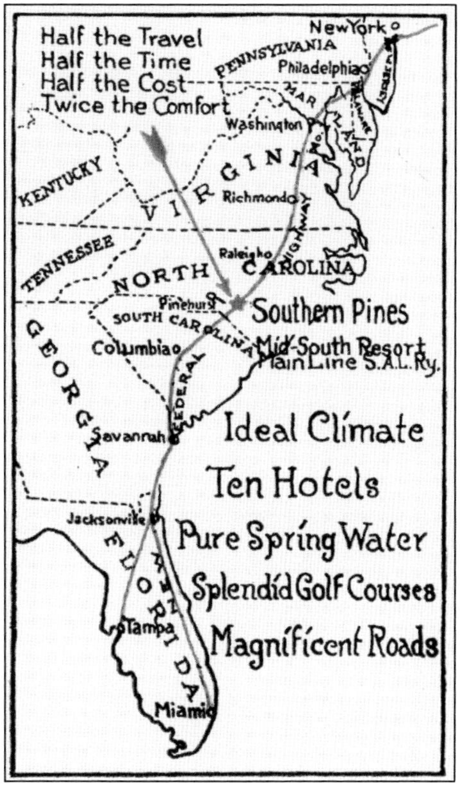

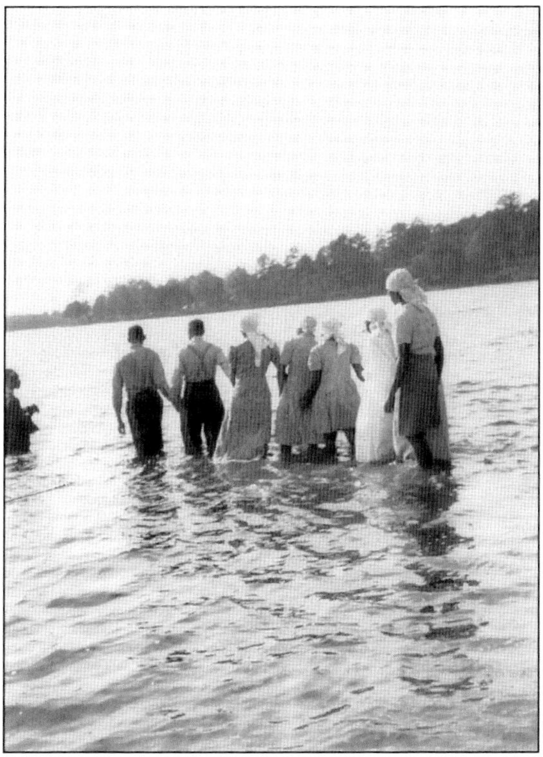

These people are getting an old-time baptism in one of Moore County's many lakes and ponds that come from natural springs. Southern Pines postcard photographer E.C. Eddy took this snapshot, which is part of his daughter Ellenore Eddy Smith's collection.

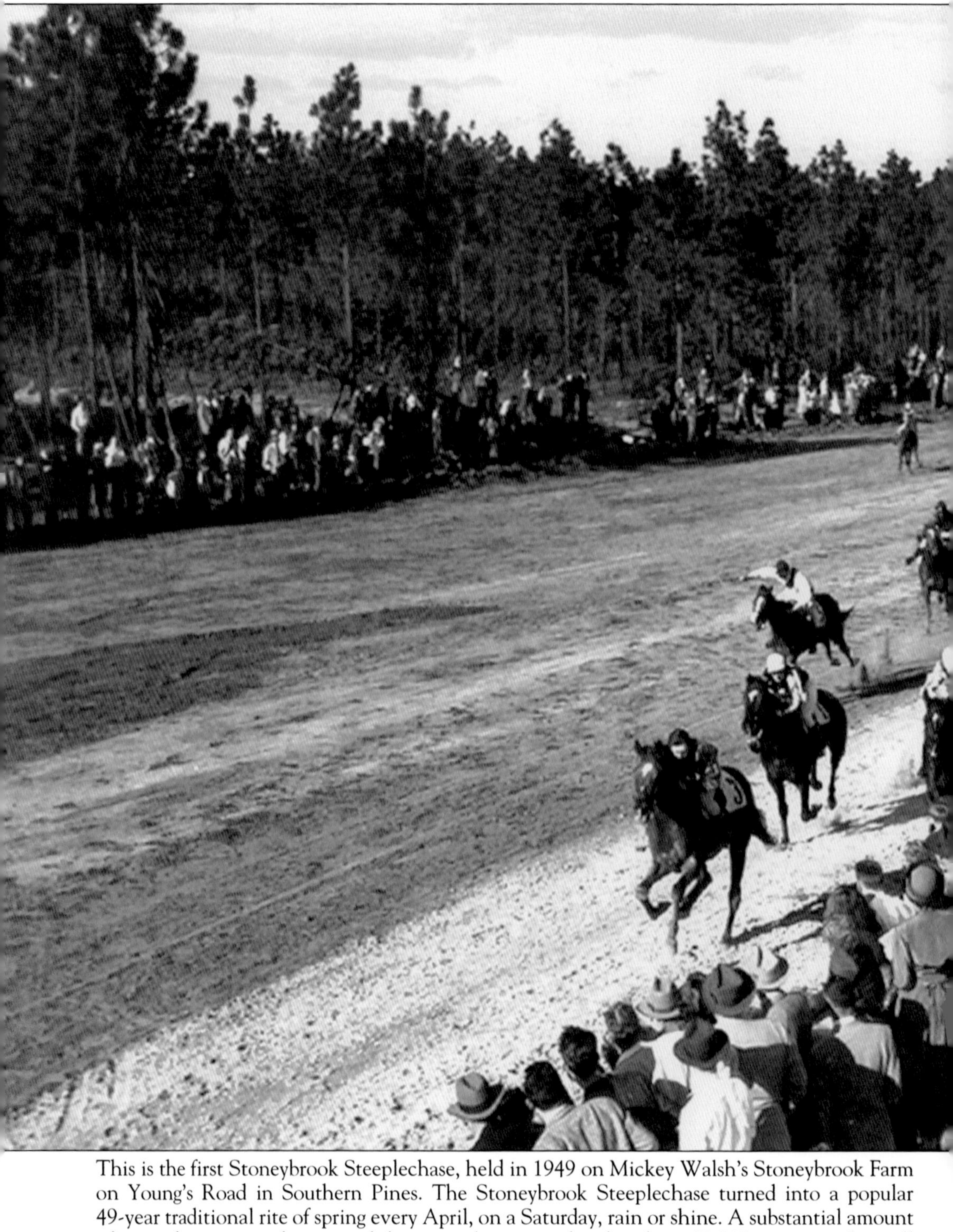

This is the first Stoneybrook Steeplechase, held in 1949 on Mickey Walsh's Stoneybrook Farm on Young's Road in Southern Pines. The Stoneybrook Steeplechase turned into a popular 49-year traditional rite of spring every April, on a Saturday, rain or shine. A substantial amount of its profits went to charity, and the event drew, at its height, about 50,000 spectators from all over the Eastern Seaboard and beyond. Walsh's family continued to hold the race until 1998,

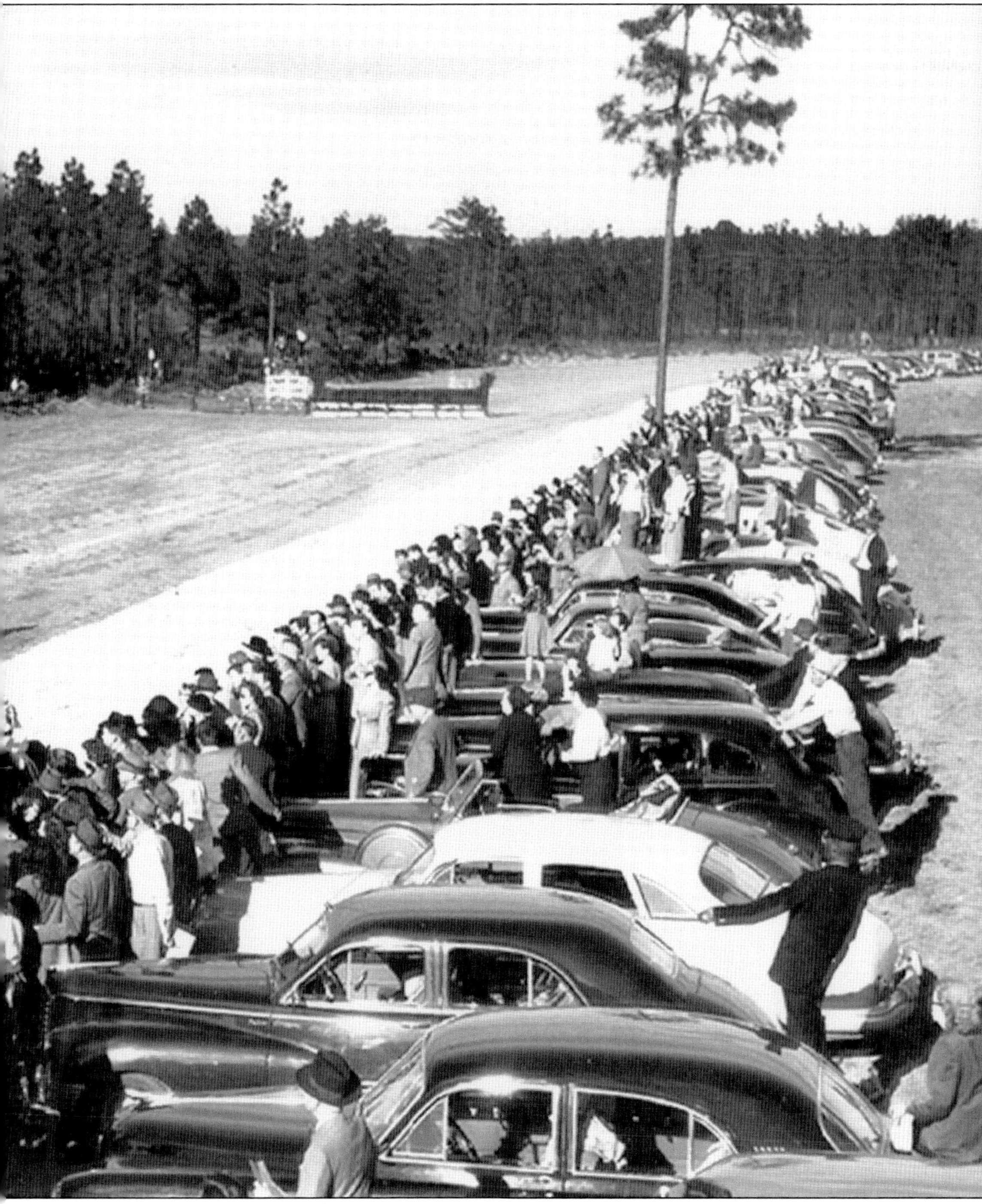

two years after his death. Mickey Walsh was an Irish immigrant who arrived in America in 1925; in 1941, he moved his Irish-born wife Kitty and their growing family to an apartment over the stable at the farm that Walsh later named Stoneybrook. Walsh's Stoneybrook Steeplechase replaced the Sandhills Steeplechase, which had been a tradition in Southern Pines for eight years.

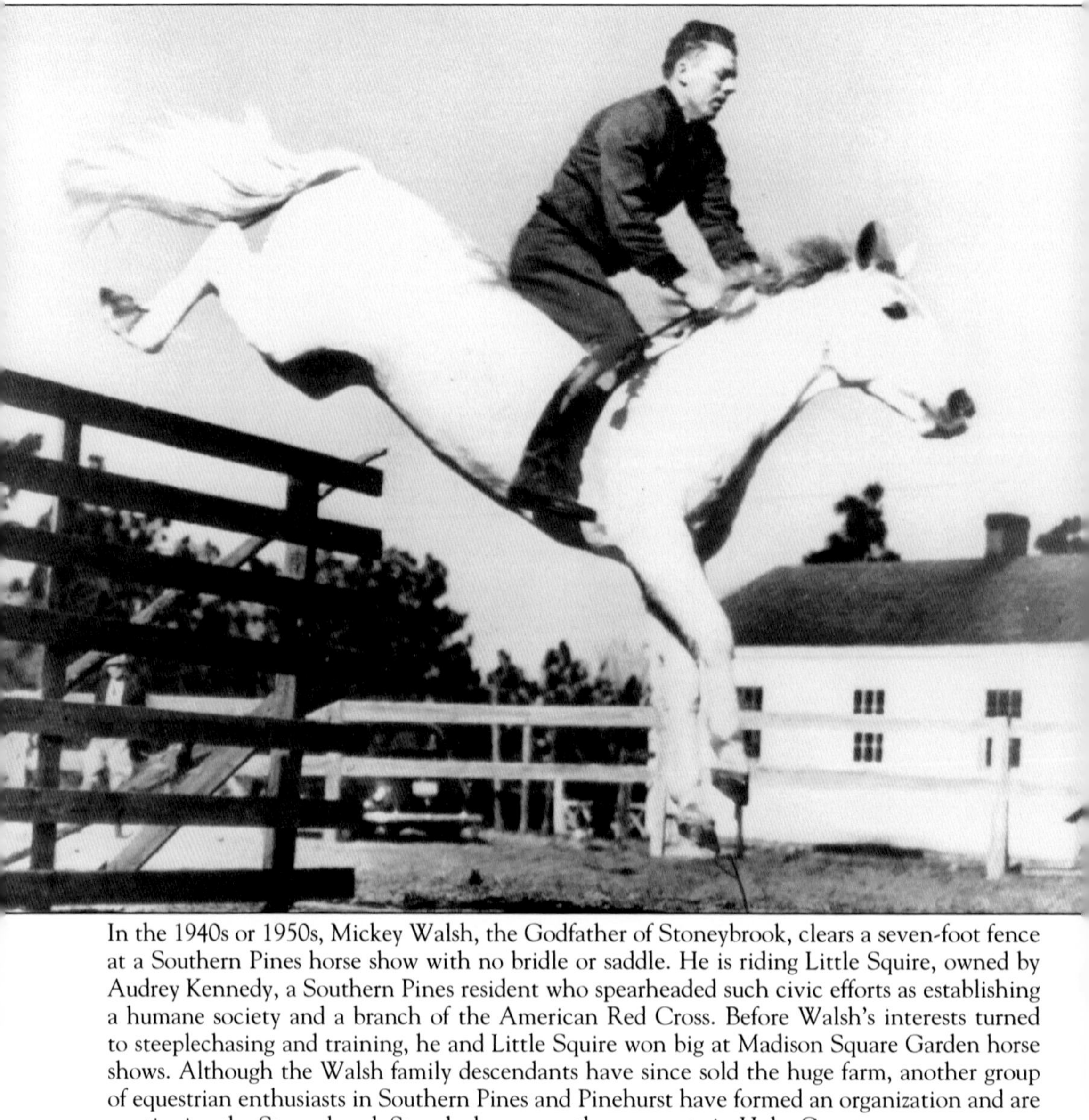

In the 1940s or 1950s, Mickey Walsh, the Godfather of Stoneybrook, clears a seven-foot fence at a Southern Pines horse show with no bridle or saddle. He is riding Little Squire, owned by Audrey Kennedy, a Southern Pines resident who spearheaded such civic efforts as establishing a humane society and a branch of the American Red Cross. Before Walsh's interests turned to steeplechasing and training, he and Little Squire won big at Madison Square Garden horse shows. Although the Walsh family descendants have since sold the huge farm, another group of equestrian enthusiasts in Southern Pines and Pinehurst have formed an organization and are continuing the Stoneybrook Steeplechases on other property in Hoke County.

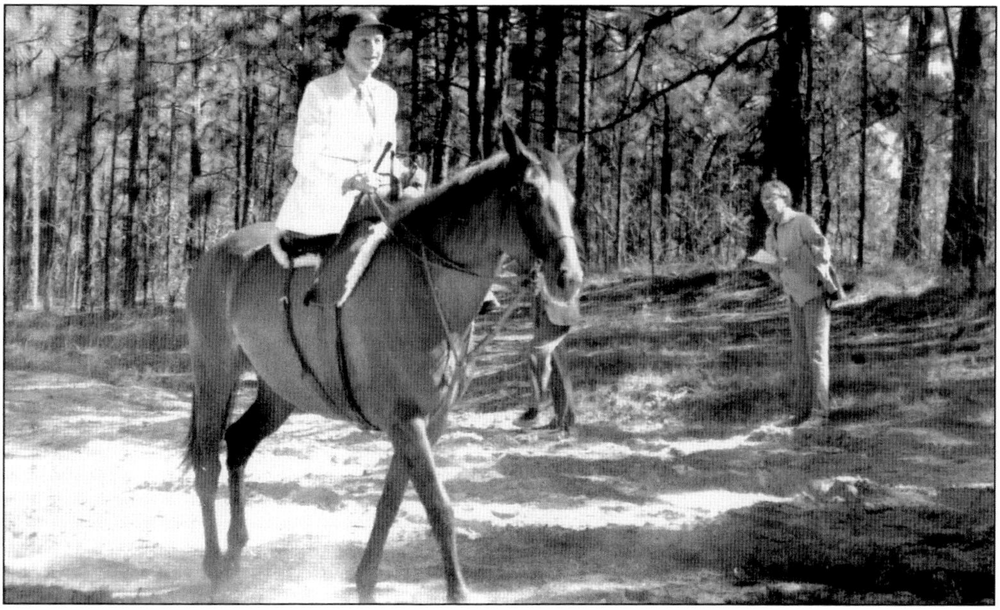

In the oldest times of Southern Pines, ladies walked, rode in carriages and carts, and, when on a horse, rode astride. Famed area photographer Emerson Humphrey captured Mrs. Gardiner Fiske enjoying a ride in the old-fashioned way. She was one of the last ladies to ride side-saddle.

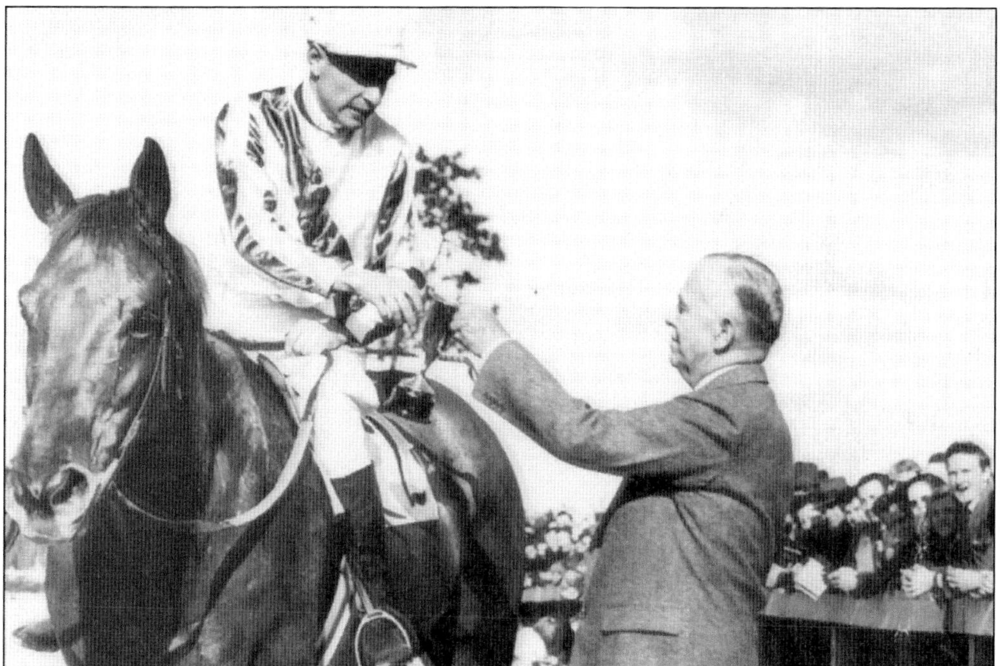

Gen. George Marshall presents a prize to a Stoneybrook winner. Marshall, a hero of World War II and the creator of a plan to reconstruct post-war Europe, was a resident of the Sandhills during his retirement in the 1940s and 1950s. Many former military generals retired in Southern Pines, partly because of the proximity to the Fort Bragg military base where some had served and others had friends.

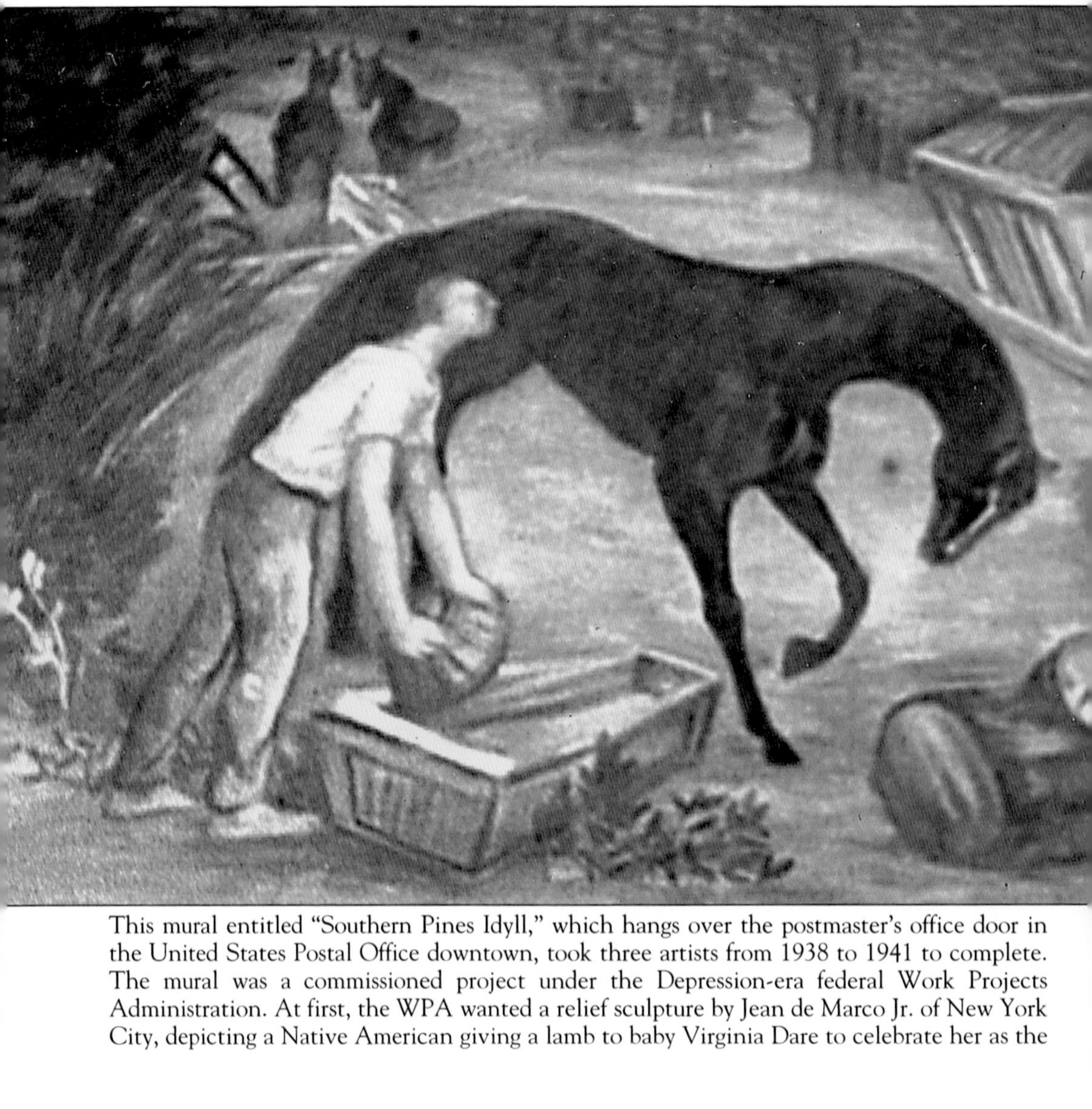

This mural entitled "Southern Pines Idyll," which hangs over the postmaster's office door in the United States Postal Office downtown, took three artists from 1938 to 1941 to complete. The mural was a commissioned project under the Depression-era federal Work Projects Administration. At first, the WPA wanted a relief sculpture by Jean de Marco Jr. of New York City, depicting a Native American giving a lamb to baby Virginia Dare to celebrate her as the

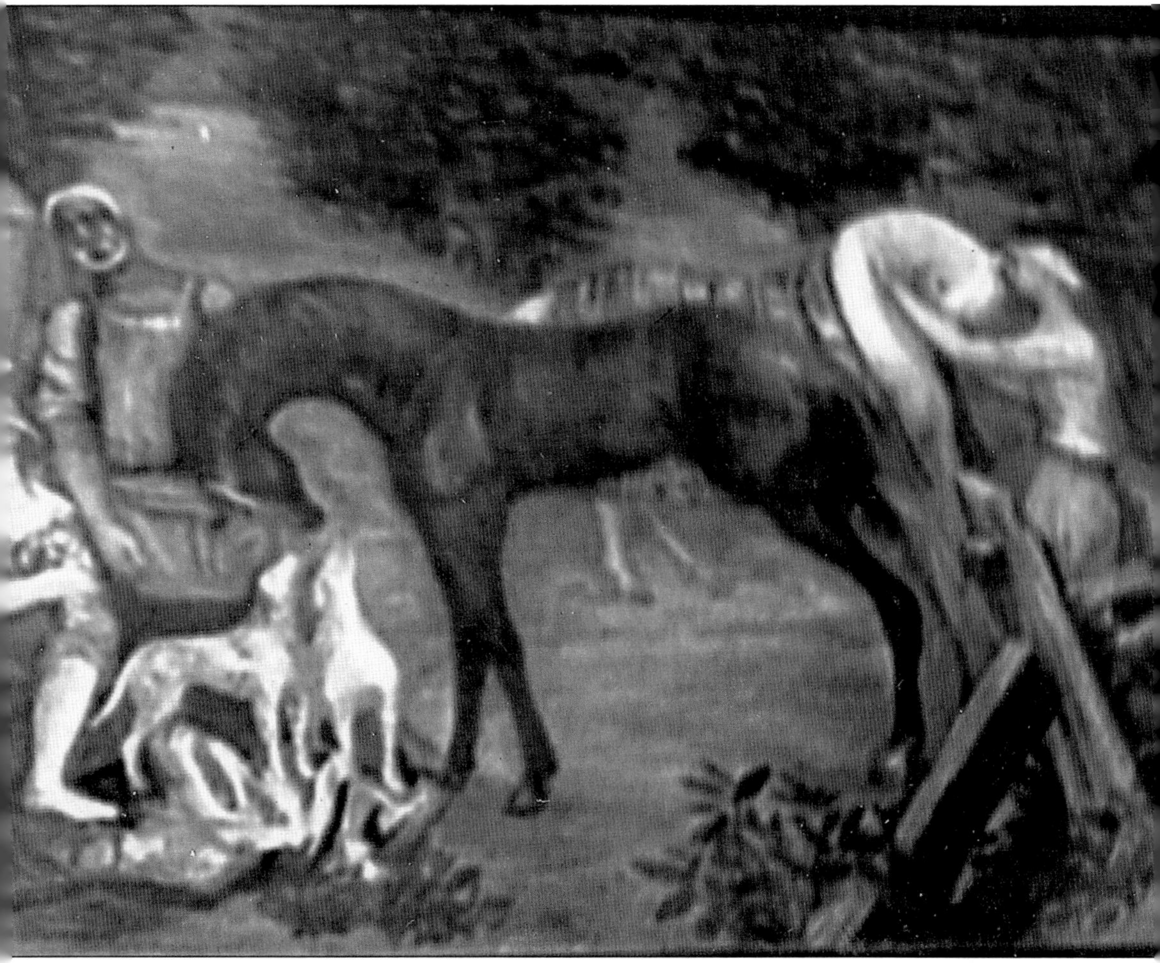

first English child born in the New World. That idea was thwarted by Southern Pines architect Aymar Embury II. Then a flat painting was decided upon and researched by artist Dunbar Beck, but Beck bowed out of the project. Josef Presser of Philadelphia completed the project at last. His mural shows peaceful Southern Pines scenes of the early days.

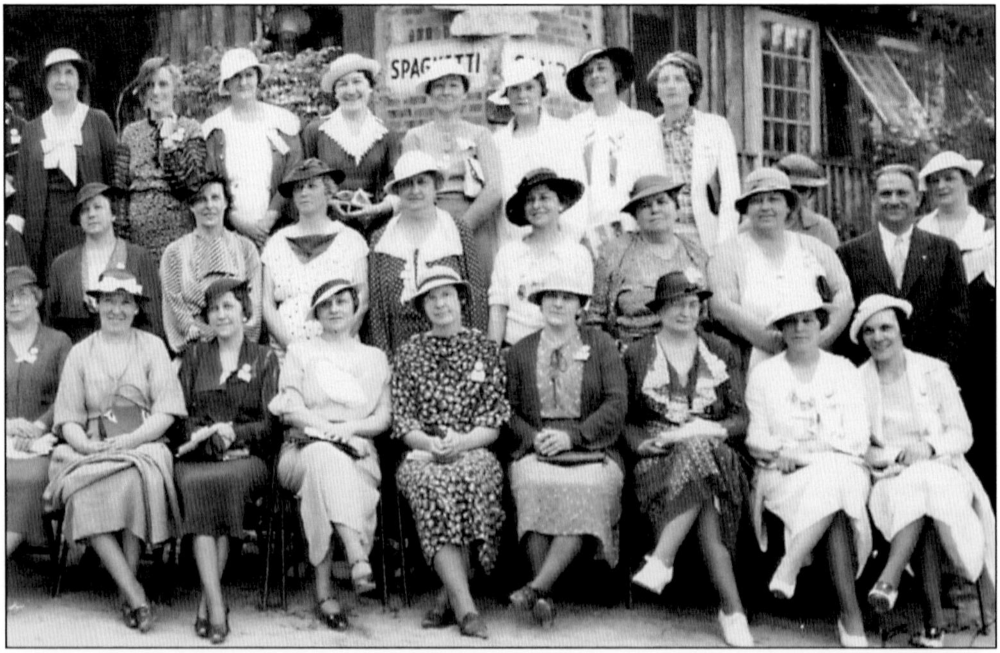

Southern Pines ladies dressed in their finery pose for a get-together in 1934 at the Spaghetti Camp, an eatery on the outskirts at an old hunting lodge run by Angelo Montesanti. He arrived in Southern Pines in 1912 to cook for the tourists. The Montesantis eventually settled in Southern Pines. From 1946 until the 1970s, Angelo's son Dante ran one of North Carolina's very few four-star restaurants, named Dante's, on Broad Street.

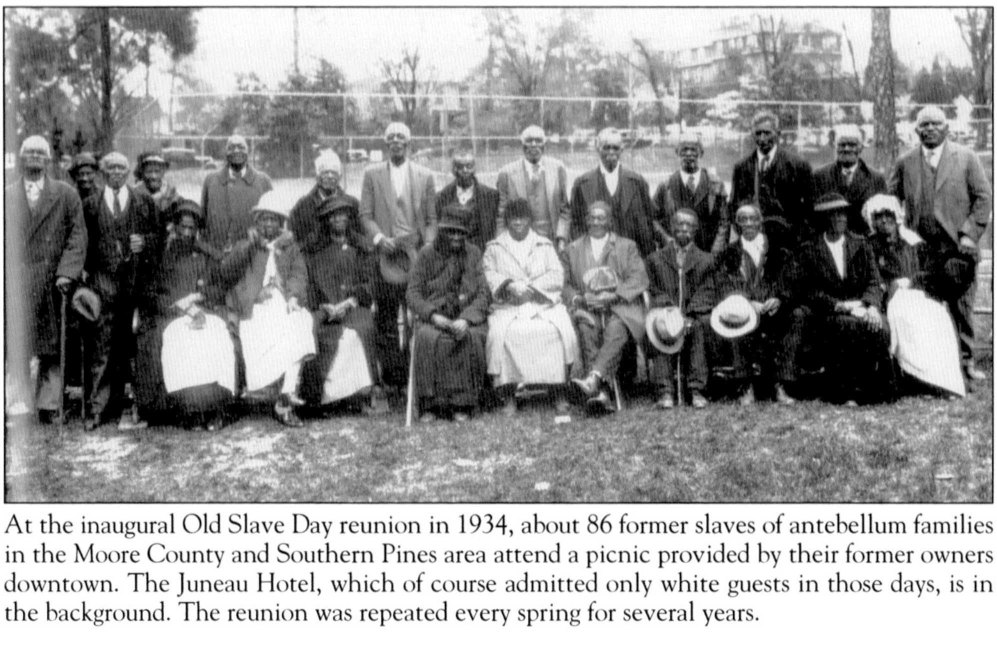

At the inaugural Old Slave Day reunion in 1934, about 86 former slaves of antebellum families in the Moore County and Southern Pines area attend a picnic provided by their former owners downtown. The Juneau Hotel, which of course admitted only white guests in those days, is in the background. The reunion was repeated every spring for several years.

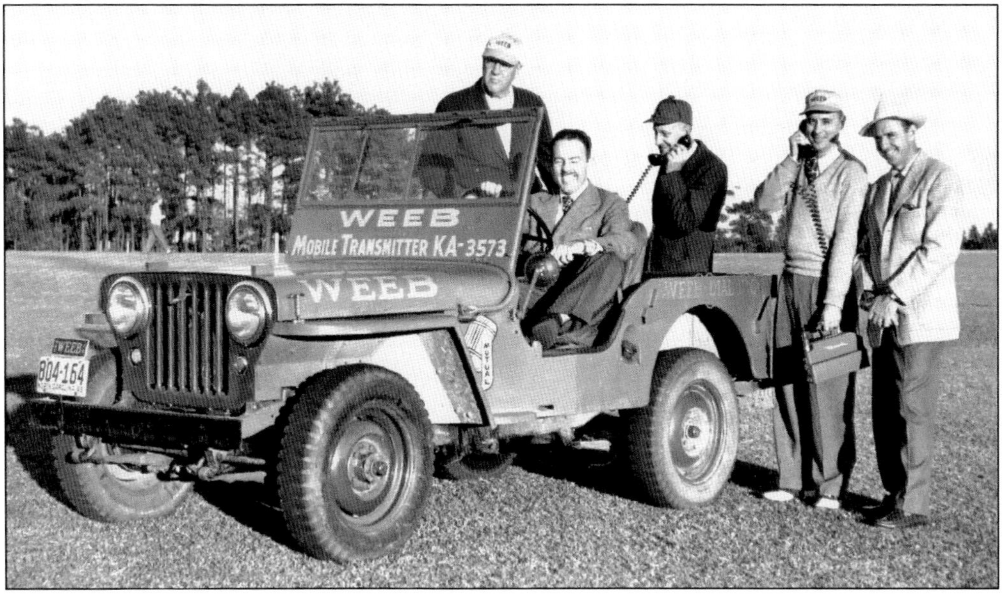

Jack Younts (second from far right) started the first radio station in Southern Pines and all of Moore County. During Station WEEB's first broadcast—in 1949 from this jeep—golf great Sam Snead (far right) participates in the play-by-play of a game at the Pinehurst Country Club to a six-station hookup. Other participants, from left to right, are Pinehurst resident and golf commentator Bob Harlow, Greensboro journalist Jim Reid, and Southern Pines resident Arch Coleman, who became a regular WEEB commentator.

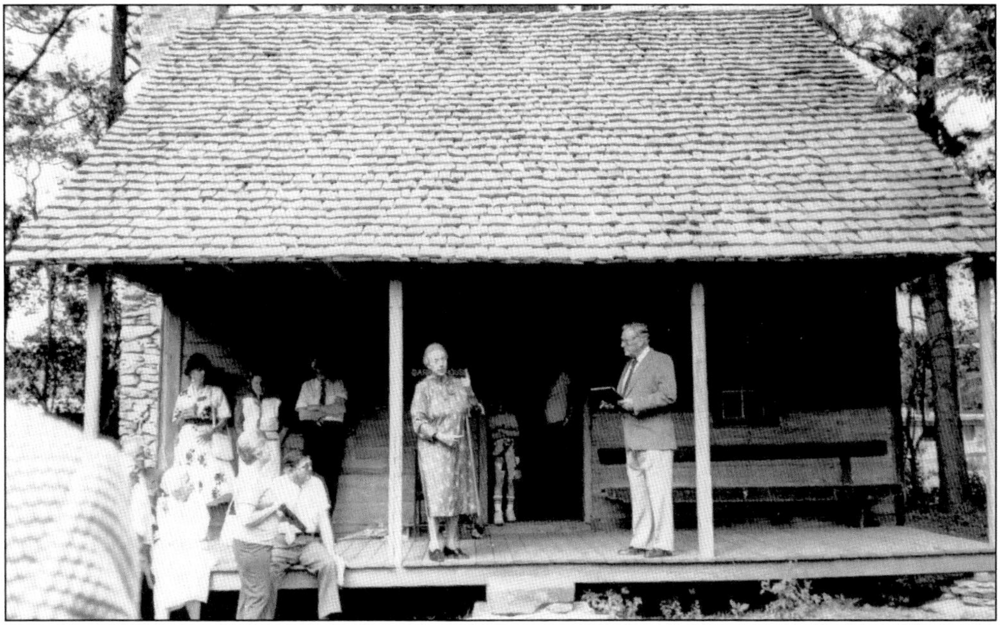

The Moore County Historical Society was formed in 1946 under the leadership of Elizabeth "Buffie" Ives of Illinois (center), one of the many visitors to Southern Pines who decided to stay. Here, the society members enjoy an open house on the porch of the Garner House, an old pioneer cabin that the society has moved to the grounds where the Shaw House is also preserved. Both houses date to the 1830s.

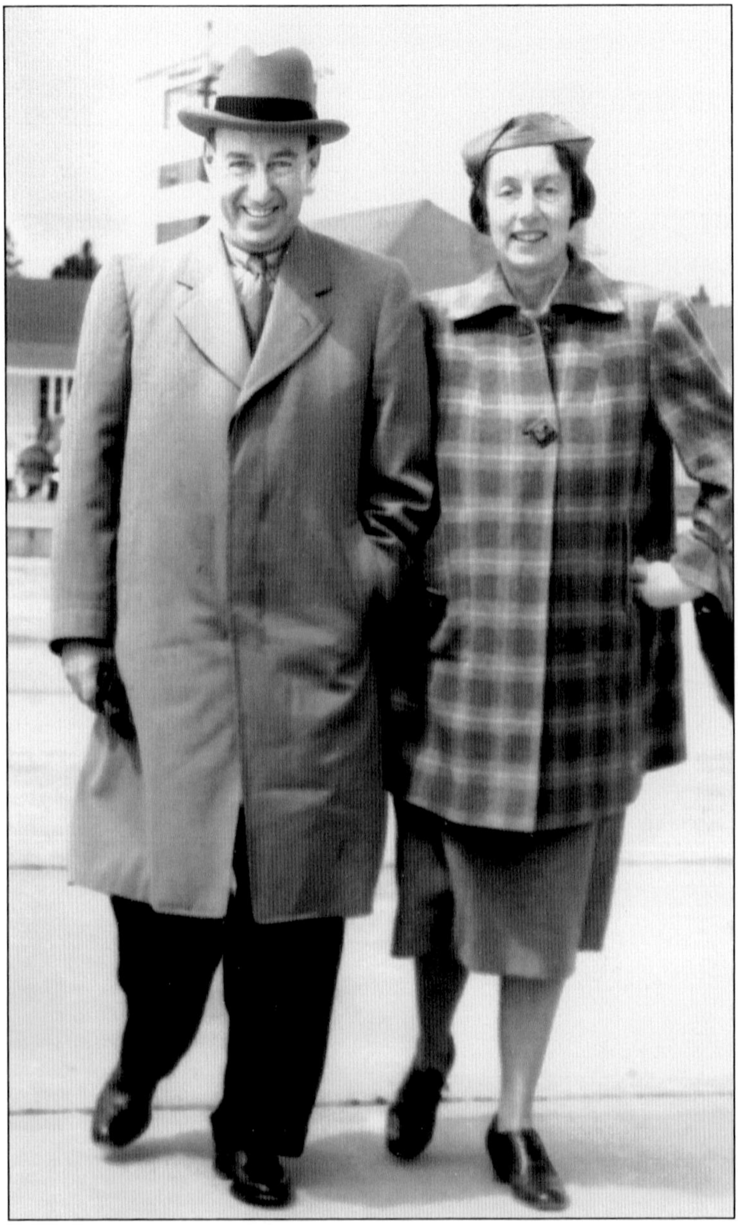

Pictured here are Buffie Ives and her brother, Adlai Stevenson, in the fall of 1952 when Stevenson was running for President of the United States against Republican candidate Gen. Dwight D. Eisenhower. Adlai Stevenson was the governor of Illinois and a frequent visitor to his sister's restored Paint Hill Farm home outside Southern Pines in the 1940s and 1950s. Mrs. Ives and her husband, Ernest, were winter residents for years. According to an article from *The Raleigh News and Observer*, Elizabeth Ives's cousin was Alben Barkley, Vice President of the United States in 1949. The Iveses brought pre–Civil War structures from Jackson Springs and a cotton gin near Mt. Gilead to Paint Hill Farm. In 1939, Mrs. Ives became interested in historic restoration in North Carolina. The name "Paint Hill," as the story goes, came from rocks where Native Americans would take red powder to paint their bodies. Mrs. Ives lived until the 1990s at Paint Hill.

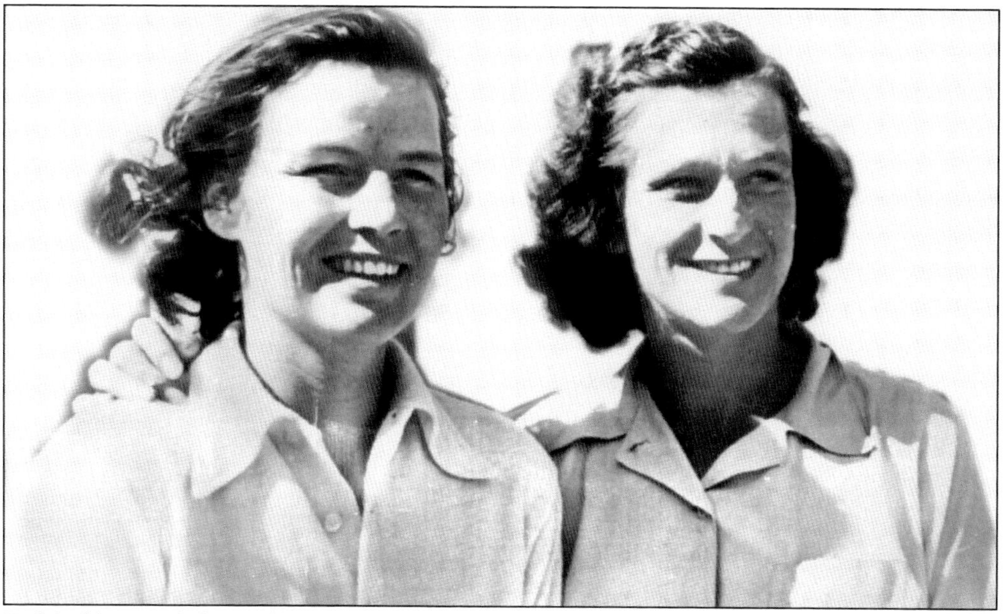

Titleholders in ladies golf, Peggy Kirk Bell (left) and Babe Didriksen Zaharias, stars of the 1950s, pose together in one of many publicity photos probably taken in Southern Pines at Pine Needles golf resort. Bell and her husband, Warren, purchased the resort, and it is still family-owned and operated. Mrs. Bell is currently active in international and national golf events and owns the sister resort, Mid Pines.

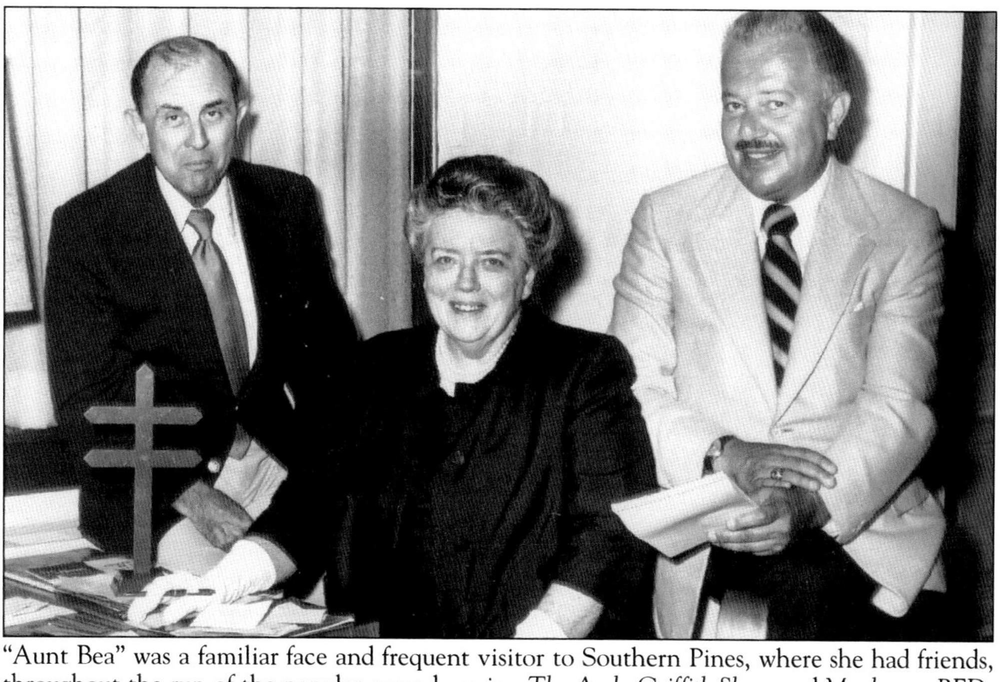

"Aunt Bea" was a familiar face and frequent visitor to Southern Pines, where she had friends, throughout the run of the popular comedy series, *The Andy Griffith Show* and *Mayberry, RFD*. She resided in Pittsboro in nearby Chatham County. Few could recall the actress's real name although everyone could recognize her face. Dr. Alfred Siege, director of the Moore County Health Department, is on the right.

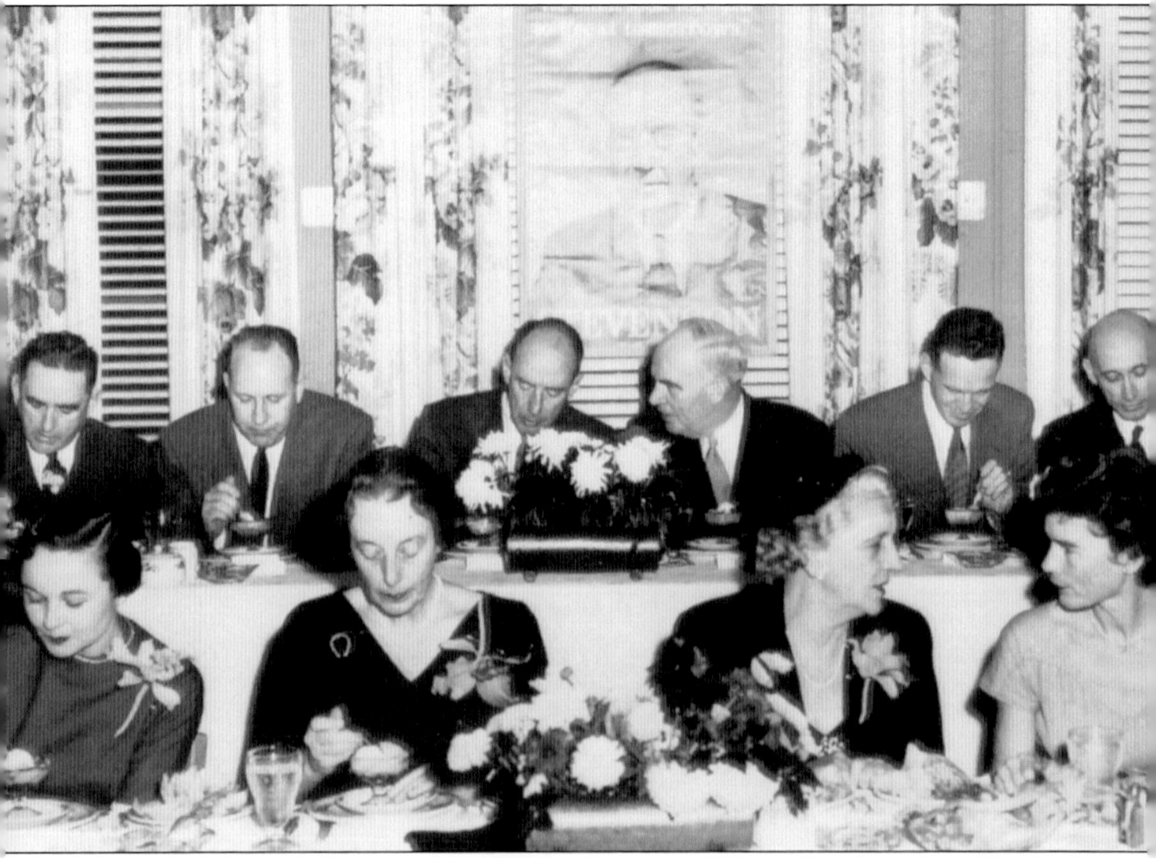

Presidential politics have arrived in Southern Pines in 1952 with Democratic candidate Adlai Stevenson (third from left in the back row), who is attending a fund-raising banquet, no doubt enthusiastically promoted and sponsored by his sister, Buffie Ives (front row, second from left). In the picture, Stevenson confers with his dinner partner, North Carolina governor Luther Hodges, also a Democrat. Stevenson, the governor of Illinois, did not win the election but did go on to serve as America's ambassador to the United Nations before his death in the 1960s. Mrs. Ives was a powerhouse: she helped to beautify her adopted town, she assisted Audrey Kennedy in forming a branch of the American Red Cross, and she helped form the Moore County Historical Society, which is still active as the Moore County Historical Association.

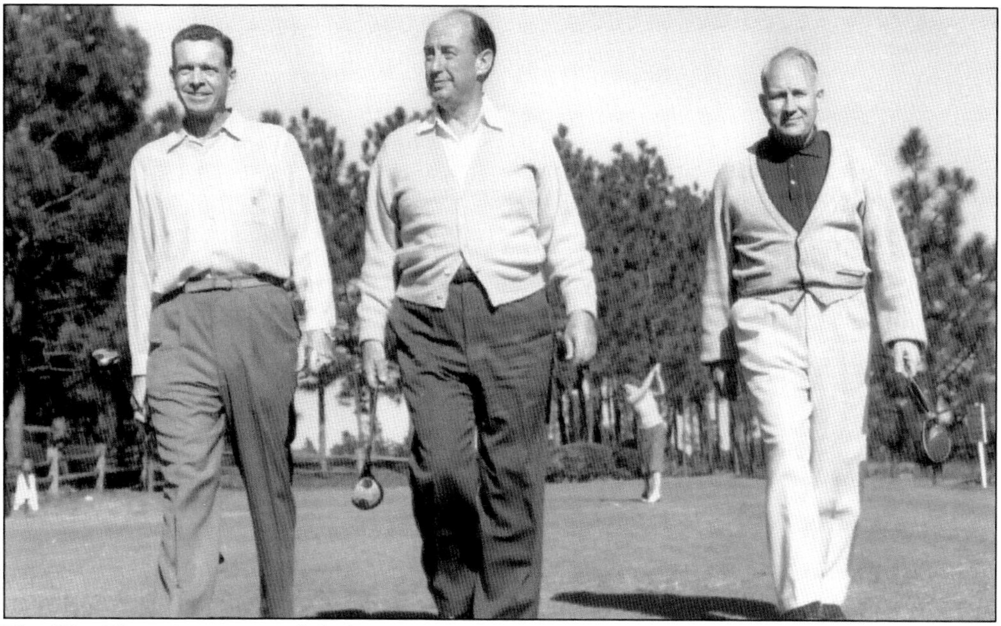

The "Big Three" movers and shakers enjoy a game of golf one afternoon in the 1950s. Pictured at left is Voit Gilmore, a prominent businessman who led the way in peacefully integrating downtown movie houses and restaurants when segregation was declared illegal by the high courts. Gilmore was eventually elected as a state senator. Adlai Stevenson is pictured center, flanked on the right by Lamont Brown, town attorney for Southern Pines.

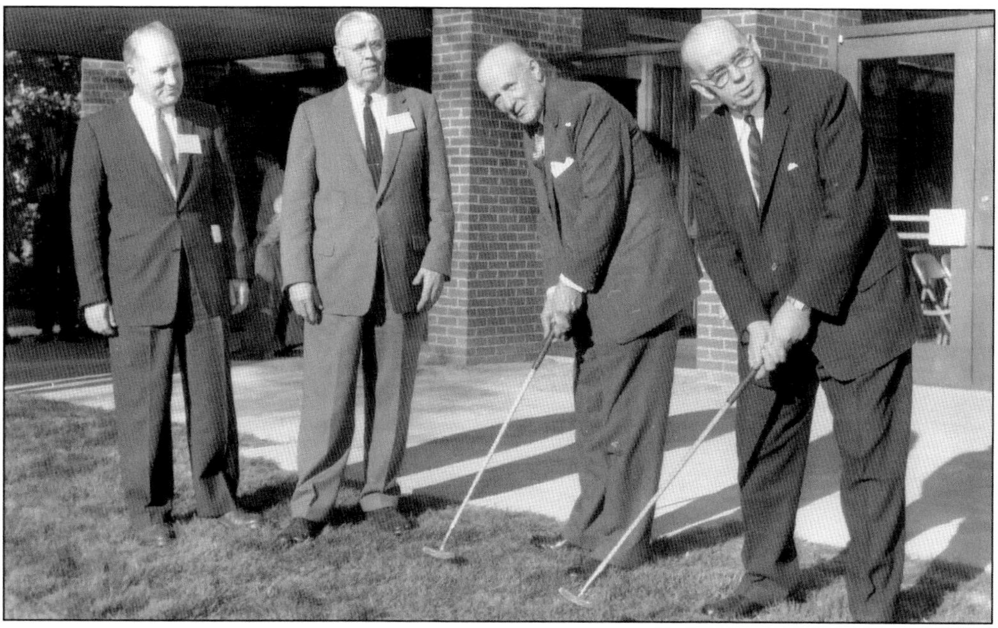

In 1958, Southern Pines municipal services moved from a former residence into a new, modern building on Broad Street, where it remains today. Town attorney Lamont Brown (left) helps dedicate the new town hall with Southern Pines mayor Walter E. Blue. Demonstrating the town's major status are special guests Carolina Power & Light Company CEO Louis V. Sutton and State Treasurer Edwin Gill (right).

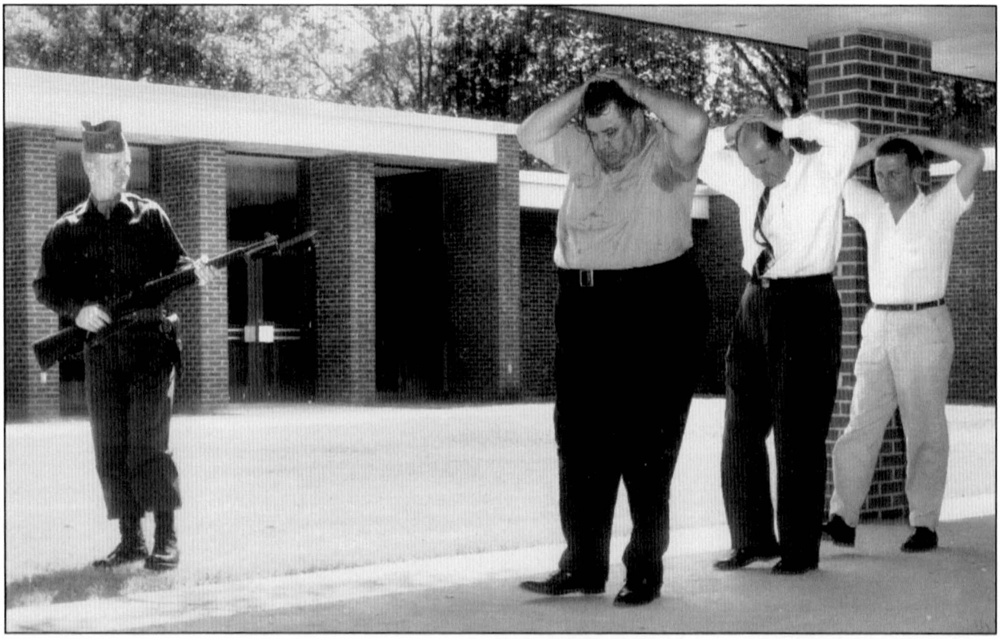

War games are conducted at the new town building not long after it was finished. Fort Bragg sent over its finest soldiers to "occupy" Southern Pines, with the cooperation of the town government, of course. Here, a soldier escorts Police Chief Ed Newton, Mayor Bob Ewing, and Town Manager Louis Scheipers into custody. Newton was a descendant of the original Shaw family, whose property eventually became Southern Pines.

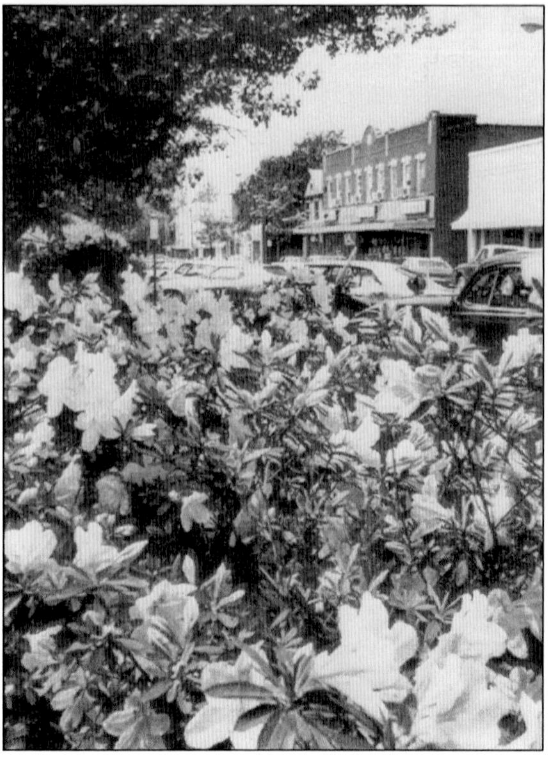

The Southern Pines Garden Club, the oldest of several active clubs in the area, was the result of Helen Boyd Dull's efforts at beautification in the early 1900s. The club was organized in 1947 by a group that included Mrs. Robert McMillan, Mrs. Leon Seymour, and Mrs. W.D. Campbell. In 1948, the club held its first house and garden tour. The tour, which continues to be held every April, draws visitors from all over the state and several bordering ones, as well.

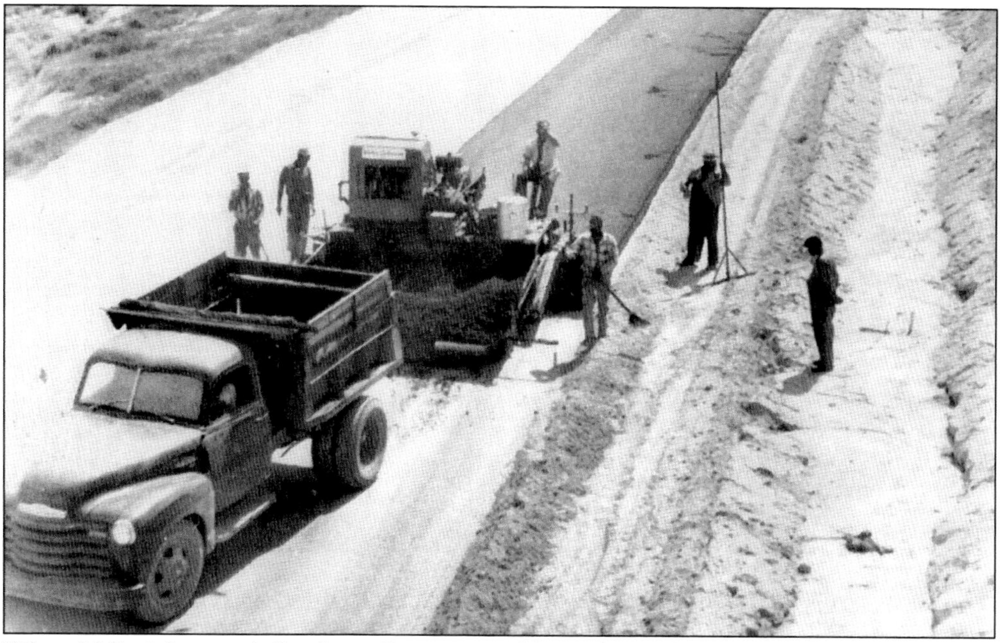

When U.S. 1 bypassed Southern Pines in 1955, it changed traffic patterns, fostered the growth of shopping centers, and created a physical racial divide between East and West Southern Pines. The streets previously connecting the east and west sides of town became overpasses and bridges.

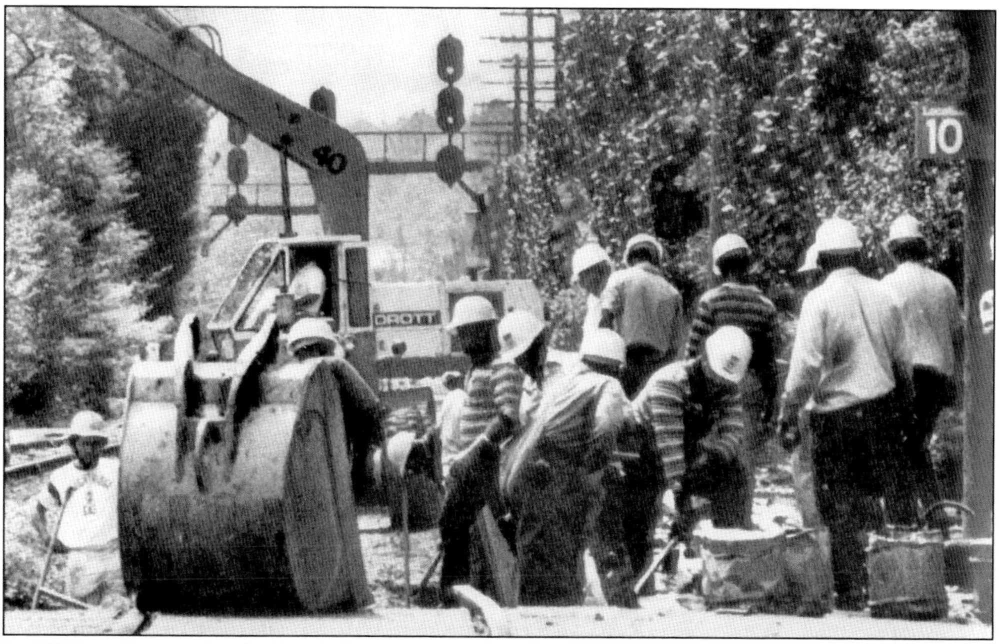

In 1955, railway officials decided to remove the ornamental vegetation alongside the railroad tracks in Southern Pines. Evelyn Rhodes, a member of the Southern Pines Garden Club, is said to have flung herself between the workers and the trees. Today, the rescued plants and evergreens remain amid magnolias, azaleas, camellias, dogwoods, and daffodils. The greenery blocks the view of the tracks from the passersby.

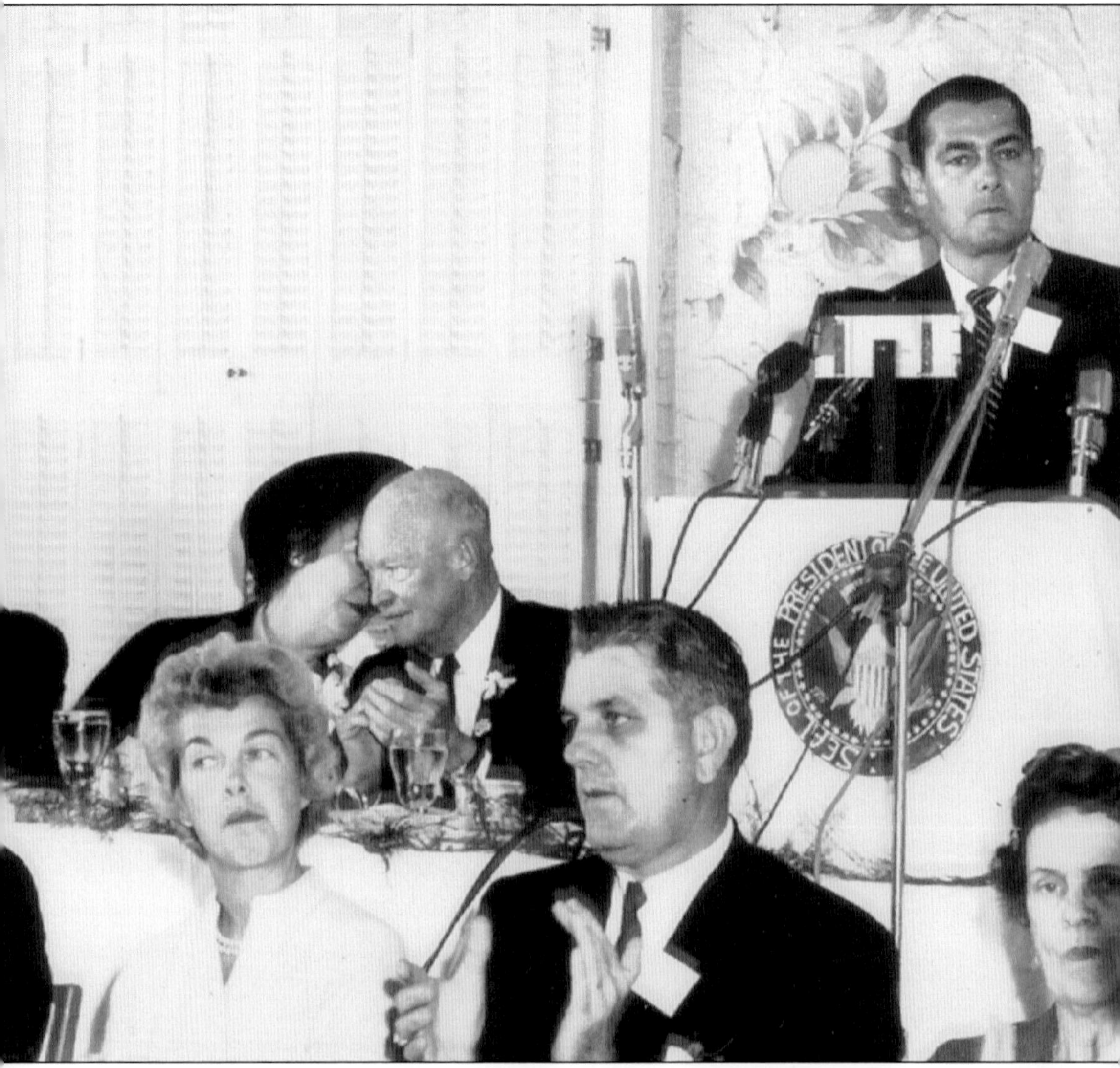

A GOP banquet in the 1950s for a Republican candidate for U.S. Congress has drawn Republican President Dwight D. Eisenhower. "Ike," who beat Adlai Stevenson in 1952 and was re-elected in 1956, sits to the left of the speaker's podium while a woman who might be First Lady Mamie Eisenhower whispers in his ear. Southern Pines resident and dentist Bruce Warlick emceed the party rally to elect Charles Jonas to Congress. In those days, Moore County was ruled by the Democrats, although a small Republican contingent worked stalwartly for their candidates, who almost always lost a partisan election in Moore County. Many years after this picture was taken, North Carolina elected its first Republican governor since Reconstruction. James Holshouser Jr., who took office in the early 1970s, served for a time as Moore County attorney, and is now a resident of Southern Pines.

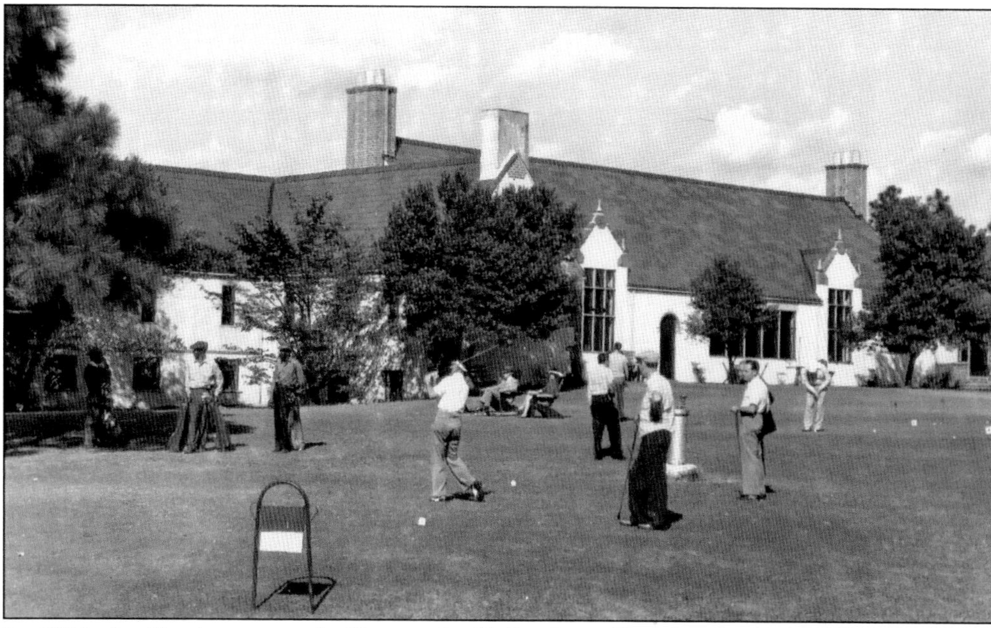

In 1909, the Boyds supported efforts to build Southern Pines's very first golf course, in the Weymouth Heights area. The first clubhouse was in an old dwelling, but in 1912, a new one was built around it. The old house was then used as the kitchen. The third and longest-lasting was the 1924 vintage Southern Pines Country Clubhouse, visible in the background of these players. This structure burned down in 1969. It was replaced by a modern clubhouse with a pool.

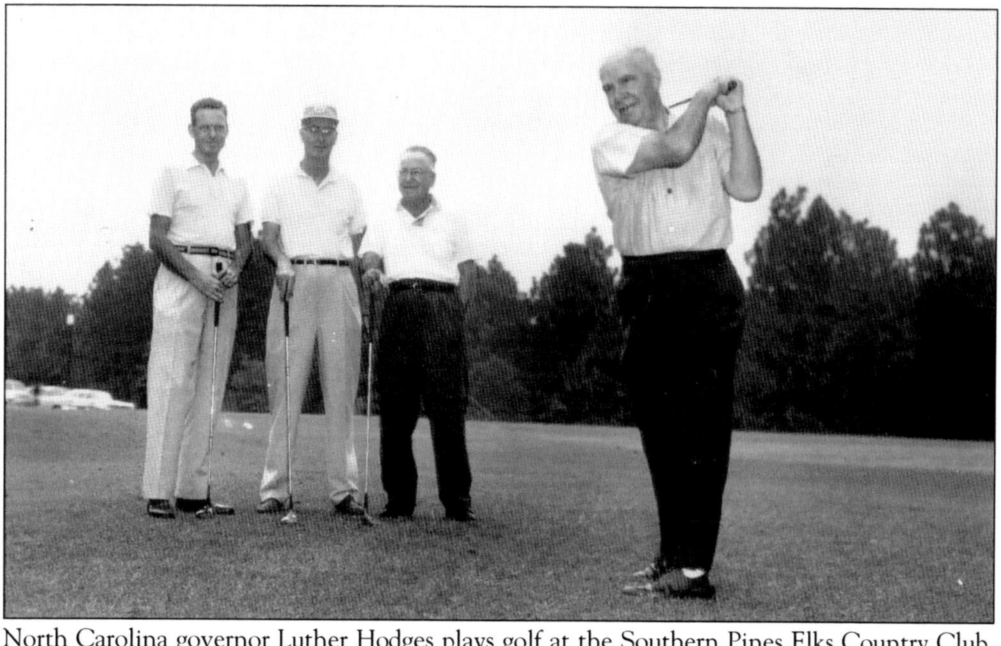

North Carolina governor Luther Hodges plays golf at the Southern Pines Elks Country Club, where he was a frequent visitor during his term in the early 1950s. Voit Gilmore looks on from the left, with A.C. Dawson, a Southern Pines City School superintendent, and William P. Saunders. The course was originally designed by Donald Ross, who is best known for designing the No. 2 course in nearby Pinehurst.

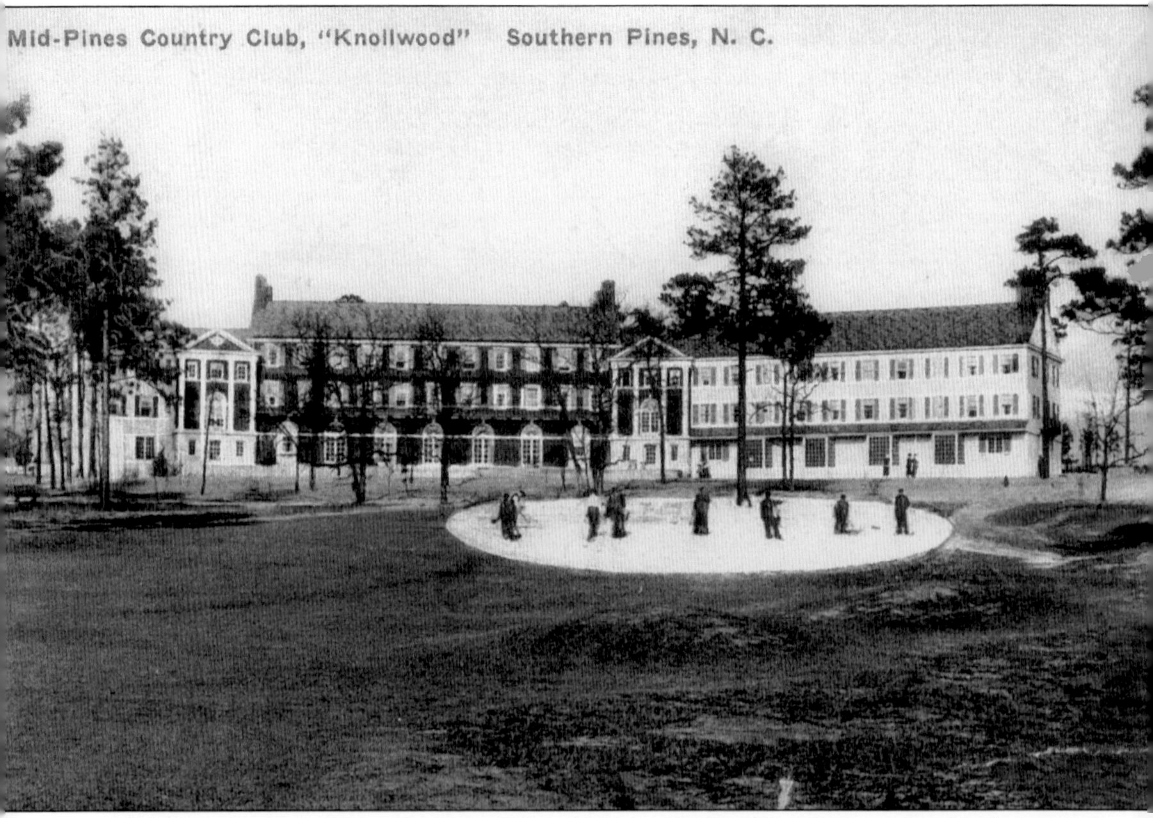

Mid Pines Country Club, which opened in 1921 on Midland Road, was originally designed as a private club, social center, and principal attraction of Knollwood, a new development on the northwest side of Southern Pines that competed with Weymouth Heights to attract the affluent to its beautiful estates. Investors in Knollwood included Leonard Tufts, the son of Pinehurst's founder, and Donald Ross, the famous golf course designer. Aymar Embury II of New York and A.B. Yeomans of Chicago put their stamps on the development, featuring winding, park-like lanes along which homes were to be built. They patterned it after a historic Virginia estate. Embury designed the Mid Pines clubhouse, and Ross designed the golf course. During the Depression, Mid Pines lost its status as a private club and, like other resort hotels, was taken over by the military in World War II. In post-war times, Mid Pines made a stunning recovery.

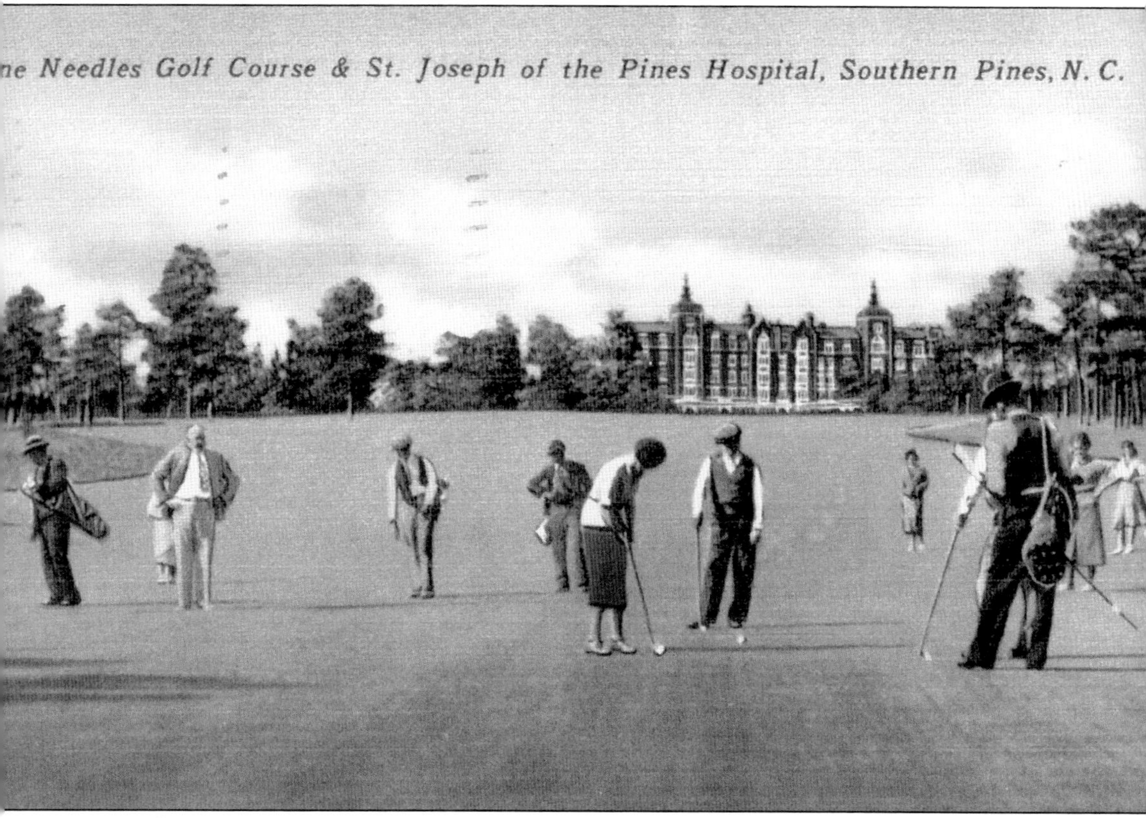

Pine Needles Inn opened in 1928 just across Midland Road from Mid Pines. Its course, too, was designed by Donald Ross. For a short time, it was the hot spot for prominent visitors to lodge, but it fell on hard times. Early in 1942, the Air Force Technical Training Command took over Knollwood Airport, Pine Needles, and Mid Pines. Equestrian events continued to be popular for a time during the Depression, but they, too, came to a halt with World War II. After the war, the inn was sold to the Catholic Diocese of North Carolina and opened in 1948 as St. Joseph of the Pines Hospital. In 1953, Warren and Peggy Kirk Bell bought the golf course at Pine Needles in partnership with Julius Boros, Mr. and Mrs. Frank Cosgrove, and their daughter, Jean, who owned Mid Pines. Boros, at the peak of his PGA career, was the Mid Pines touring pro during the 1950s. In 1955, the Bells bought out their partners for Pine Needles. A new lodge and clubhouse was built to a more modern taste.

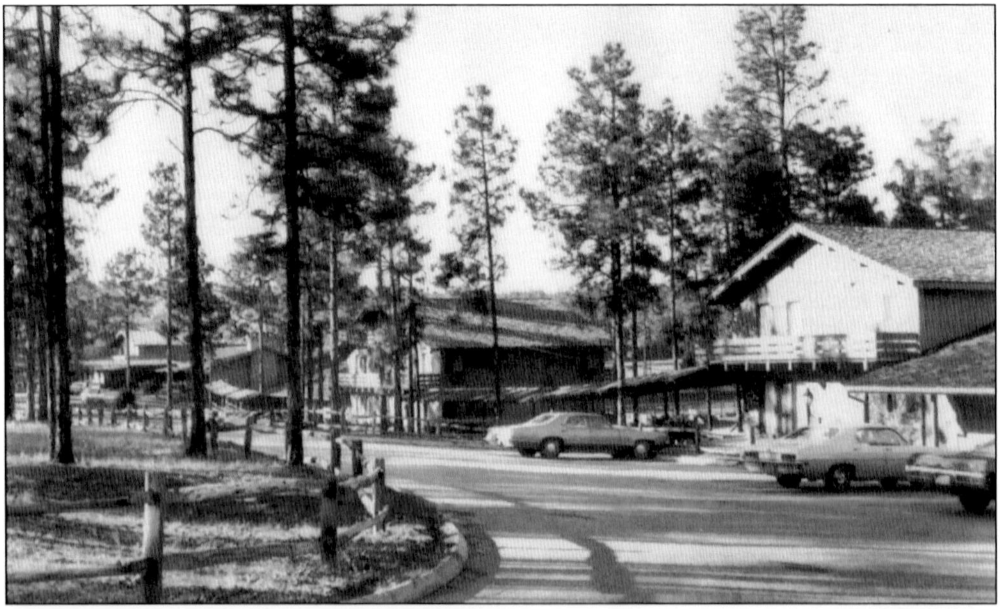

The new Pine Needles Lodge and Golf Club began to take its present form in 1957, when the Bells built the first of several chalet-style lodges, designed and managed by Warren Bell. Bell always insisted on keeping the Lodges and Country Club, as it was called then, small and catering exclusively to golfers. Since Warren Bell's death, Peggy Kirk has operated both Pine Needles and Mid Pines, which she acquired in the 1990s. They regularly host prestigious tournaments.

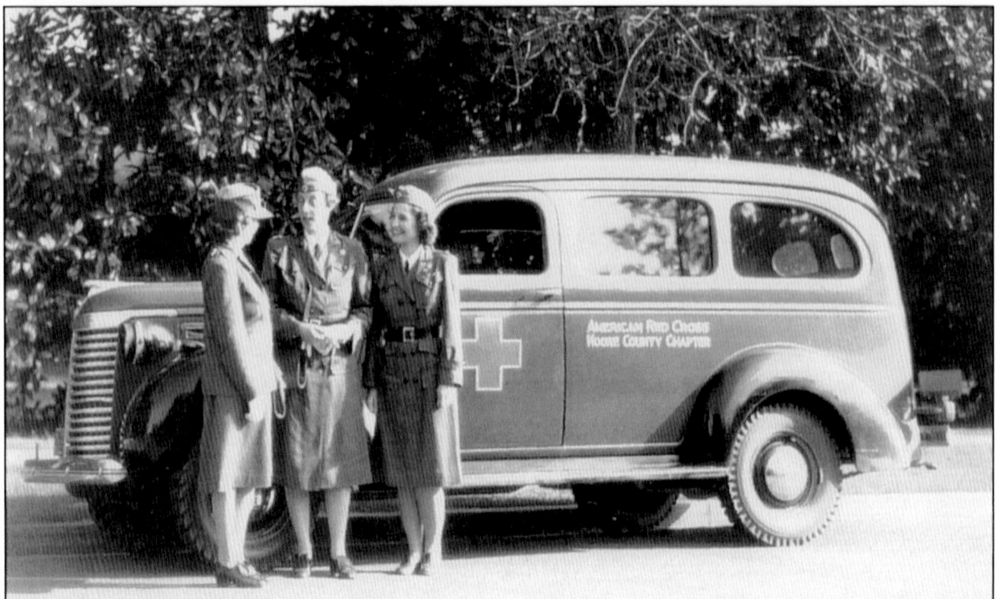

Society leaders Audrey Kennedy (left), Elizabeth Ives (center), and Barbara Betterly (right) led the Moore County Chapter of the American Red Cross. As the town grew, they anticipated the need for disaster relief. The Red Cross is just one of several volunteer organizations that Kennedy and Ives organized for Southern Pines and the surrounding area.

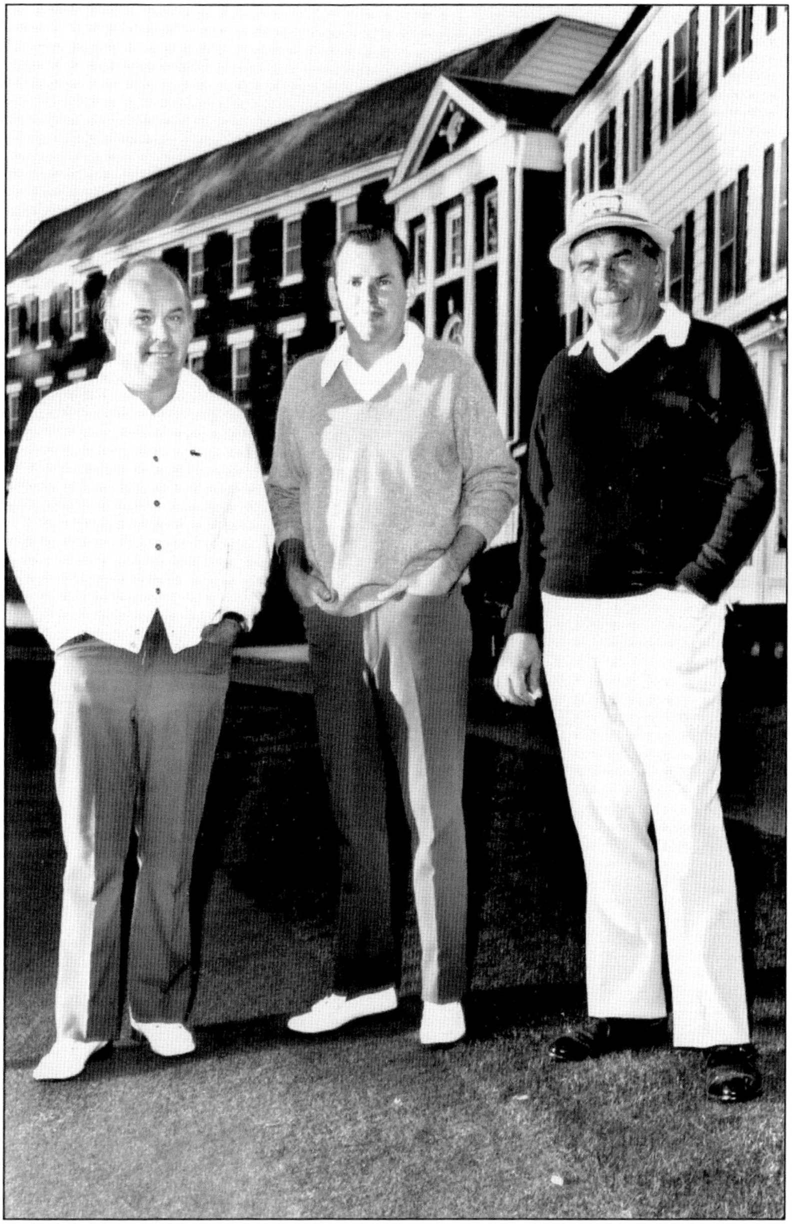

Three of the Boros men enjoy a warm day in front of the famed Mid Pines Country Club after World War II, when the club came into a new, prosperous era under Frank Cosgrove's family ownership. Pictured from left to right are Ernie Boros, his cousin Jim Boros, and golf pro Julius Boros, Ernie's brother. Under the Cosgroves, Mid Pines was known for many years for its warmth and family atmosphere. They knew the hotel business and assembled a good, loyal staff. Guests came back year after year and still do. Frank Cosgrove's daughter, Jean Cosgrove Stevenson, became the social director and carried on the tradition when Mid Pines changed hands and, for a time, came under the ownership of Quality Inns. Quality Inns did not keep it permanently. Mid Pines, purchased by Peggy Kirk Bell, paired with Pine Needles; the two resorts became the twin jewels in the golf resort crowns decorating the Southern Pines end of Midland Road.

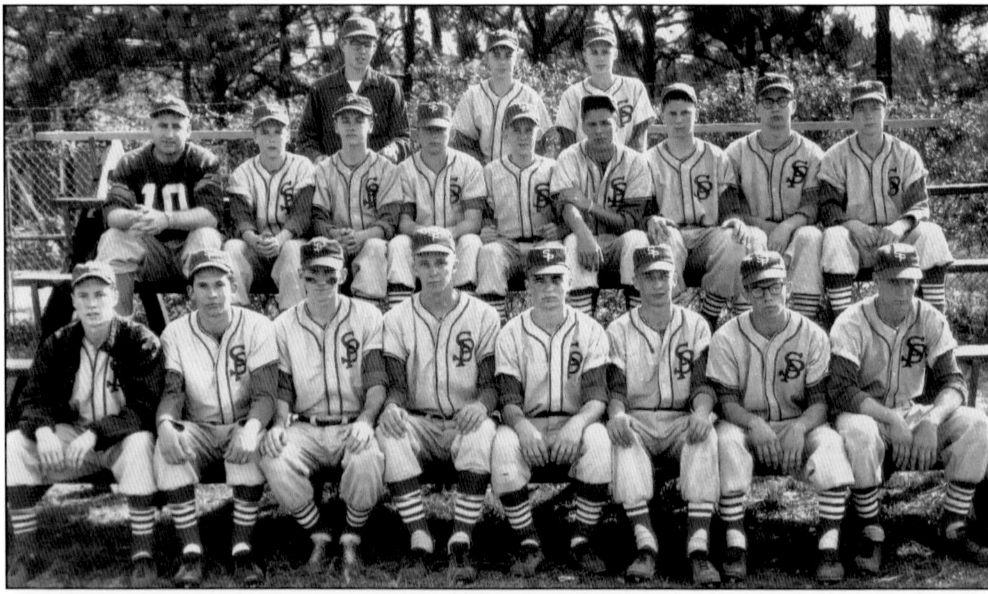

The East Southern Pines High School boys baseball team in 1959 is spirited, suited up, and ready for action. At the time of this photo, the high school had five years before the all-white city system would be consolidated and then racially integrated into a county-wide public system.

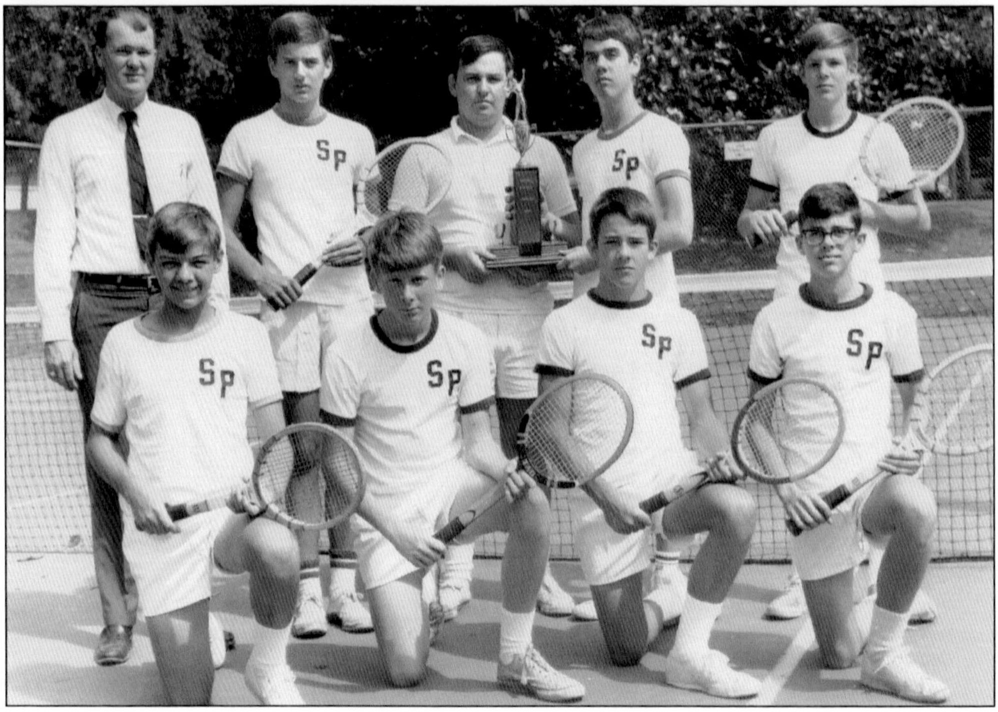

Tennis is a major sport in Southern Pines. This East Southern Pines High School boys tennis team, coached by Vernon Crumpler, includes two future tennis pros: Tommy Thompson (back row, far right) and Rick Kobleur (front row, far left). Crumpler was one of several teachers and coaches who went to work for the new consolidated and integrated high school that opened several years later. Other team members are unidentified.

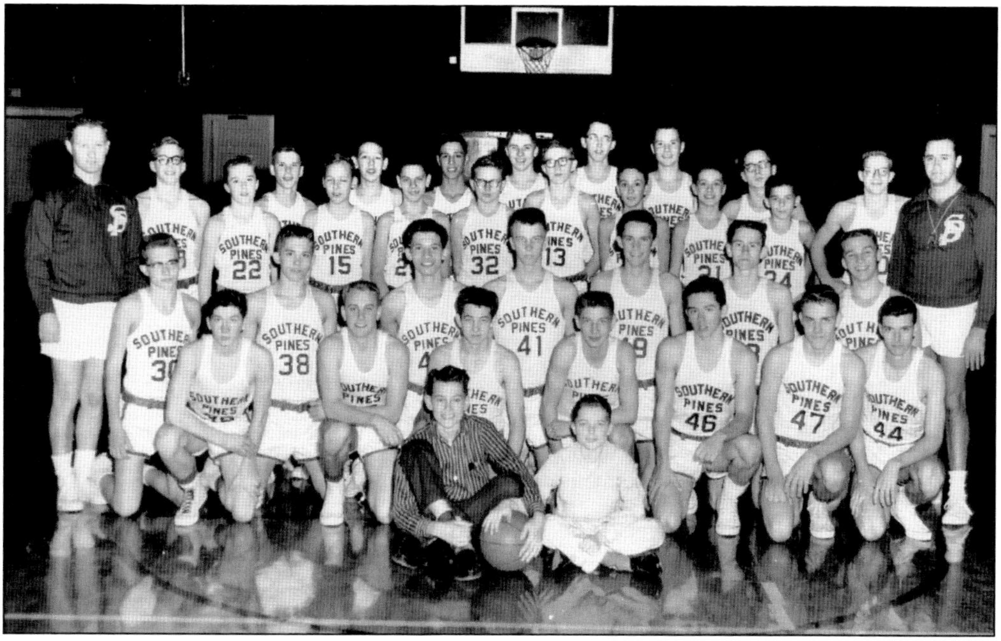

East Southern Pines boys basketball team members line up in 1958 for the formal shot. While the city schools were operating with their own school board, the teams were simply called Southern Pines. Later, when the high school moved to a new consolidated campus on the other side of town, middle school athletic teams called themselves the Blue Knights.

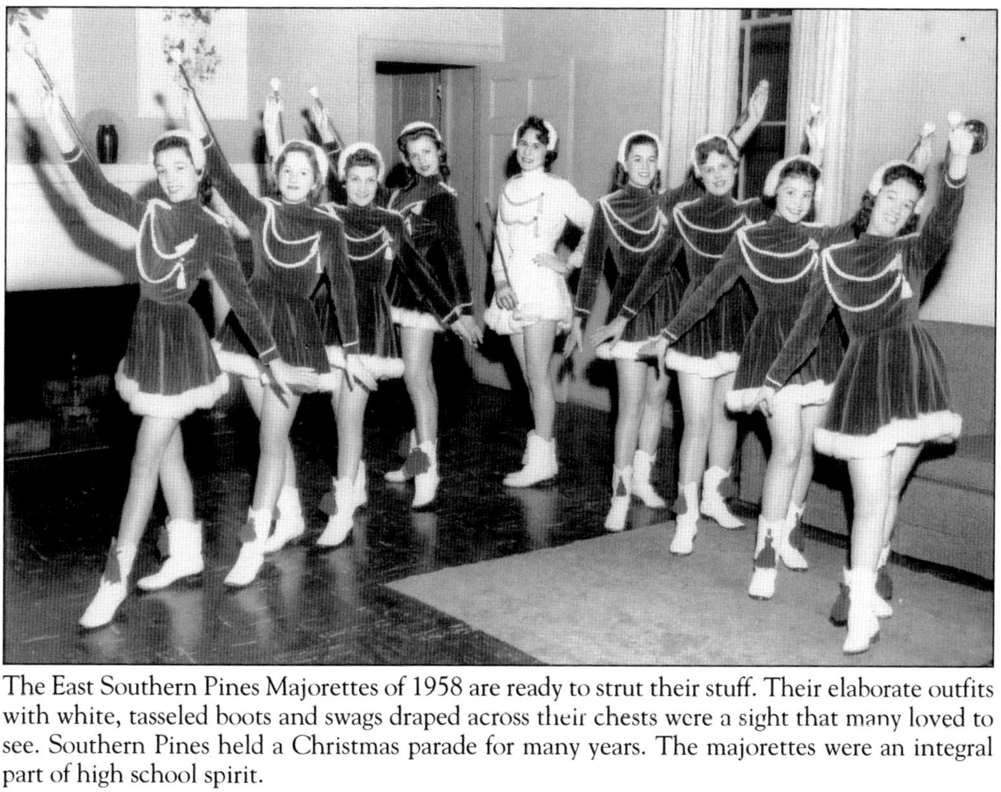

The East Southern Pines Majorettes of 1958 are ready to strut their stuff. Their elaborate outfits with white, tasseled boots and swags draped across their chests were a sight that many loved to see. Southern Pines held a Christmas parade for many years. The majorettes were an integral part of high school spirit.

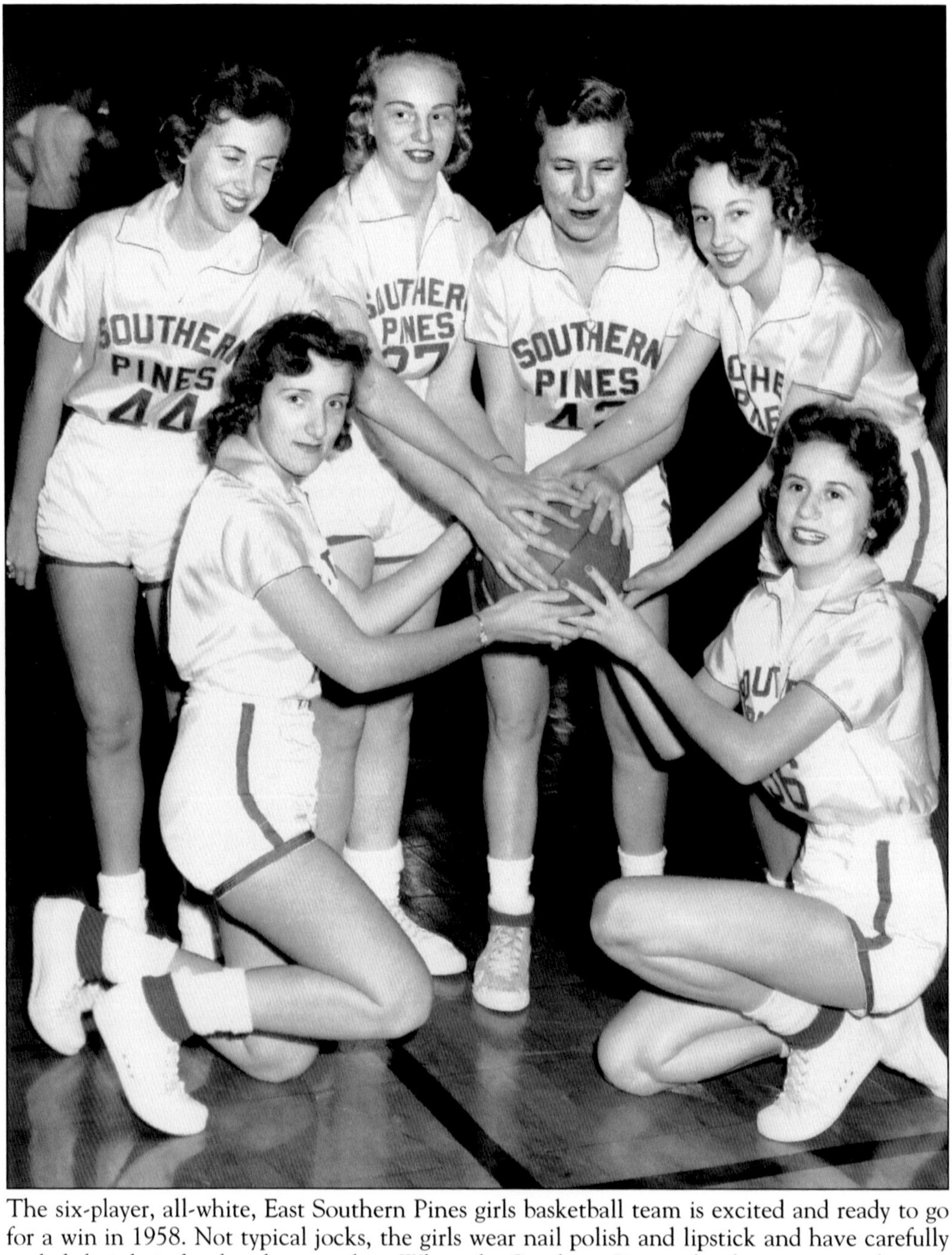

The six-player, all-white, East Southern Pines girls basketball team is excited and ready to go for a win in 1958. Not typical jocks, the girls wear nail polish and lipstick and have carefully curled their hair for the photographer. When the Southern Pines schools were merged into a county-wide public system, a consolidated, racially-integrated high school serving Southern Pines, Pinehurst, Aberdeen, Pinebluff, and West End opened on U.S. 15-501, on the west side of Southern Pines. Pinecrest High School replaced seven separate high schools in southern Moore County. The new high school had a football team, basketball and tennis teams for both sexes, baseball, softball, and golf and soccer teams for both sexes. Students coming from different communities were reluctant at first to accept the "strangers" in the new student body, all of whom lived just a few miles away.

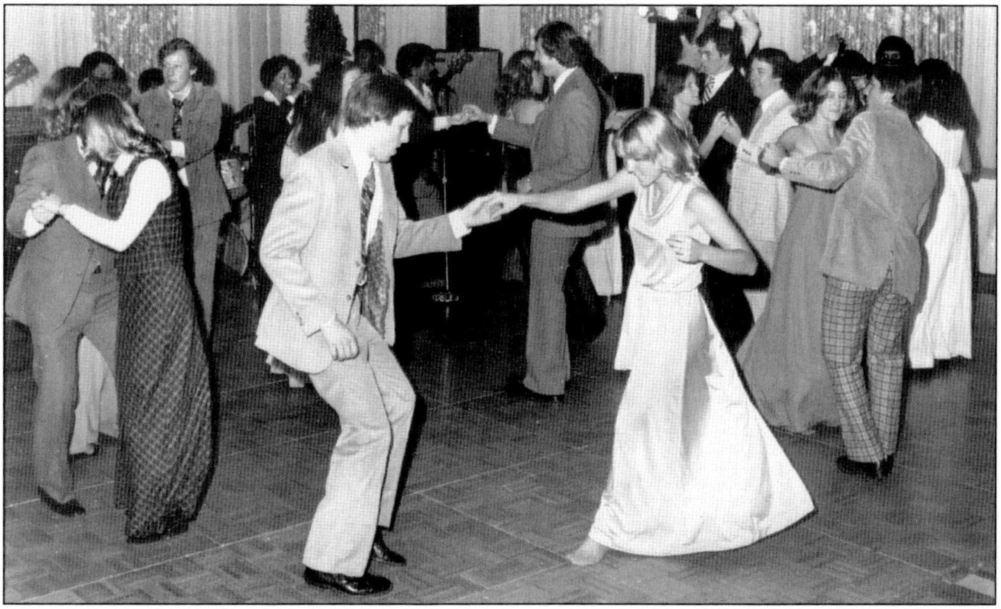

The last prom for these Southern Pines seniors marks the end of an era. Soon, high school classes will blend with other students from other, very different communities into a much larger, racially-integrated, consolidated high school named Pinecrest.

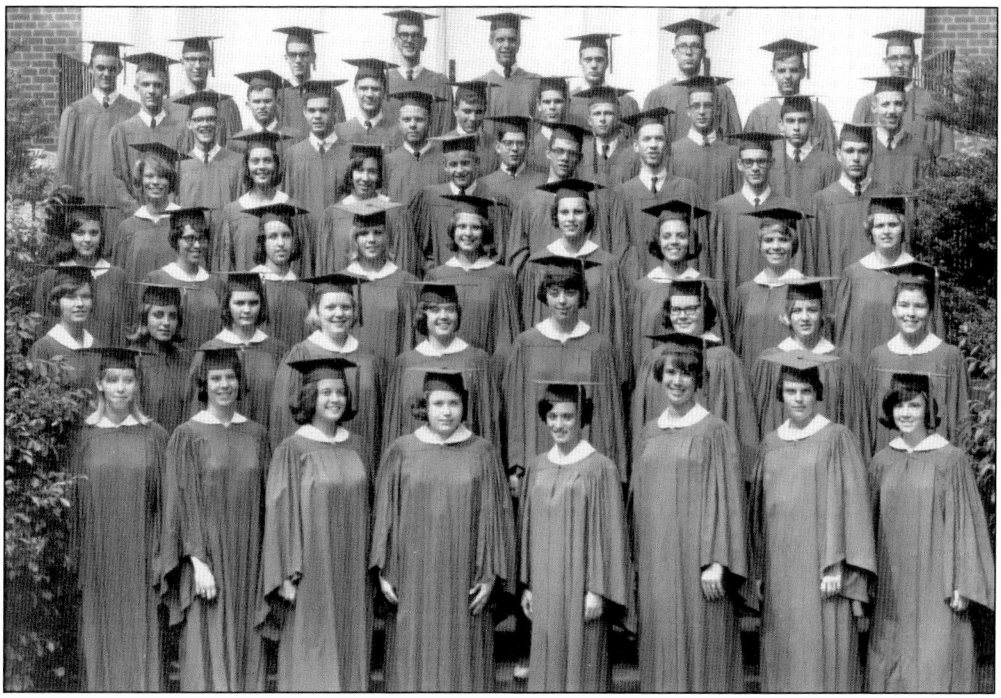

The 1965 graduating senior class from Southern Pines High School is happy to be getting on with life but probably feels some nostalgia. After all, this is the year city-county public school consolidation was decreed in Moore County. It would be several more years before a new consolidated high school was built and ready to open, replacing Southern Pines High and its just-under-60 senior class with a 1,700-student campus.

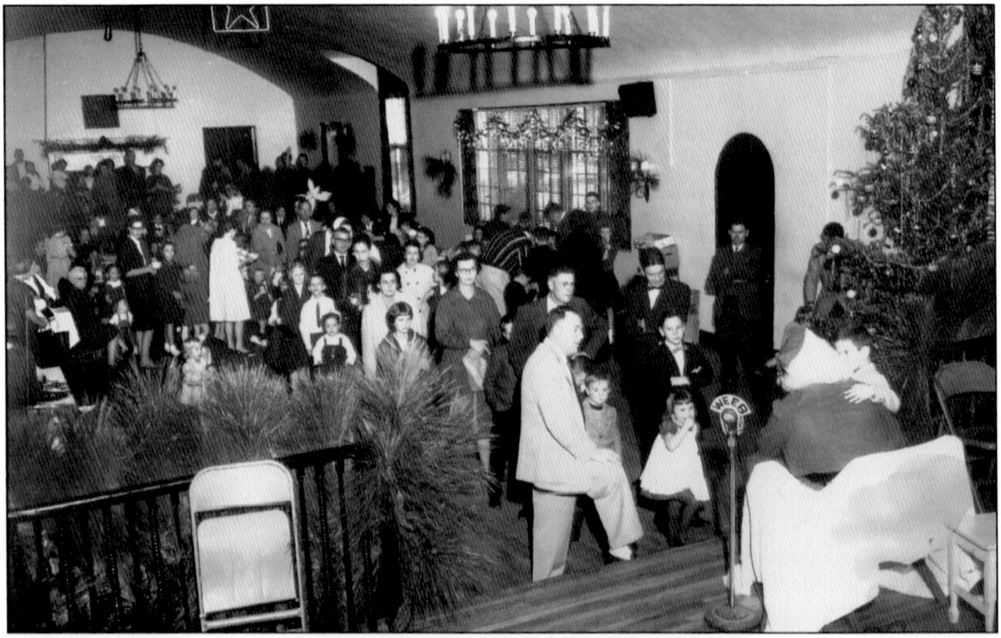

A Southern Pines tradition was the Christmas party in the old Southern Pines Country Club. Before the clubhouse burned in 1969, this yuletide was broadcast live by the town's one and only radio station of the day. Santa speaks directly into the WEEB microphone, as does his little visitor, who tells the whole listening audience whether he has been bad or good.

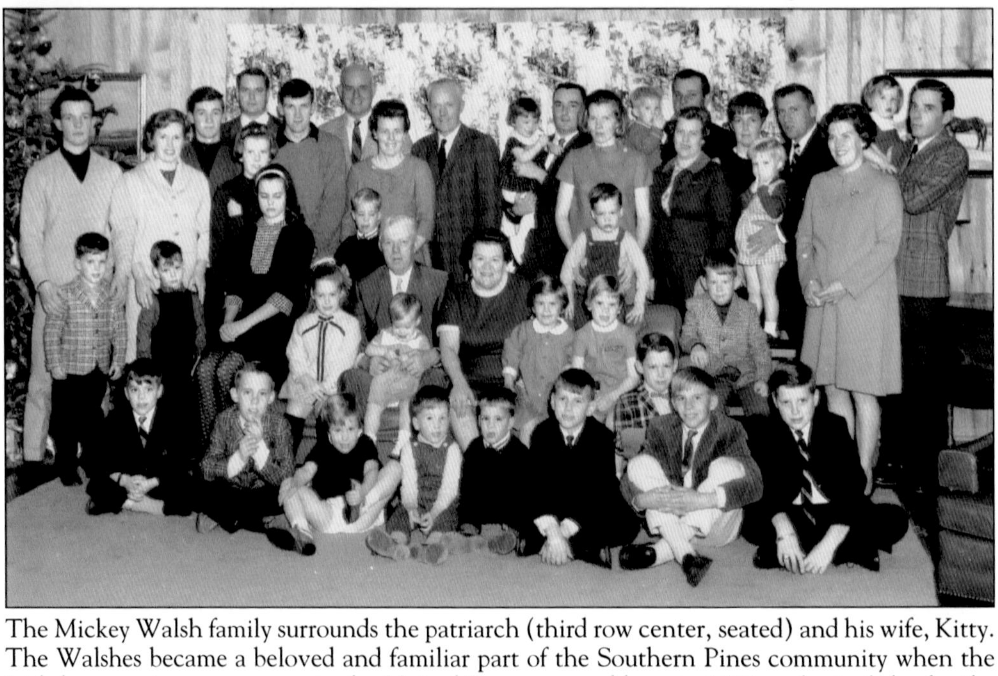

The Mickey Walsh family surrounds the patriarch (third row center, seated) and his wife, Kitty. The Walshes became a beloved and familiar part of the Southern Pines community when the Irish horse-trainer, a top one in the United States, moved here in 1941 and raised the family. He also brought greatness and fame to Southern Pines by establishing the 49-year Stoneybrook Steeplechase tradition, every April on a Saturday, rain or shine. It was dubbed by some as the biggest outdoor cocktail party in the world.

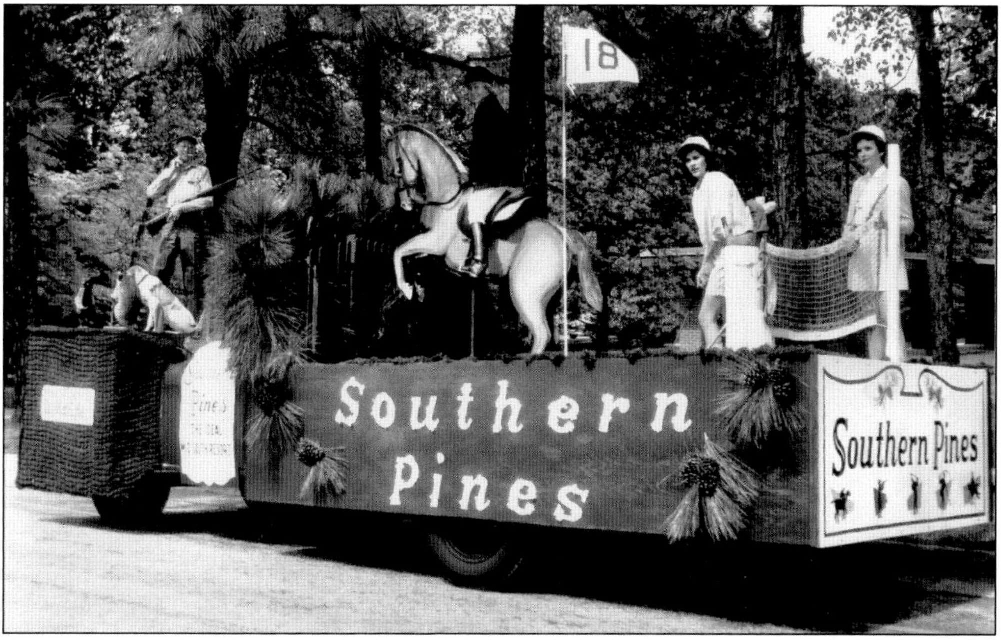

For many years, Southern Pines had a Christmas parade. This 1950s float captures all the attractions of the town touted as "the ideal Mid-South resort." At the far right, the hunter cradles his gun while smoking a cigarette with his hunting dog and stuffed raccoon at hand. The tableau is completed by a woman in a riding habit astride a leaping merry-go-round horse and girls posing with golf clubs and tennis racquet.

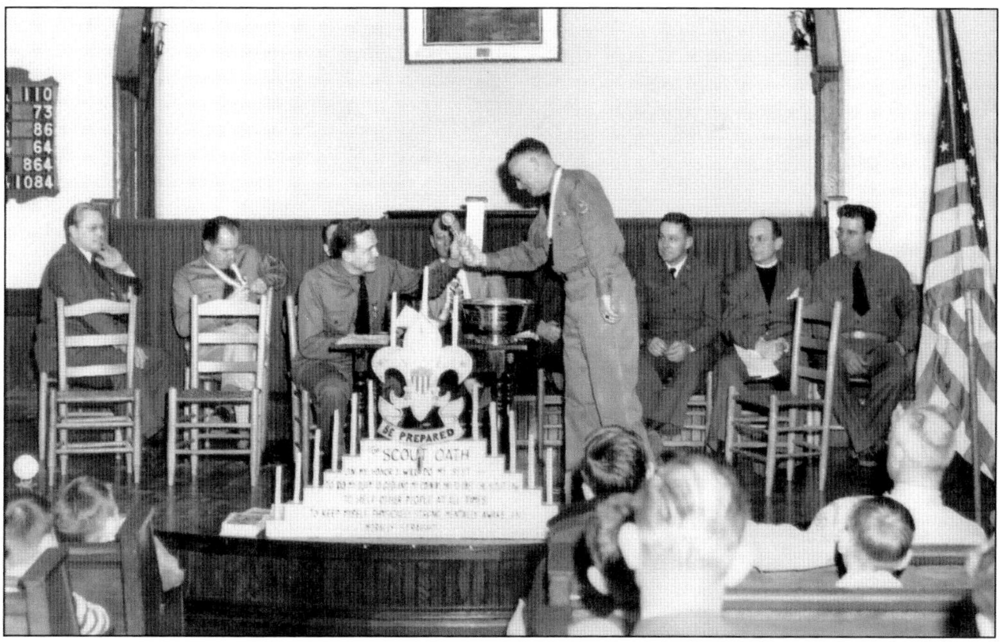

The Boy Scout Awards Ceremony is a big event in the lives of the boys, their families, and the scout leaders, showing that Southern Pines is not only a resort community but also a quiet, wholesome place to raise children. This ceremony is held in a church sanctuary, appropriate for a way of life that, for many, is sacred.

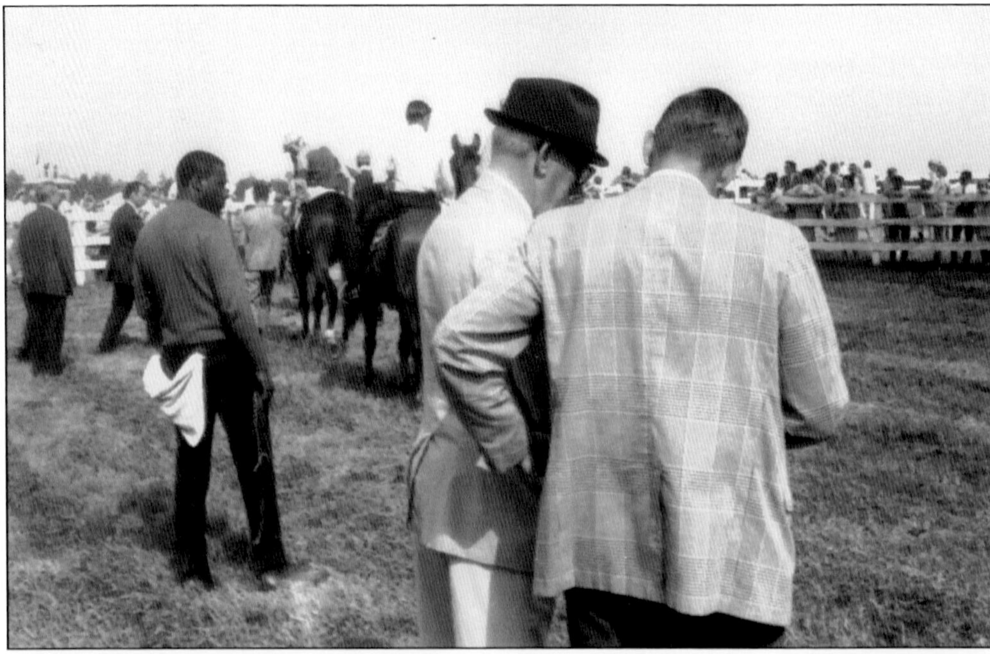

Raceway touts attending Stoneybrook Steeplechase for the horse racing check odds on this or that trainer and this or that horse. Betting is illegal in North Carolina as a form of gambling, but friendly informal bets make it more fun. Some betting is on who will buy the next drink, not for vast sums of money.

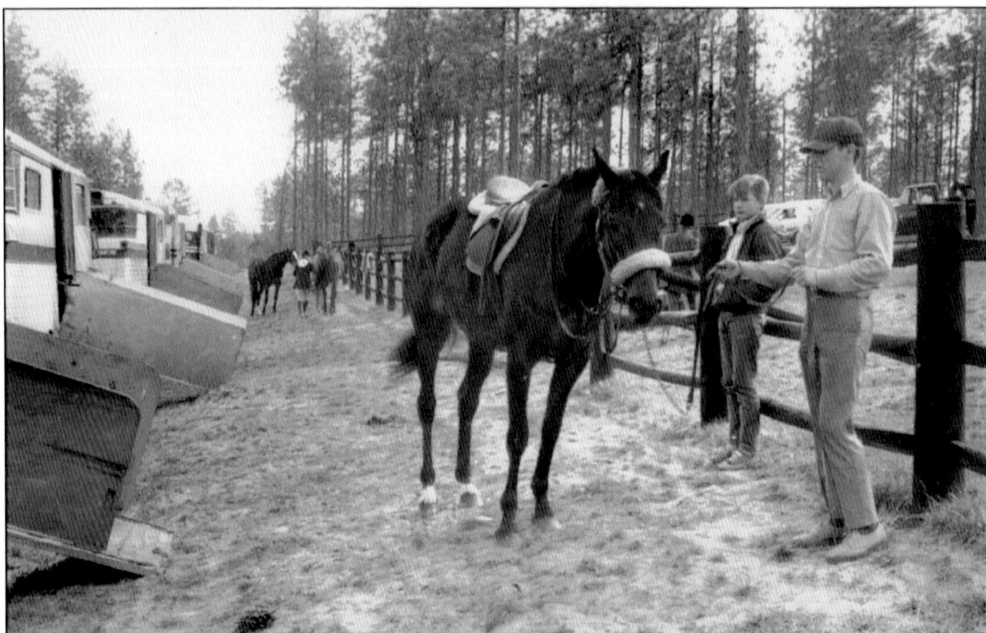

The horses line up, straight out of their trailers, getting ready for one of the Southern Pines area's frequent parades of equestrian field events, trials, and competitions. These events bring the thoroughbreds and their trainers to Horse Country every spring. They are en route to the North for late spring and summer events and competition.

Dooley Adams, a famous horse trainer in the international world of equestrian competition, leads a horse with its youthful jockey in front of spectators at one of the annual Stoneybrook Steeplechases. Adams's name is a legend; it comes up whenever the talk turns to horses. He still resides in Southern Pines.

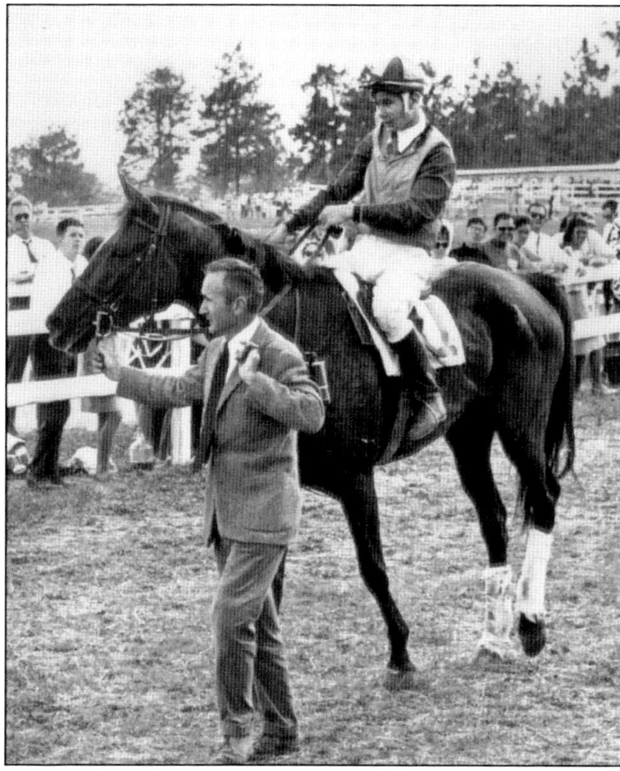

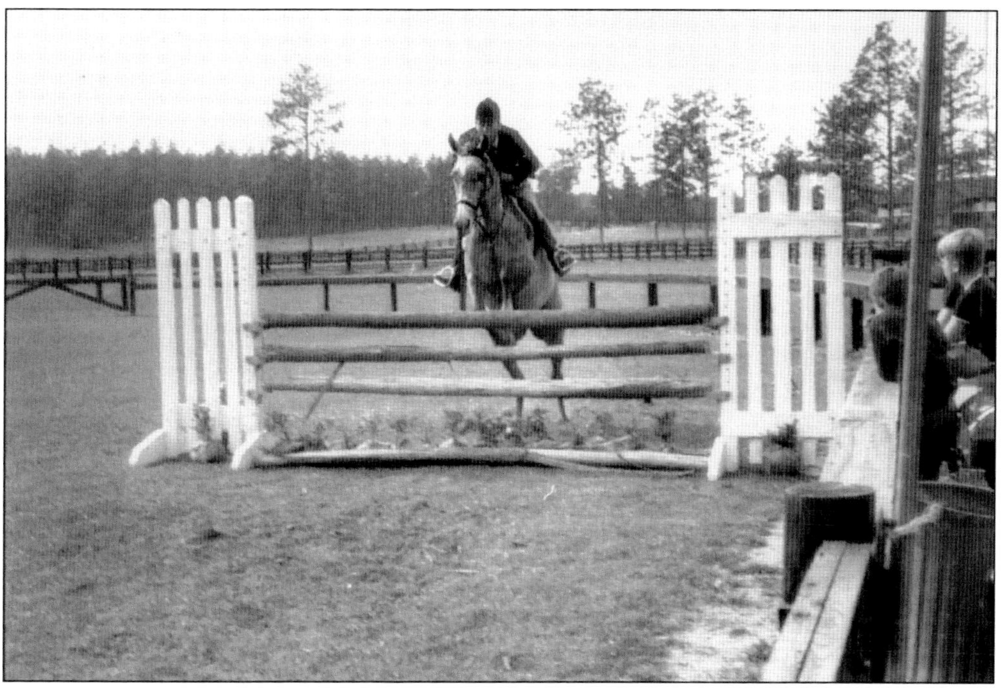

Stadium jumping is a big event in Southern Pines Horse Country. This more manicured form of horsemanship demonstrates the rider's control and handling of the horse, as well as the horse's quality of training, movement, and form.

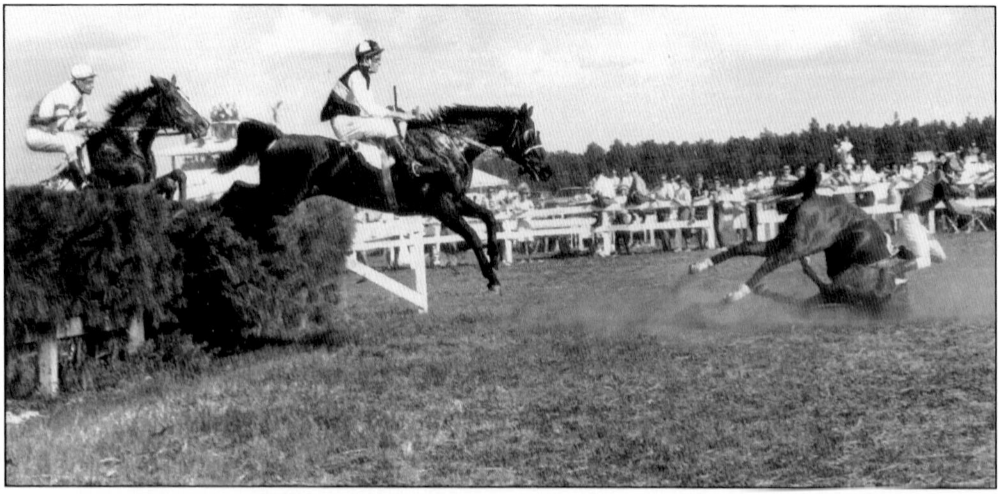

A spill for the horse and rider after leaping over the obstacle during the Stoneybrook Steeplechase makes that form of racing dangerous. A horse sometimes stumbles if he is off-balance making the jump in mid-gallop. Any number of other reasons could also cause such an accident. Sometimes the horse and rider get up to race again, but sometimes serious injury to the animal results in it being euthanized. A rider's life is full of falls.

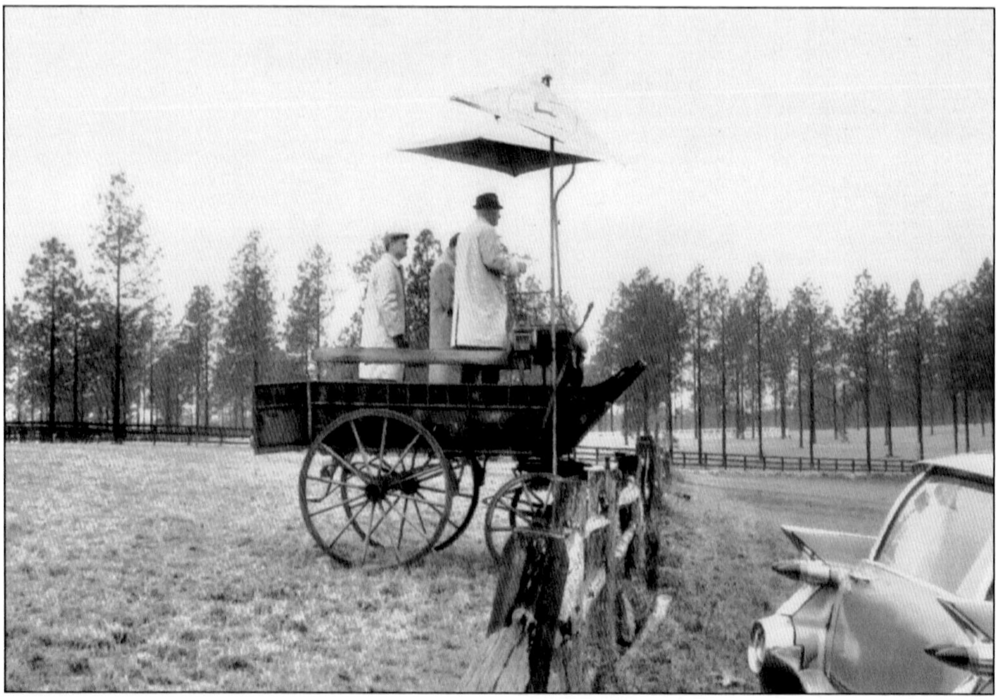

The judges of the hunter field trials in Southern Pines Horse Country have mounted their own "judges' stand," made out of an old wagon, so they can better view the action from far away over the distant fields. The trials are a cold weather, late winter event calling for warm clothes and tolerance for long hours in the rain, wind, and occasionally, sun.

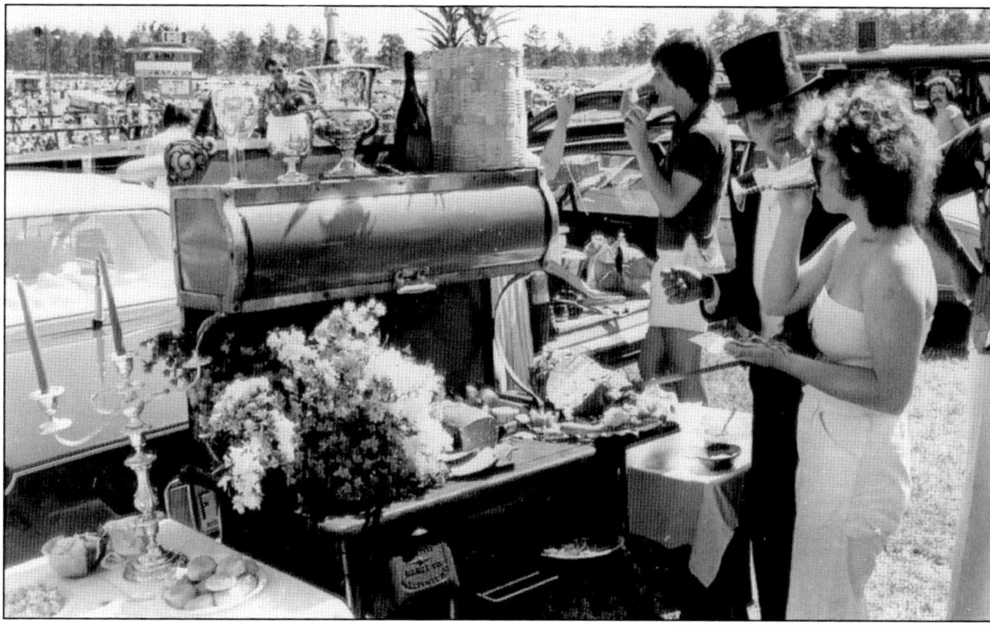

Stoneybrook race-goers sometimes go to just have a picnic, eat and drink, socialize, and only secondarily, watch the horse races. People like this couple sometimes bring elaborate get-ups to advertise a business, but even if it is more business than pleasure, they entertain the crowd almost as much as the horses do. At Stoneybrook it is not unusual to see someone like this man dressed in top hat and tails, enjoying champagne with a tailgate picnic, completed with candelabra.

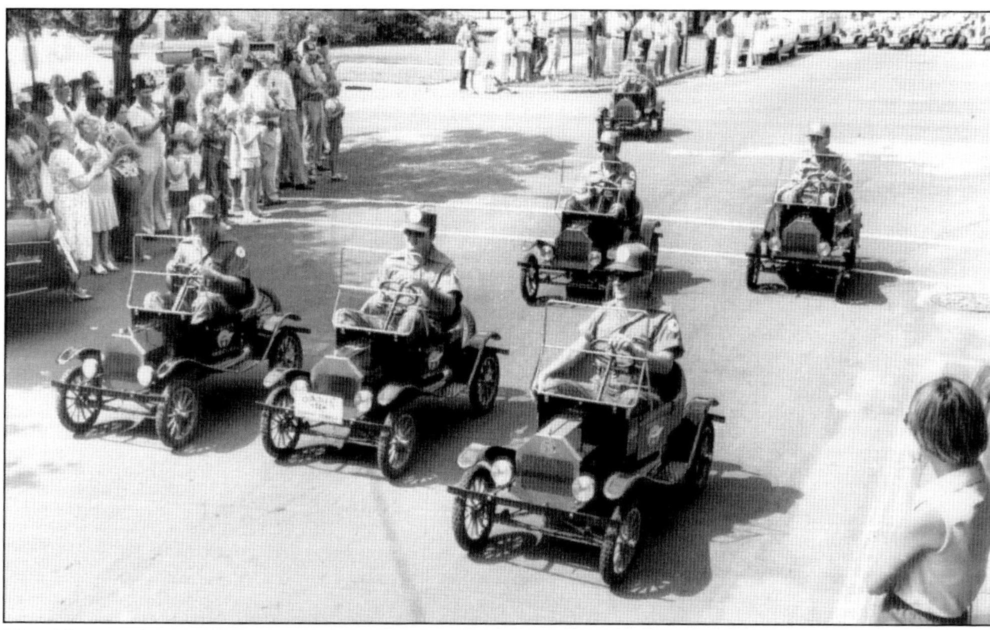

The Shriners's parade entertains many on the streets of Southern Pines. There is a parade for almost every occasion. Southern Pines's Broad Street has always been suitable for parades, because the one-way, double-laned streets on both sides of the railroad tracks are extra wide. These parading Shriners drive Model Ts that amuse an enthusiastic crowd.

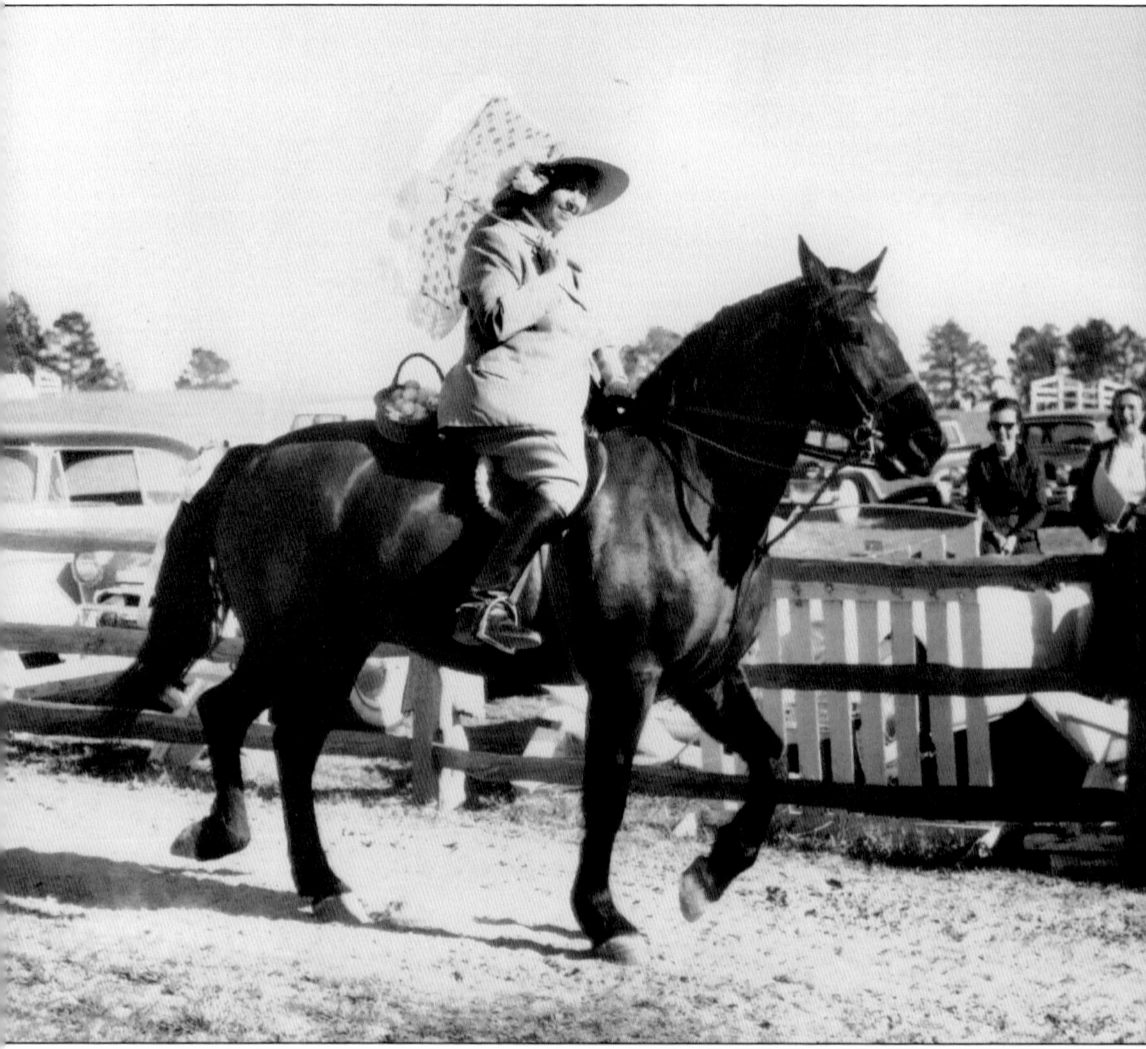

Just for fun, this jolly woman capers around Stoneybrook in the 1950s with a parasol and an Easter basket and hat to complement her riding habit. The rider is Betty Dumaine, a prominent lady who participated in many charities and was an accomplished horsewoman.

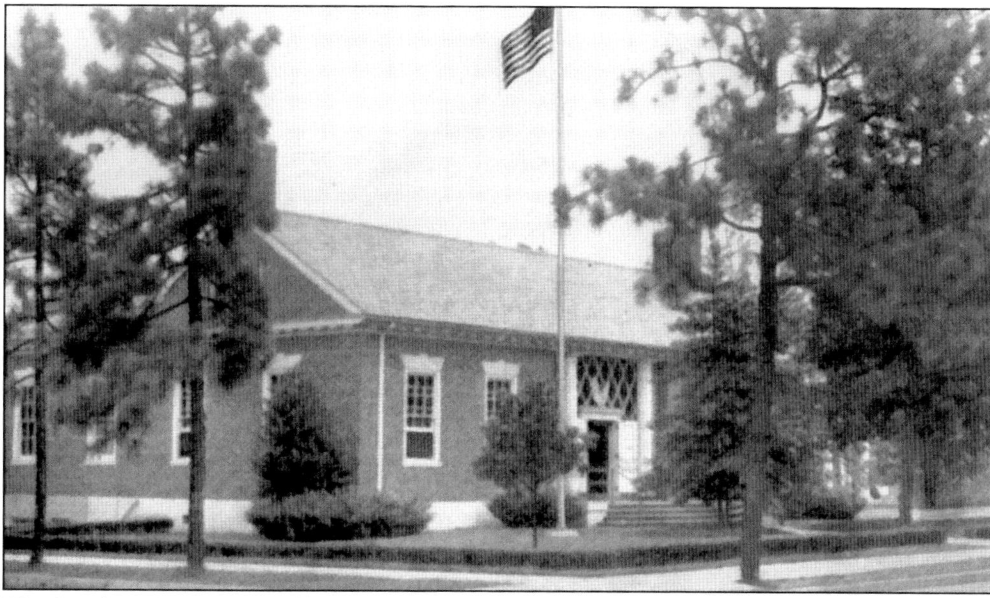

The Southern Pines Post Office was built in 1937 by the federal Public Works Administration on its present site on Broad Street. Before that time, the postal service moved from one place to another and was once located in the town's first school building. In 1904, the post office was in the Belvedere at the corner of West Pennsylvania and North West Broad Street.

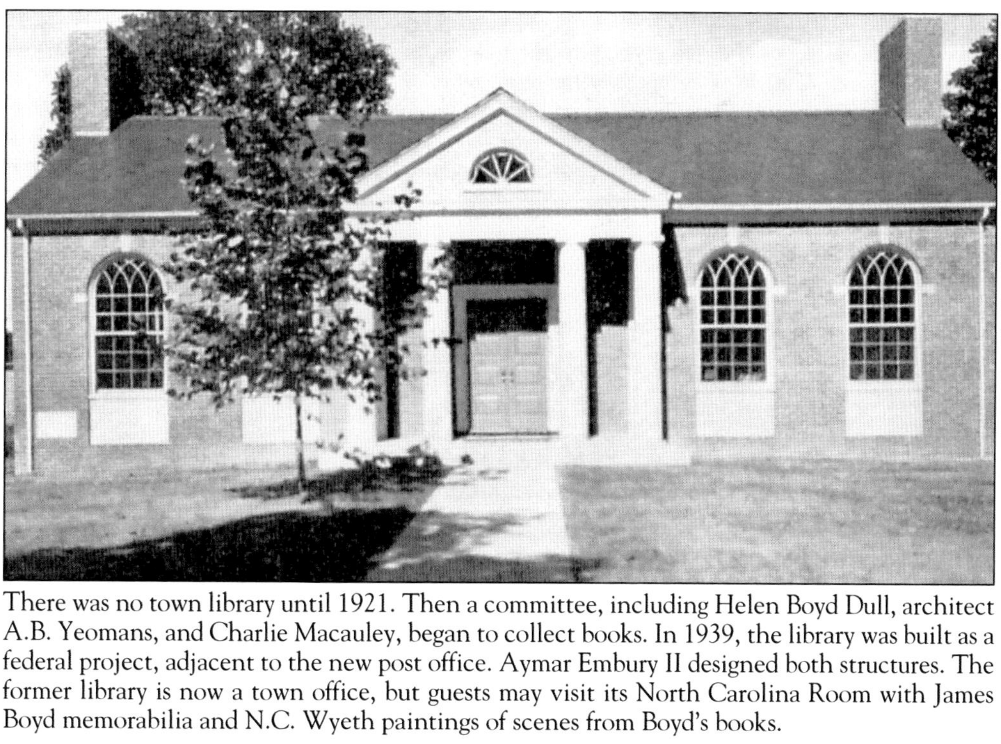

There was no town library until 1921. Then a committee, including Helen Boyd Dull, architect A.B. Yeomans, and Charlie Macauley, began to collect books. In 1939, the library was built as a federal project, adjacent to the new post office. Aymar Embury II designed both structures. The former library is now a town office, but guests may visit its North Carolina Room with James Boyd memorabilia and N.C. Wyeth paintings of scenes from Boyd's books.

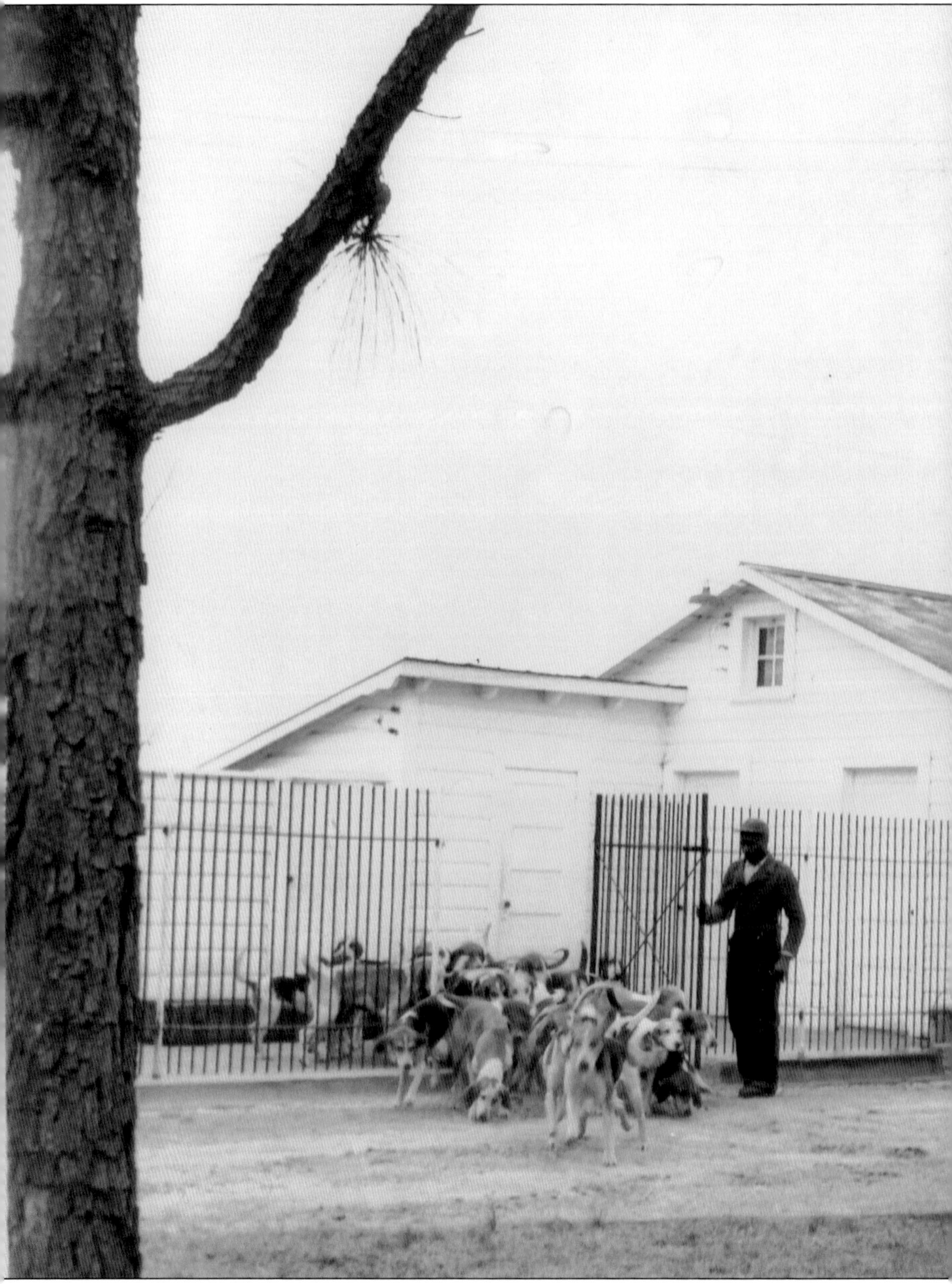

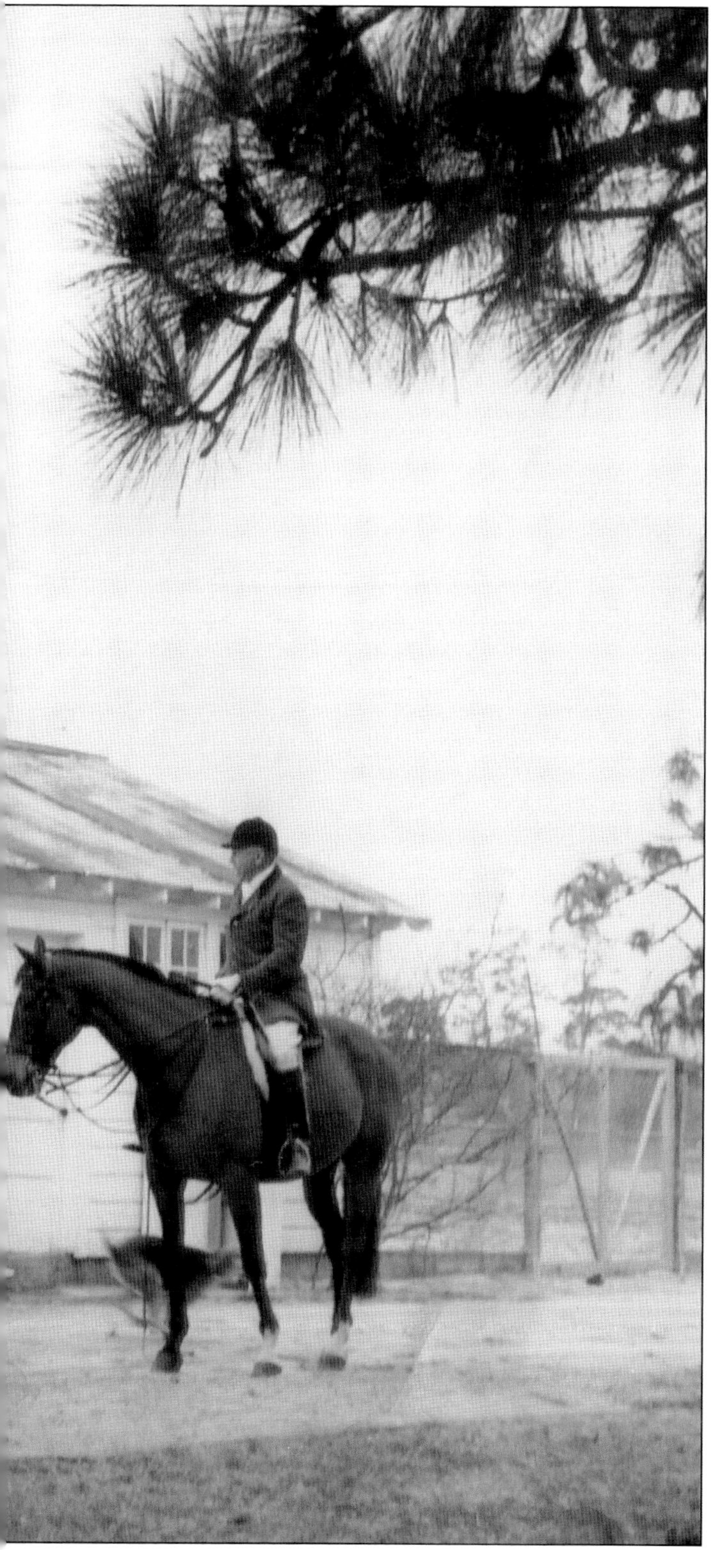

W. Ozelle "Pappy" Moss watches from his mount as a stablehand lets the excited foxhunting hounds out of their kennel for a day in the fields. The Moore County Hounds still go at it three times a year, starting on Thanksgiving Day. The Mosses inherited the Moore County Hounds from James and Jackson Boyd in 1942, when the founding brothers departed for service in World War II. James died in 1944. Mr. and Mrs. Moss, with various joint masters, hunted the pack after that and until Pappy Moss died in 1976. Ginnie Moss carries on as joint master with Richard Webb, former president of the Masters of Foxhounds Association of America. Participating in the oldest hunt in the Carolinas, Moore County Hounds have played an important role in foxhunting in the South.

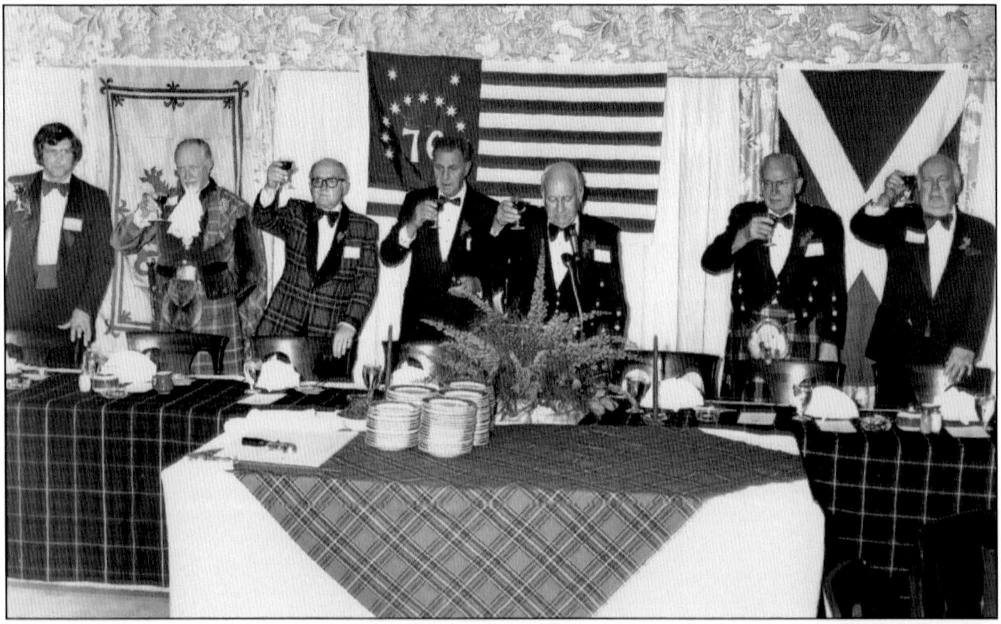

The St. Andrews Society was just one of many clubs, lodges, and other groups who enjoyed fellowship along with community service. Southern Pines town attorney Lamont Brown presides at this gathering of the kilted clan decorated with the Scottish plaids and flags that betoken the proud heritage of many in the room. The town and region in general was settled by Scottish immigrants fleeing troubles with England in the 1740s.

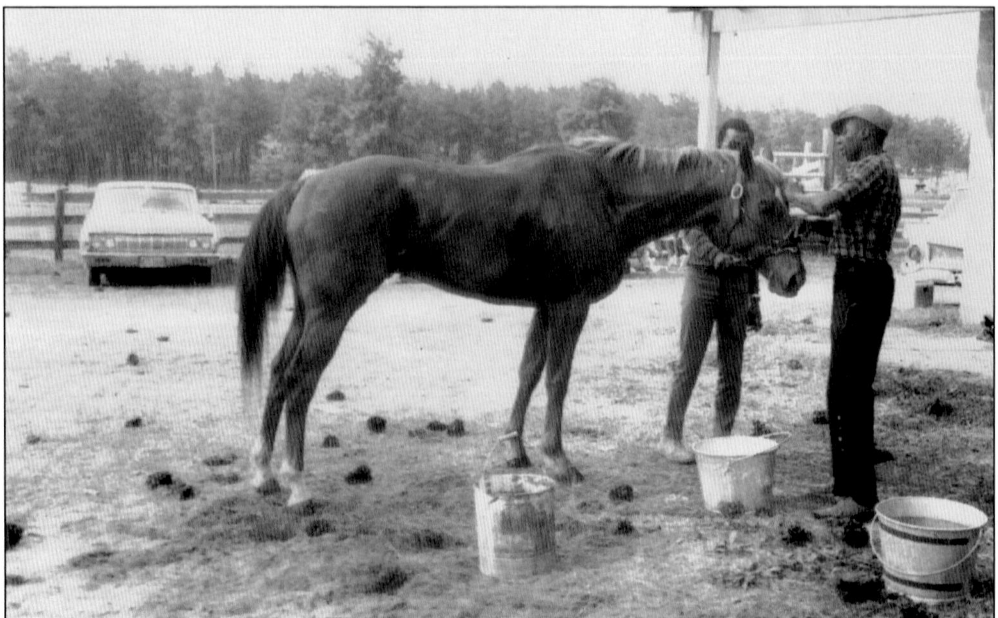

Stablehands scrub and rub down a thoroughbred behind the stables in Horse Country. The age-old scene is replayed every time a horse returns to the stable and is one of the few tasks left in the world that must be done by hand. Extra grooming, plaiting, and adorning the mane and tail go on to prepare a horse for a public event.

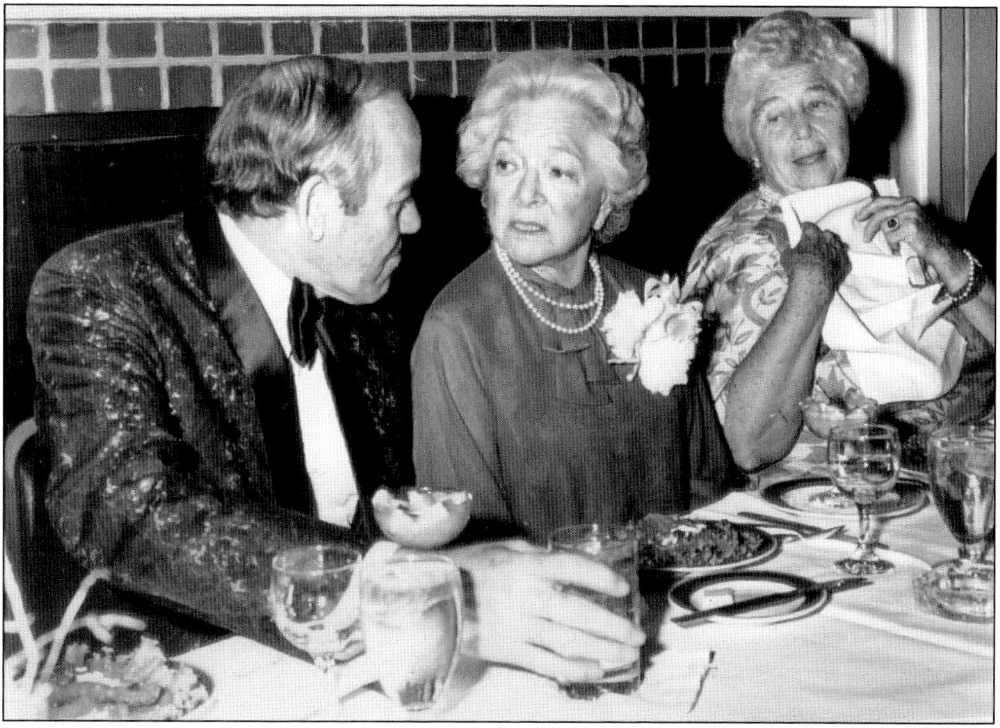

World-famous stage actress Helen Hayes visited the area, joining the list of celebrities who visit, often incognito. To her right is Betty Dumaine, an enthusiastic horsewoman who hosted a Christmas Eve tableaux in her own horse stables, a regular event to which many were invited each year. The occasion for Hayes's visit was to speak in support of the Duke University Cancer Center. The man at the left is Dr. William Shingleton, head of the Duke University Cancer Center.

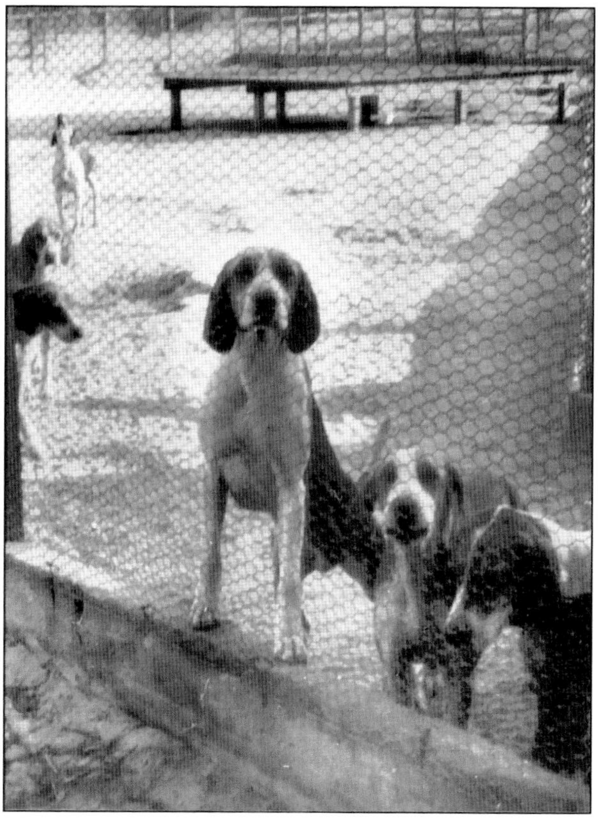

Hunting hounds look pleadingly and howl at visitors approaching their fenced compound in Horse Country. Excitable foxhounds are pack animals, and huge numbers are kept for the chase. James and Jackson Boyd gave their dogs pet names, unlike some fox hunters. These dogs have to get accustomed to being around horses.

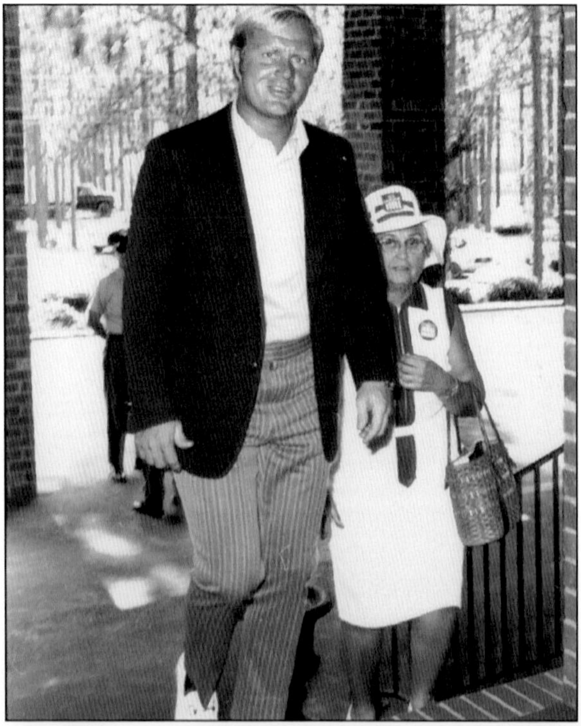

Jack Nicklaus is one of the familiar faces seen frequently in the Southern Pines–Pinehurst area. The Golden Bear has visited the famous golf courses in the area, including the Country Club of North Carolina, playing and putting his stamp on them all from the early days of his career. More recently, he designed the course for a country club that was built on Midland Road, now named the National Golf Club.

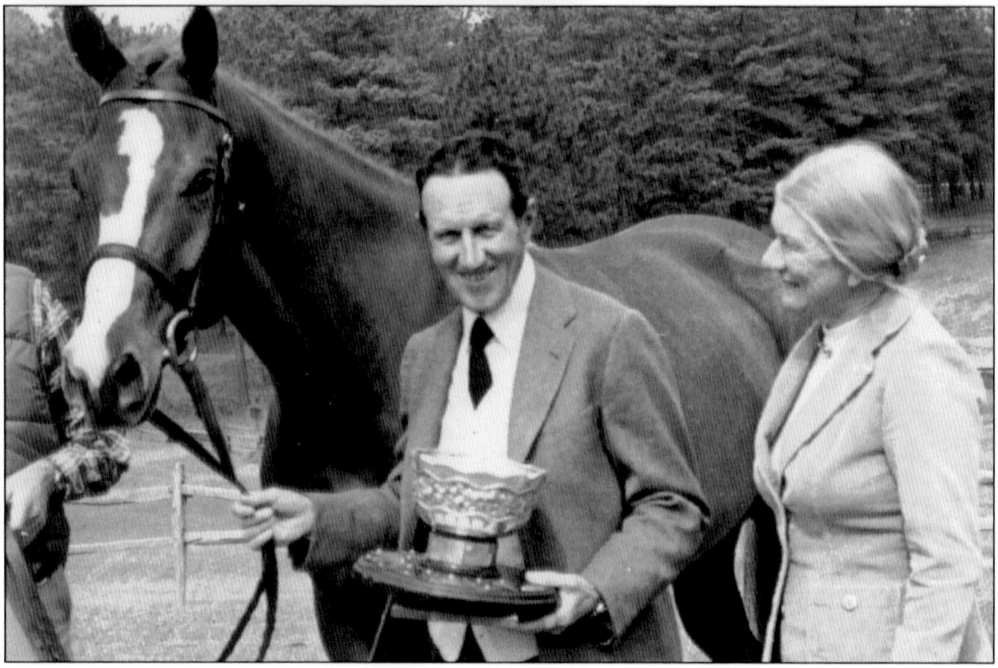

Raymond A. Firestone of Southern Pines holds the reins to his hunter, Sir Charles. He has accepted the H.E. Walsh Challenge Trophy from Ginnie Moss on behalf of the Moore County Hounds. Sir Charles was judged by the hunt committee to be the safest hunter in the field during the season. Firestone resided on a horse farm and large estate in Southern Pines for many years. Firestone brand tires has carried his family name for years.

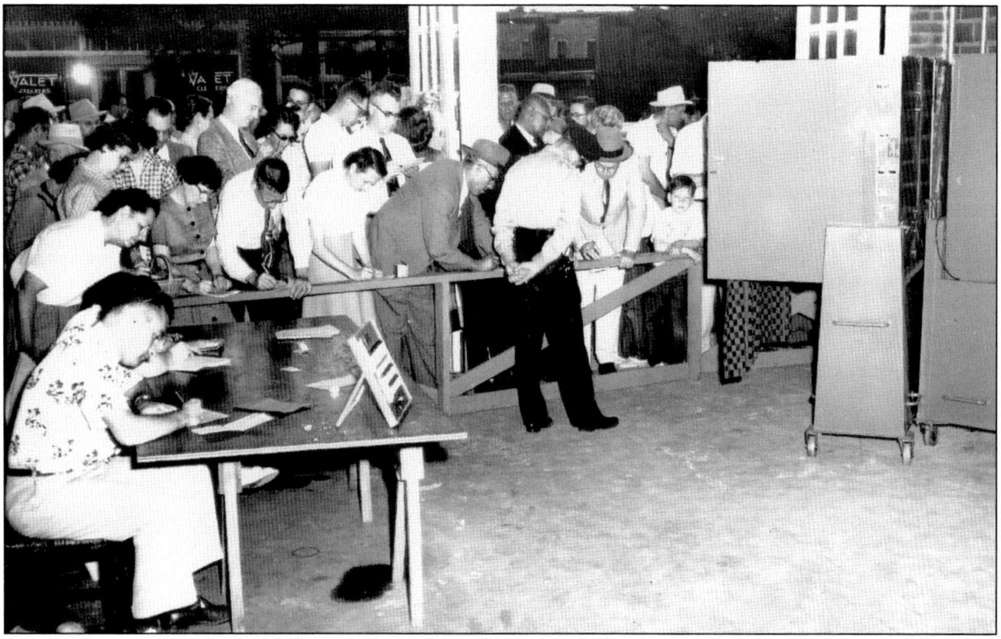

Town elections were held for years in this old-fashioned way, with paper and pencil ballots. Counting the marked ballots was also done manually. On this election day, a local election or referendum results are being counted under the gaze of a large throng of Southern Pines voters in the old fire station on East New Hampshire Avenue. A number of important referendums included a bond issue to build the state's first community college and consolidated high schools.

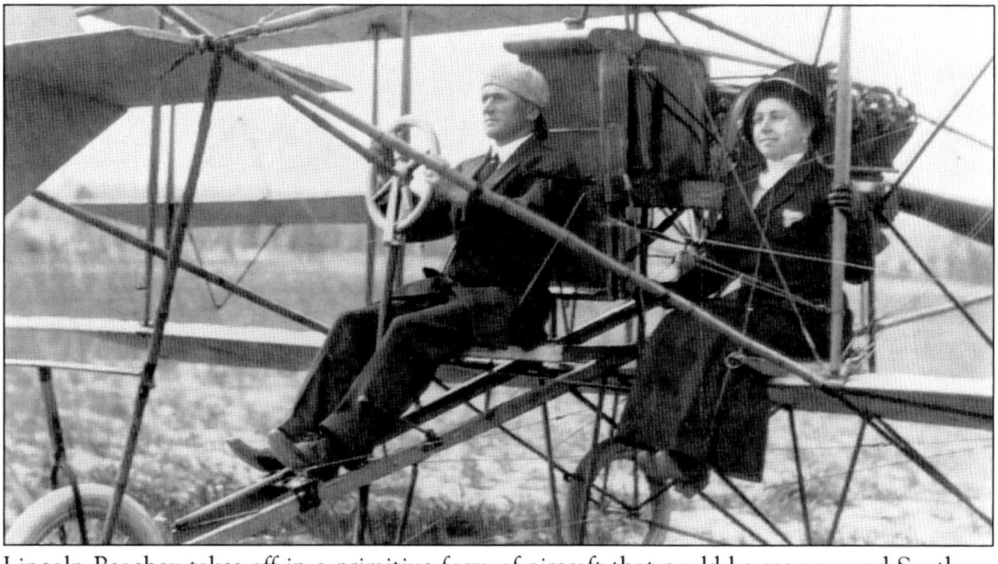

Lincoln Beachey takes off in a primitive form of aircraft that could be seen around Southern Pines, probably using a flat pasture or field. In 1928, the Knollwood Airport was built and was the forerunner of a county-owned airport equipped to handle both general aviation and commercial passenger flights. In the early days, such famous fliers as Amelia Earhart used the Knollwood runways. In fact, a framed photograph of the famous woman flier hangs in the Moore County Airport terminal building on Airport Road.

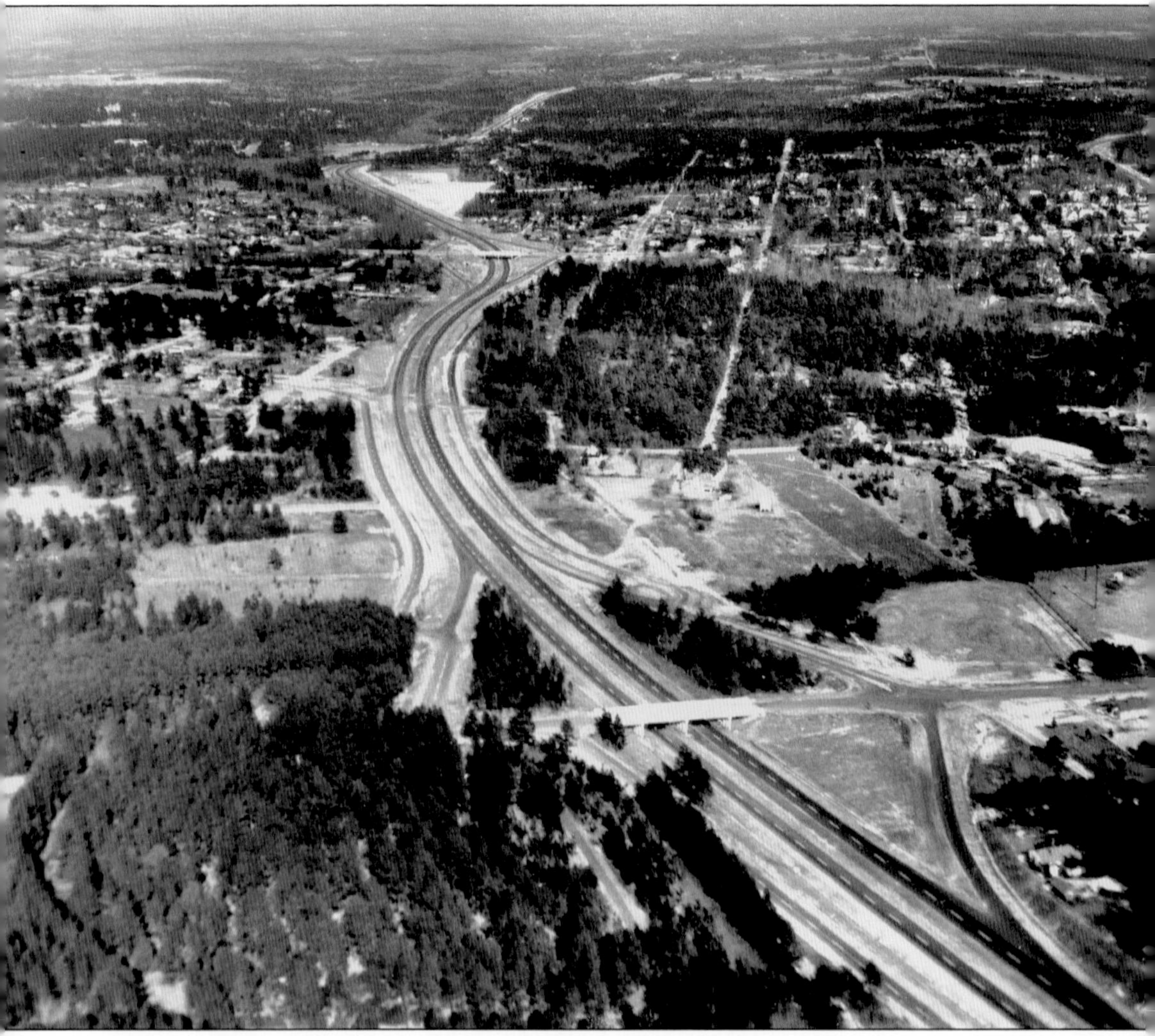

Development, population growth, and traffic volume caused Southern Pines to spread as the town entered its fifth decade. The aerial view of the new U.S. 1 Bypass, built in 1955, shows an overpass and interchange in the foreground where Morganton Road crosses the federal highway running north to south, bypassing the historic grid of downtown Southern Pines. Morganton Road is part of an ancient route used long before automobiles or white settlers with their carts and carriages arrived in the area; it still carries major traffic on the outskirts of Southern Pines west to Pinehurst. The bypass carries traffic to and from Raleigh, north to New England, and south to Florida. A Sheraton/Holiday Inn, a LobSteer, and a town fire station would be built later on the frontage. West Southern Pines can be seen to the left of the highway. A small white line crossing the highway in the distance is the West Pennsylvania Avenue overpass, which connected East Southern Pines to the African-American community.

Two

West Southern Pines

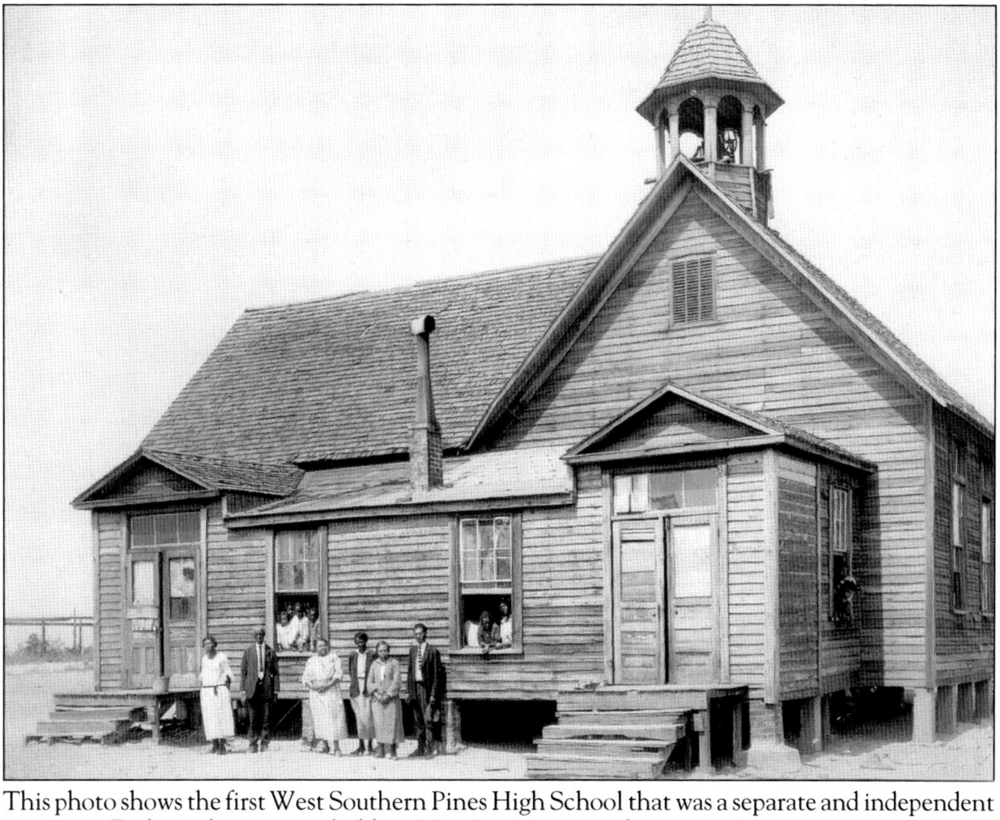

This photo shows the first West Southern Pines High School that was a separate and independent structure. Earlier, classes were held in Mrs. M. McLean's home on Gaines Street. Later, Dr. Cady and others were instrumental in getting another structure built, which was completed in 1925. Even though this school was called West Southern Pines High School, it consisted of grades 1 through 11. At the first high school commencement in 1930 were the following four members: Jasper Hill, Helen Hasty, George McKeithan, and Alberta Steele. The principal was John Simpson. All school supplies and furnishings were funded by personal contributions, and many donations came from visiting Northerners. The school also conducted various fund-raising projects, which included showing movies. In the late 1960s, West Southern Pines High School integrated and became part of the new Pinecrest High School.

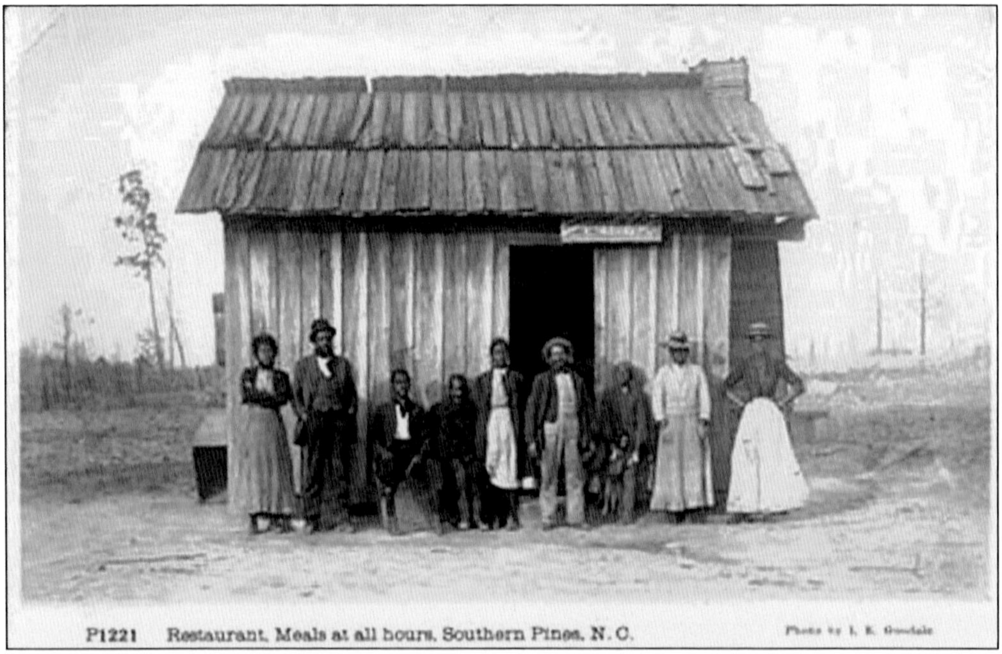

This is an early 20th century photograph of a restaurant located in West Southern Pines; the exact location is unknown. The sign hanging from the restaurant states, "Meals at all hours."

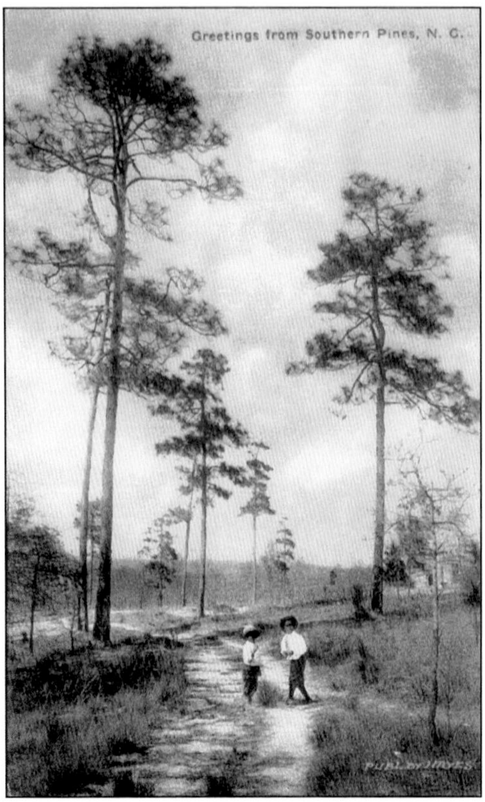

This 1920s photo shows how very little grows naturally in the sandy soil of East and West Southern Pines, except for the long-leaf pines. The sandy soil is extremely infertile and does not retain moisture. Due to this unique topography, there are frequent summer fires and farming is difficult.

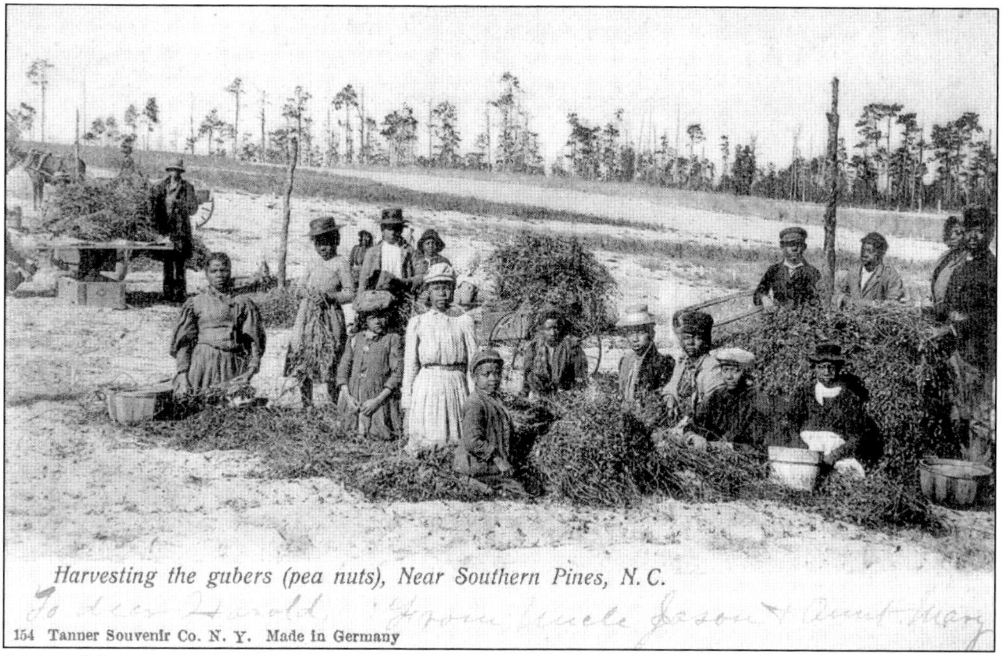

Pictured here are people harvesting peanuts in Southern Pines. The harvests were not native to the areas of East and West Southern Pines until the late 1800s when they were introduced by newcomers.

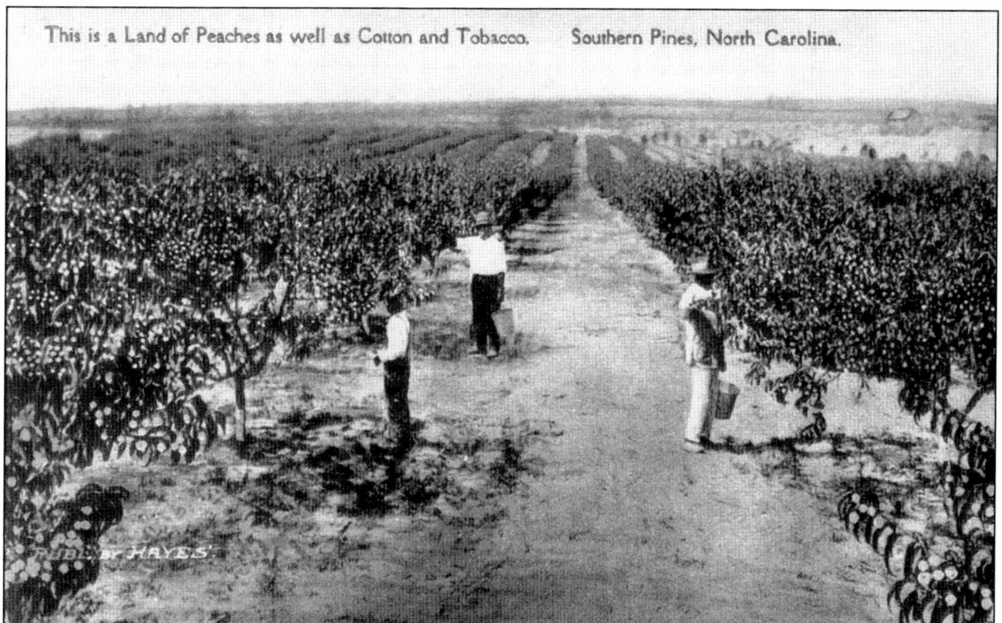

When the resorts were closed for the summer, the residents of West Southern Pines sought other ways to make a living and often held several jobs at one time. One of the many forms of employment for families was picking peaches in the peach orchards, picking dewberries, and harvesting peanuts in and around Southern Pines.

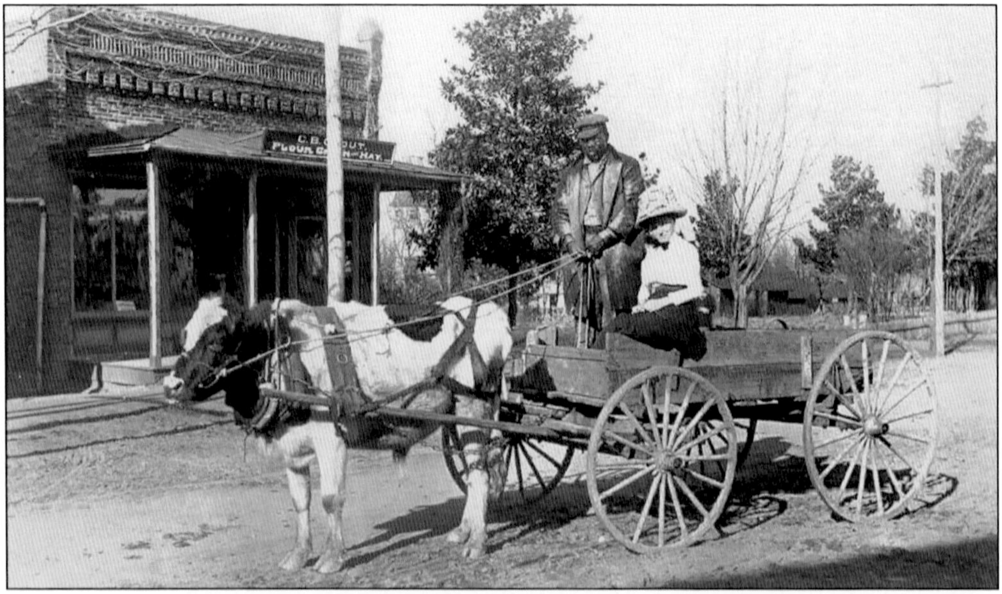

Horses, mules, and oxen were common forms of transportation in the Southern Pines area even into the 20th century. Men in West Southern Pines were listed on the 1910 U.S. Census with occupations such as farrier, owner of horse teams for deliveries, and laborer at livery stables.

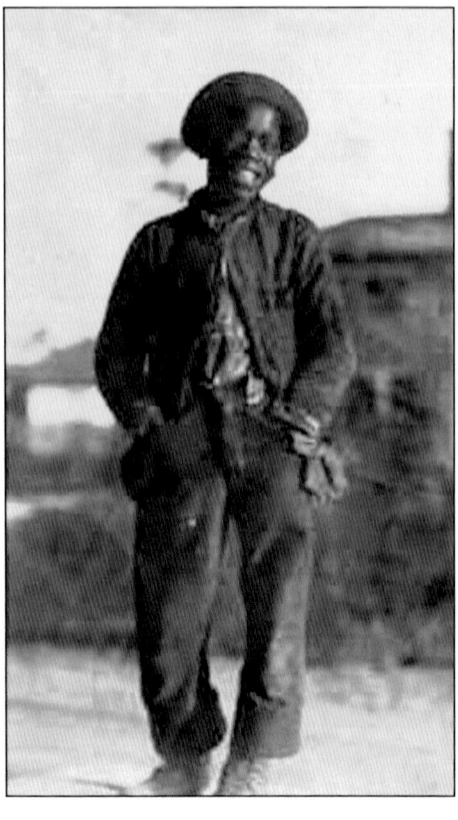

It is not clear as to why many African Americans moved to West Southern Pines, also known as Jimtown. However, many worked in the turpentine mills in the early 1900s and stayed, working in various other mills. Others came to work in the resort industry.

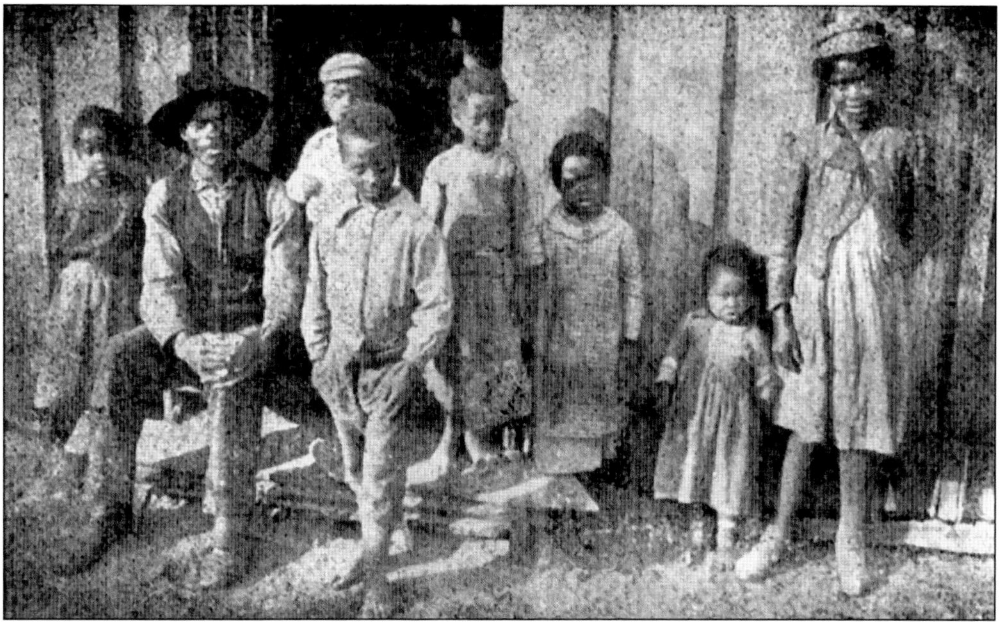

A postcard describing Jimtown touts, ". . . 500 colored people, with their own homes, shops, churches and schools."

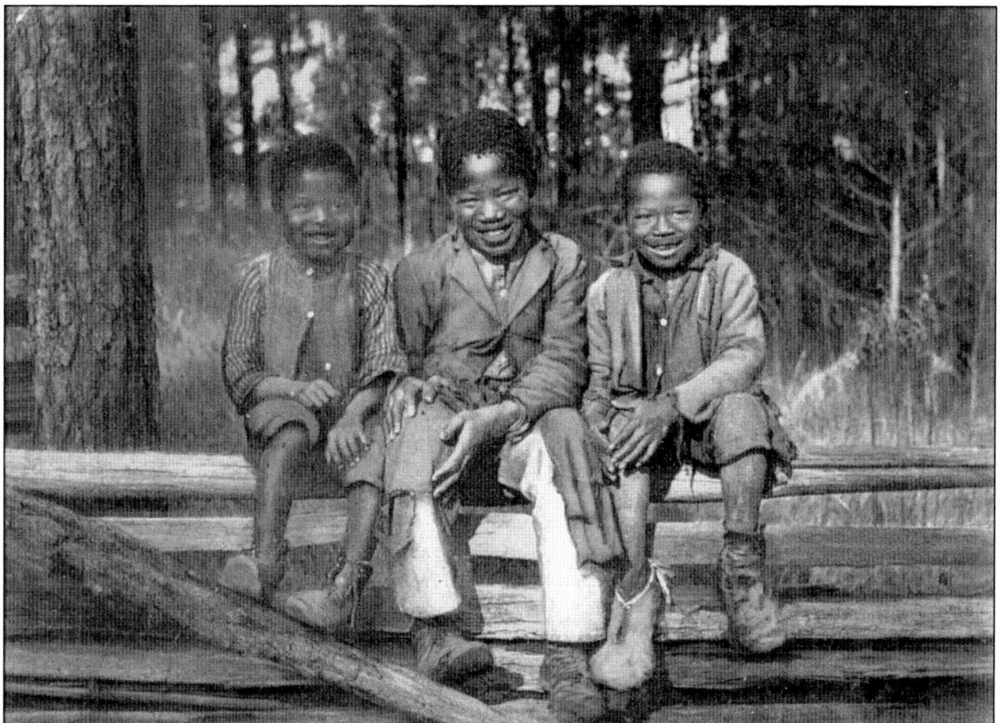

In this photograph, three unidentified children sit on a split rail fence. These fences are very common in the Moore County area even today.

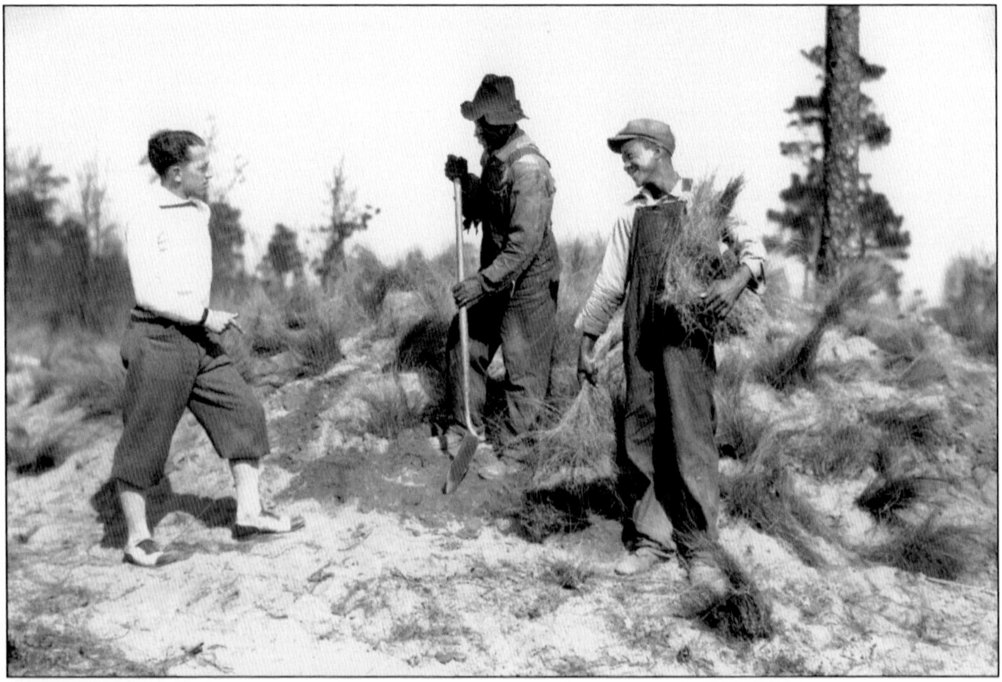

This is a photograph of the construction of the golf course at Pine Needles. George Dunlap Jr. appears to be giving advice on how the hole should be dug.

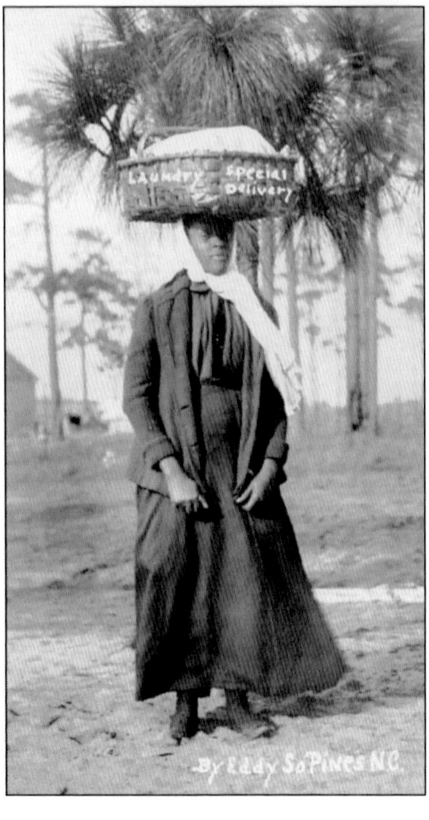

It was a very common occurrence for the women of West Southern Pines to take in laundry, sometimes in addition to other work. Many women worked as maids and cooks in the local hotels and private homes.

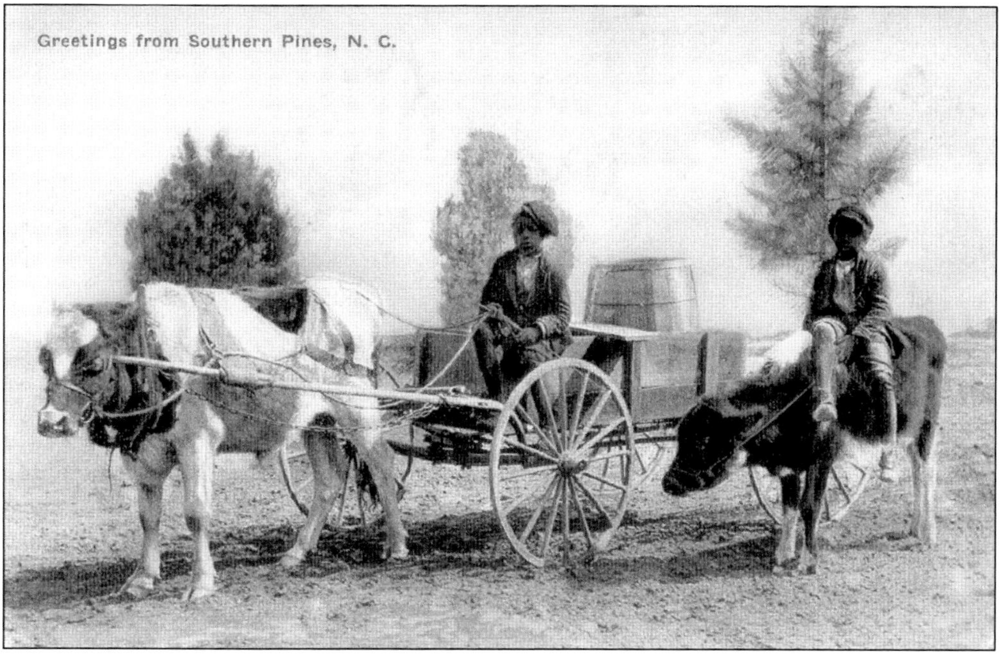

The cargo of this ox-pulled wagon is unknown, but the young men might be making a delivery for a local grocery store.

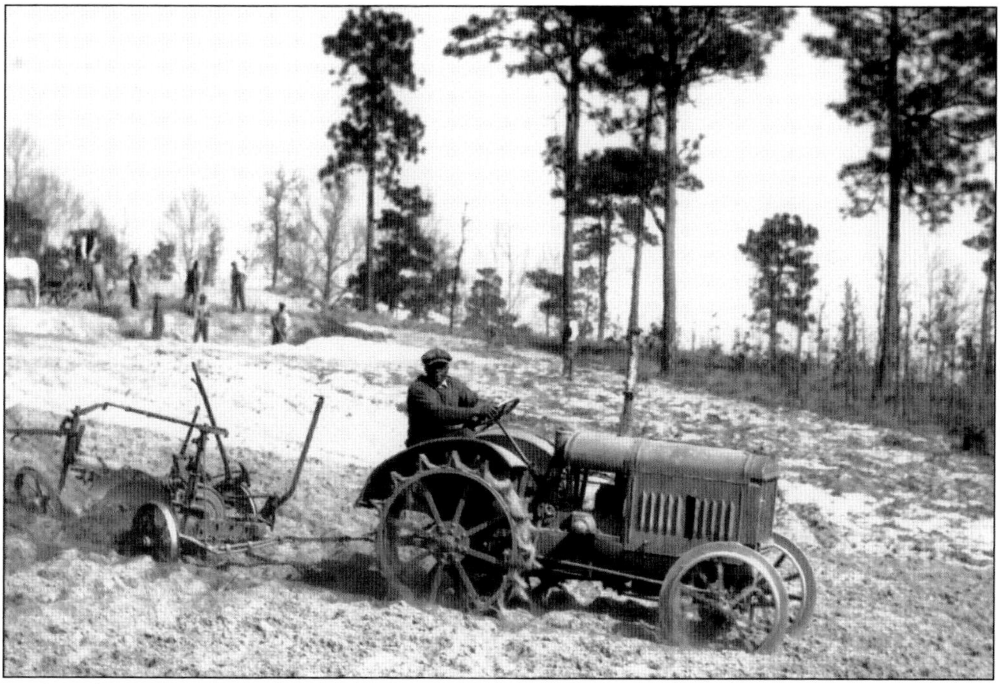

In this photograph, a tractor is used to clear land for the Pine Needles golf course in the late 1920s. This course was designed by Donald Ross, and the Pine Needles Lodge & Golf Club opened in 1928. These laborers may not have realized it at the time, but they are working on a golf course that would be legendary 70 years later with practically no changes made other than the renumbering of the holes. These workers are a part of golf history.

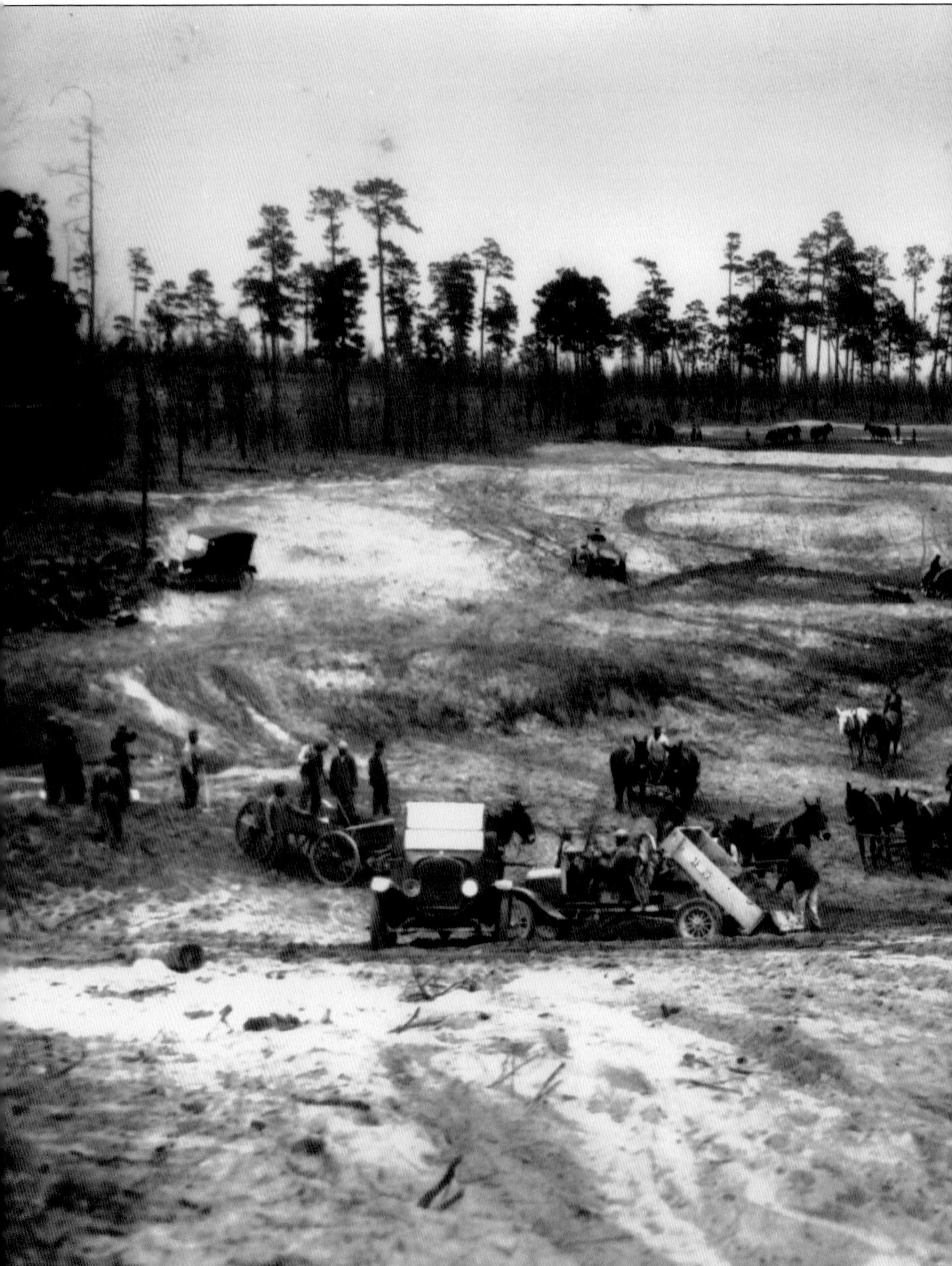

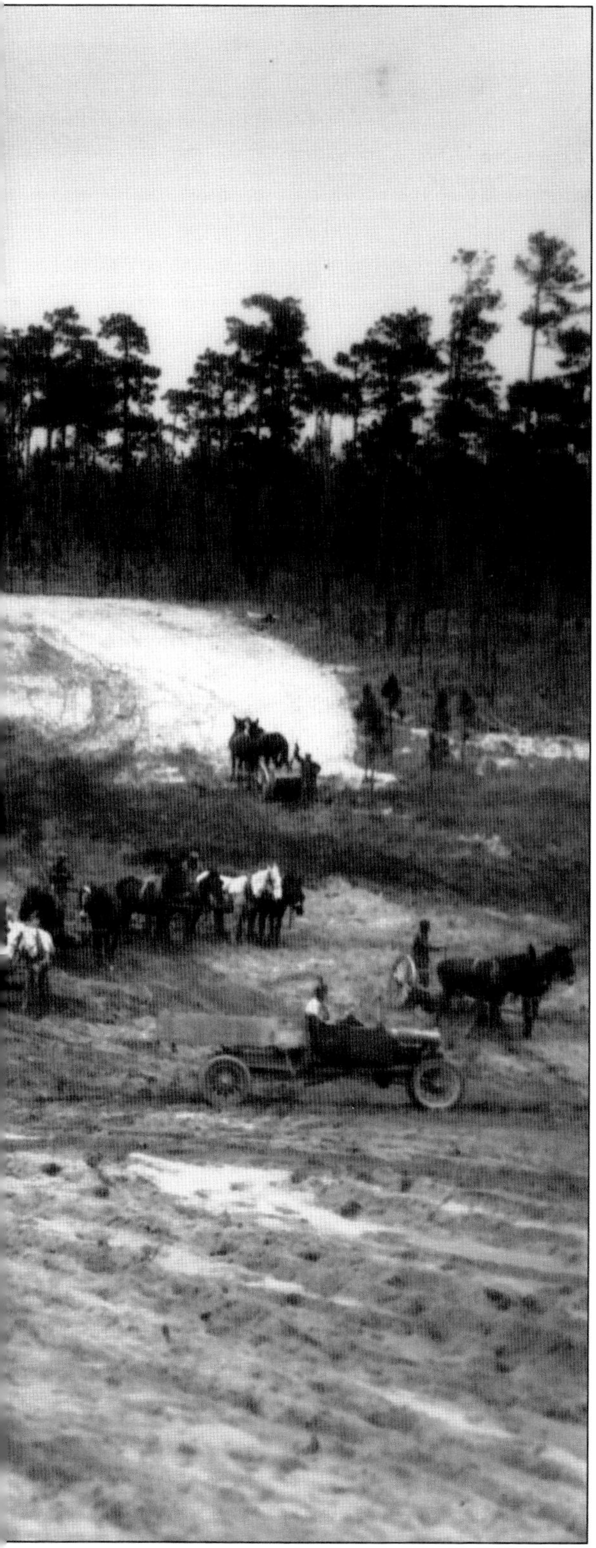

Many African-American men from West Southern Pines worked as laborers in various areas of construction. In this photograph, the men are clearing the land for the future Pine Needles golf course. In 1931, the course was closed for four years because of the economic depression. Later, it was used for combat training in World War II and also provided an army barracks for soldiers. For $15 per night, the men received meals and unlimited golf. This photograph was taken in early 1927.

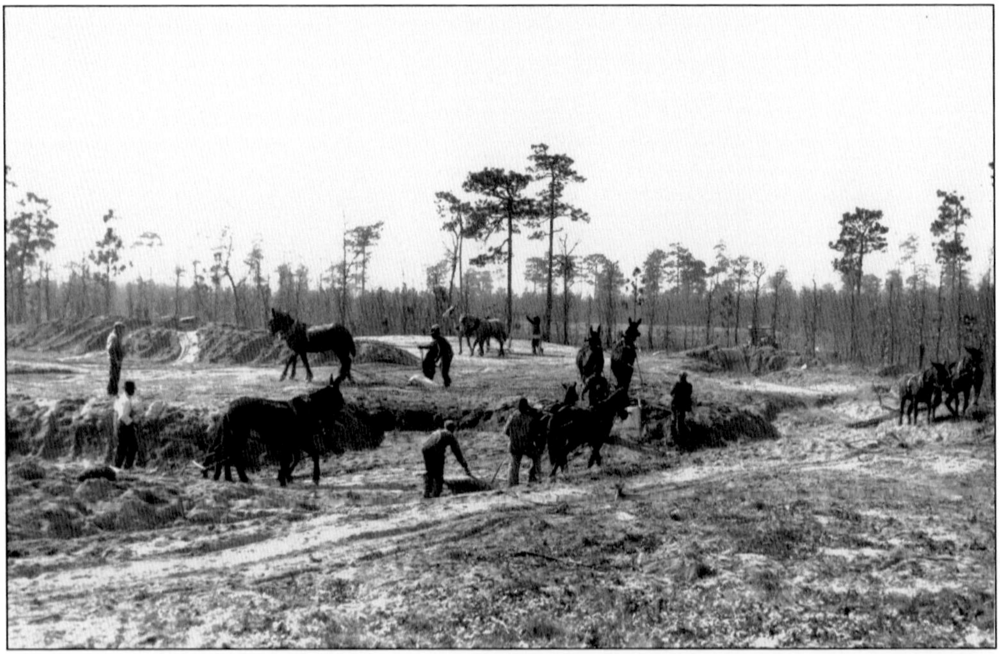

The residents of West Southern Pines were no strangers to hard work. Many came from South Carolina because of the opportunities to work in the resort community of Southern Pines.

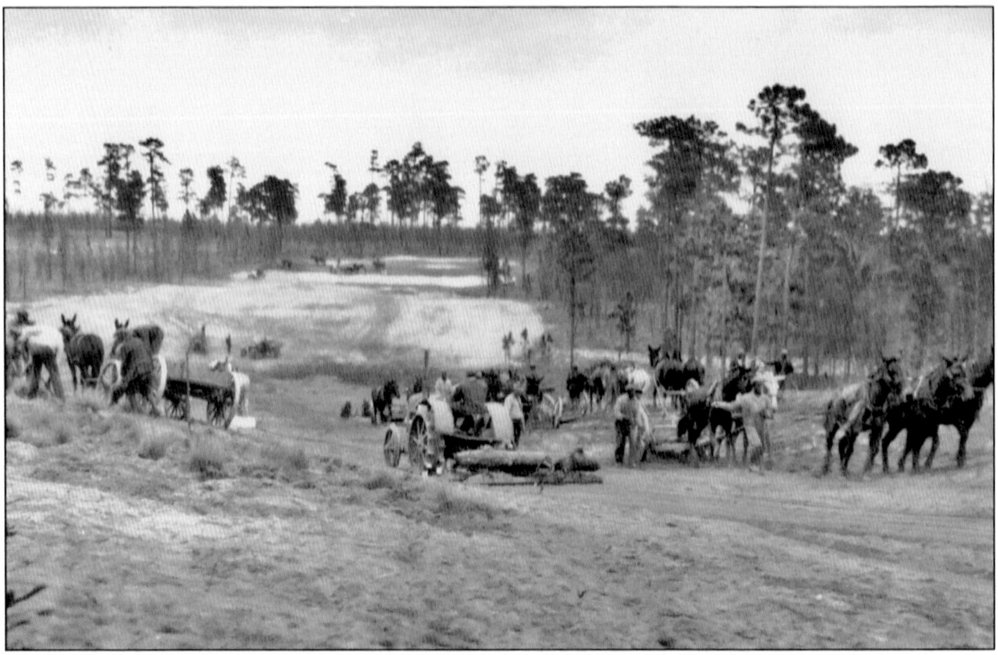

This is a photograph of workers hauling timber during the construction of the Pine Needles golf course. Mule teams seem to be the most efficient way to get the job done on this particular work day. In 1953, Peggy Kirk Bell and her husband, Warren (Bullet) Bell, purchased Pine Needles Lodge & Golf Club. Originally, this property was named "Pine Needle Inn" during the planning period, but it is said that advertisements and the news media renamed it "Pine Needles," making it plural.

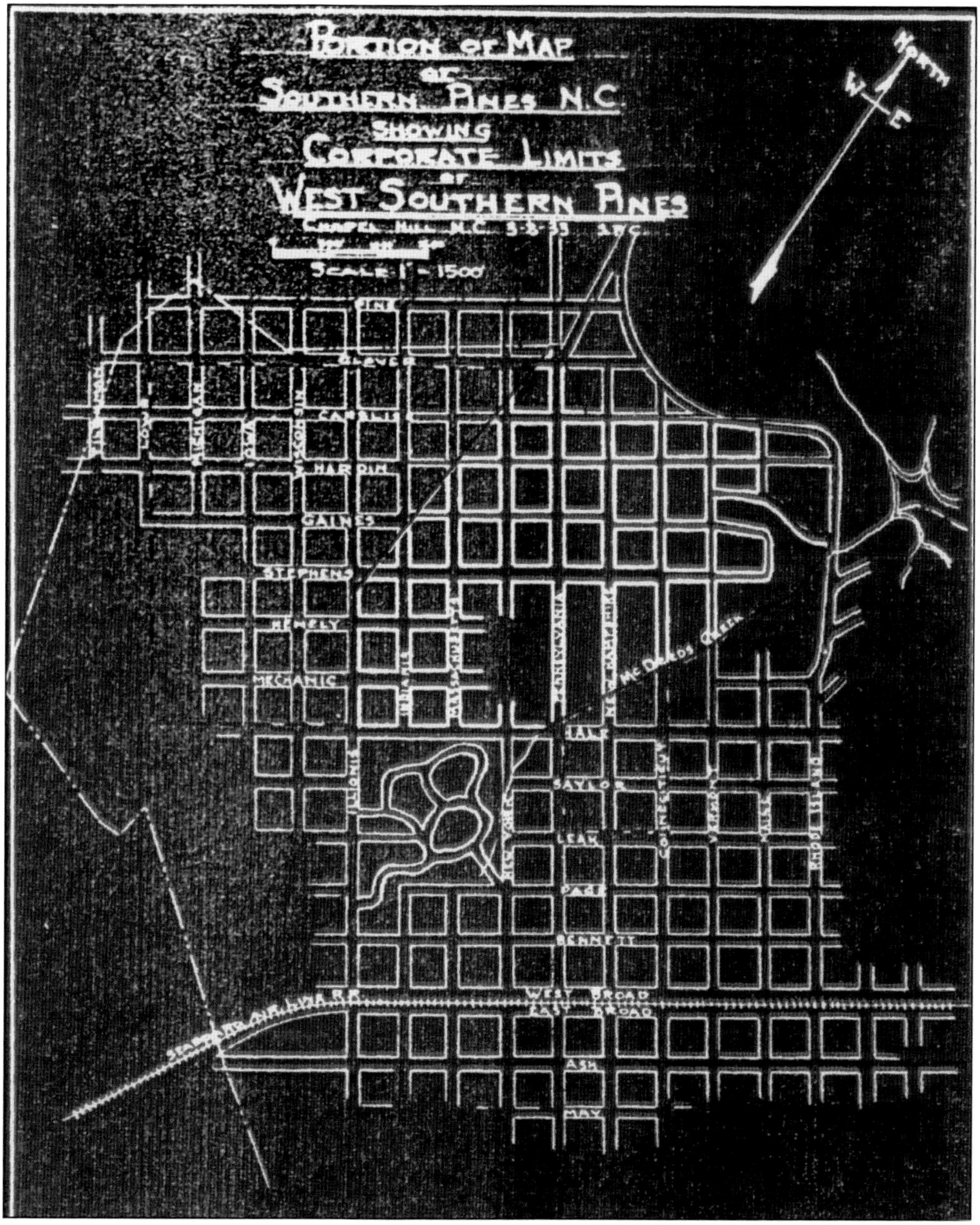

The North Carolina State General Assembly passed an act (Chapter 210, Private Laws of NC, 1923) incorporating the town of West Southern Pines in Moore County, North Carolina, in the year 1923. The first mayor was J. Pleasant Hines, and commissioners were Rev. Evander McIver, Keene Addison, Benjamin Armstrong, James Bethea, and C.F. Martin; the town marshal was Vannie Harrington. According to the charter, "It shall be the duty of the officers named in this section to meet within twenty days after the ratification of this act and organize, after being duly sworn by some one authorized to administer oaths in Moore County." The first meeting was held in the school auditorium on Friday night, March 16, 1923. At this meeting, the town attorney, J. Talbot Johnson, explained what it meant to be an incorporated town and what the charter required of them as a town.

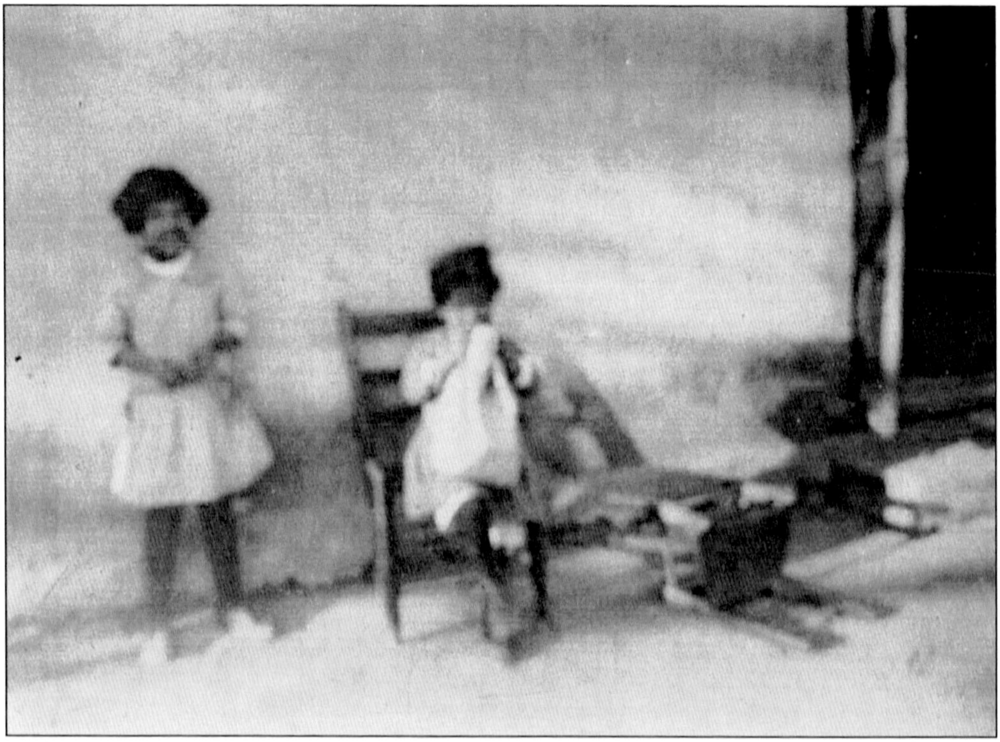

In this c. 1920s photo, Gertie and Ann Blue are outside their home at the present intersection of Pee Dee and Midland Roads. Often people would stop and ask African-American children if they wanted their picture taken, sometimes offering them a few pennies.

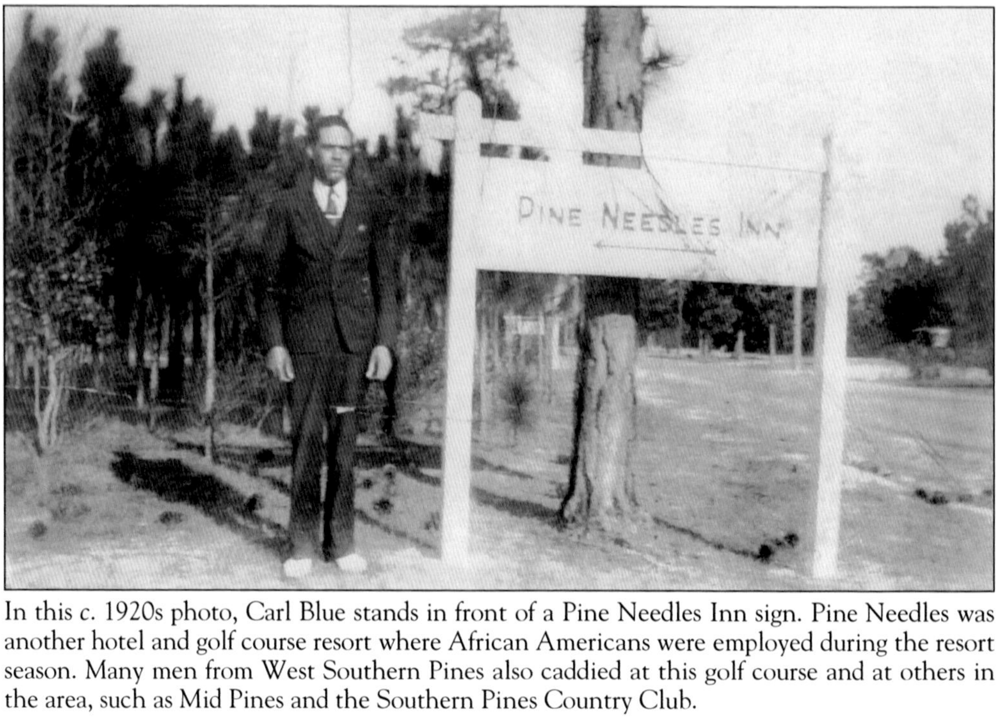

In this c. 1920s photo, Carl Blue stands in front of a Pine Needles Inn sign. Pine Needles was another hotel and golf course resort where African Americans were employed during the resort season. Many men from West Southern Pines also caddied at this golf course and at others in the area, such as Mid Pines and the Southern Pines Country Club.

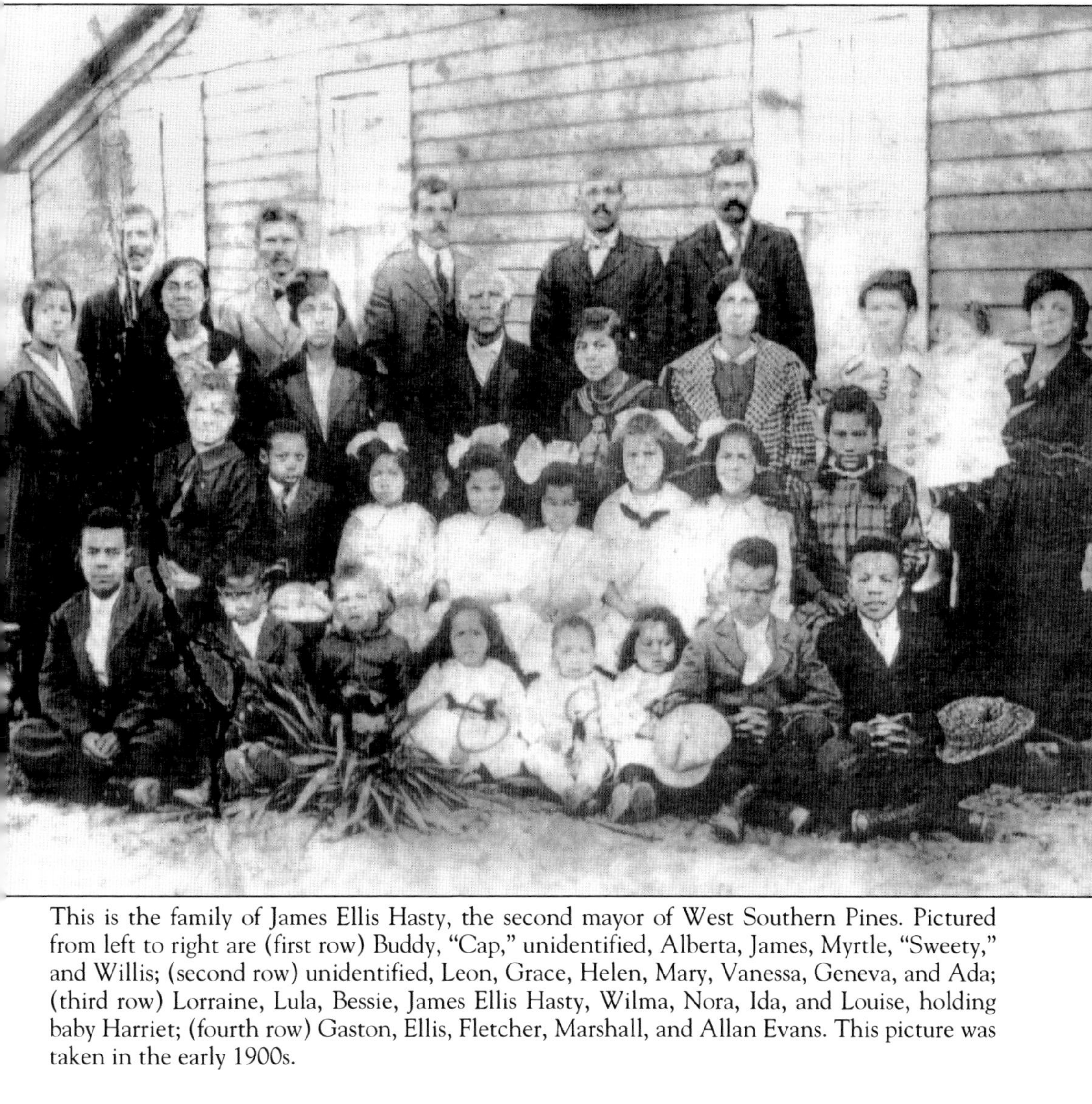

This is the family of James Ellis Hasty, the second mayor of West Southern Pines. Pictured from left to right are (first row) Buddy, "Cap," unidentified, Alberta, James, Myrtle, "Sweety," and Willis; (second row) unidentified, Leon, Grace, Helen, Mary, Vanessa, Geneva, and Ada; (third row) Lorraine, Lula, Bessie, James Ellis Hasty, Wilma, Nora, Ida, and Louise, holding baby Harriet; (fourth row) Gaston, Ellis, Fletcher, Marshall, and Allan Evans. This picture was taken in the early 1900s.

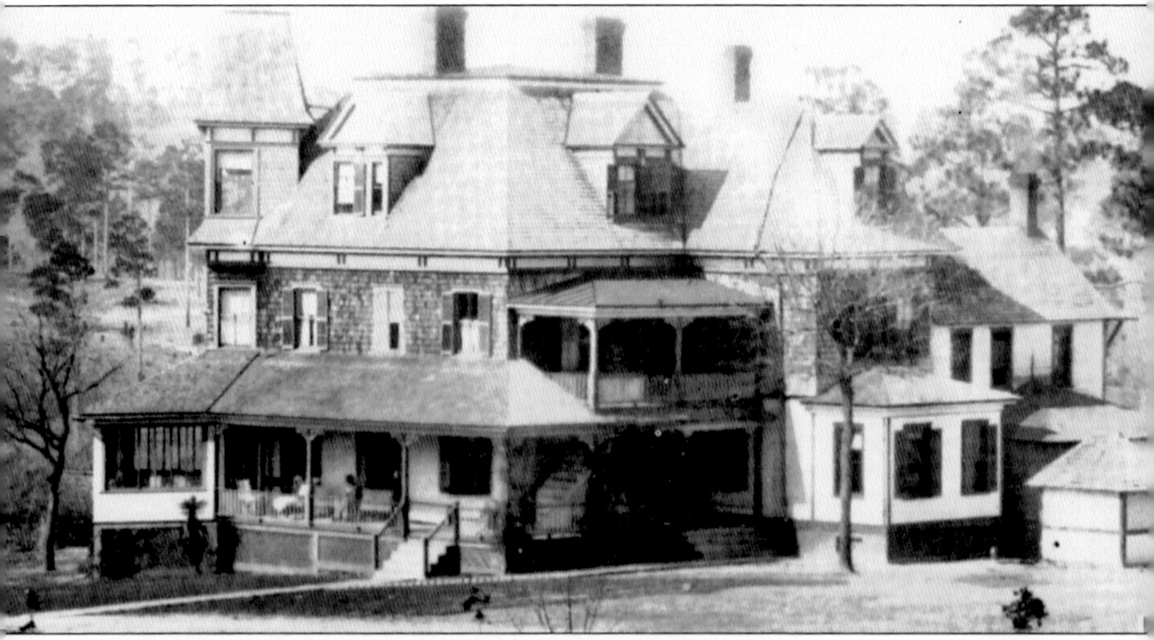

For a brief time in the early 1900s, this was a sanitarium for people of color with tuberculosis and other respiratory diseases. The advertisement claims it was ". . . the only one in the South built and equipped for the special treatment of those diseases of the throat and lungs so prevalent amongst colored people." L.A. Scruggs, M.D., was the secretary, general manager, and one of the trustees. Mrs. C.J. Pickford and John T. Patrick were also trustees. An advertisement referred to it as "The Pickford Sanitarium for Consumptive Negroes."

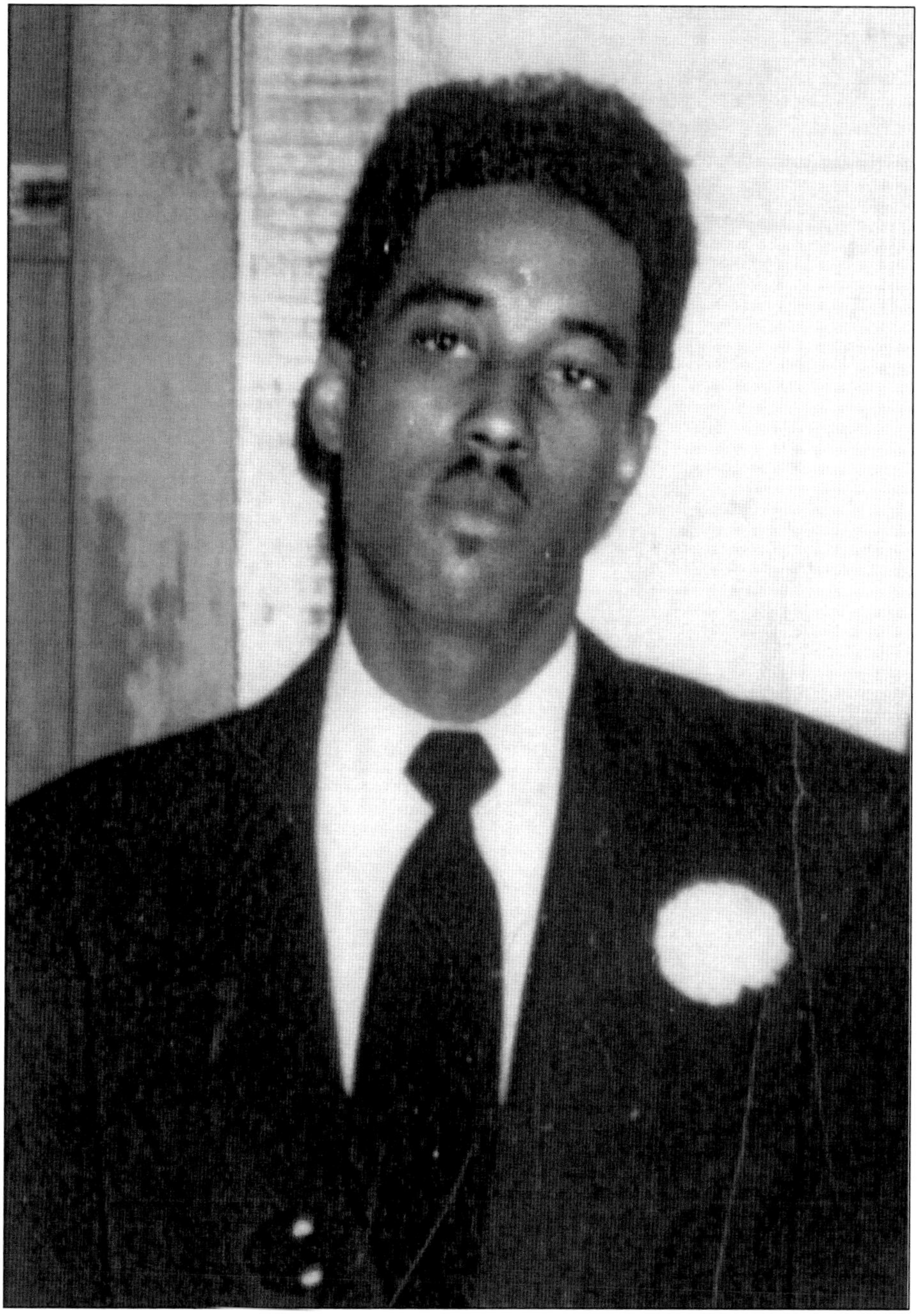

In September 1898, a missionary, Rev. Nels Bakke, sent H.L. Persson to form a school in the black community. There was considerable resistance from the white community, but the school, called "Day School House" or "St. James Elementary," prospered. Pictured here is Frank Nelson, a son of Christine and Clarence Nelson. Their family belongs to St. James Lutheran Church, one of the oldest churches in West Southern Pines. A few years before joining the church, the Nelsons enrolled their sons in the school even though there was a public school in the neighborhood. The same building served as a house of worship, Sunday school room, and the school for many years. The school closed in 1939.

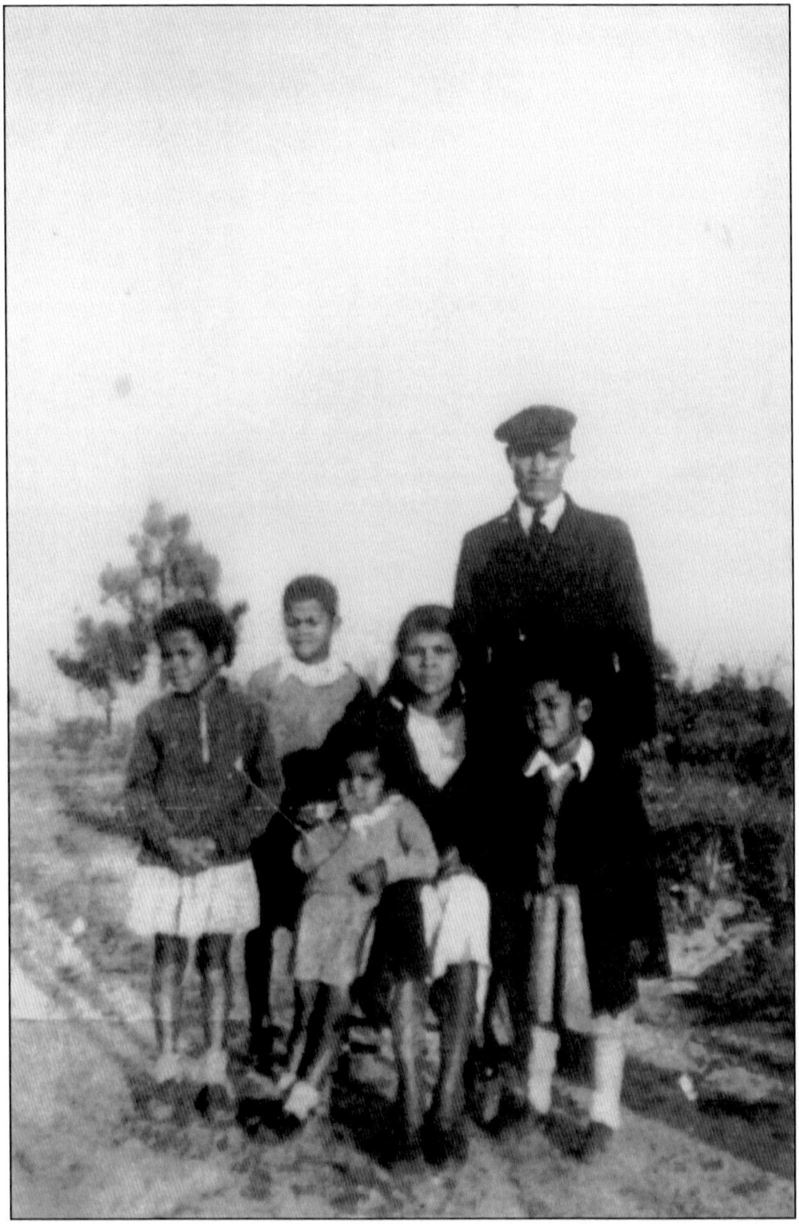

Claude and Vera Blue stand with their children, Edward, Martha, Robert, and Delores, near their home on North Carlisle Street in West Southern Pines during the 1930s. The streets were a combination of sand and clay packed down by a road paver (a machine used to smooth out some of the ruts in the road), unlike the paved roads in East Southern Pines. It would be many years before this street and others like it in West Southern Pines were paved. Mr. Blue worked as a yard/handyman, and Mrs. Vera Blue did domestic work for a retired army officer. In the winter and resort season, many African Americans worked in the hotels, such as The Jefferson Inn and Mid Pines Inn. The Blues, like other parents, worked hard to support their families and to provide a community with churches, schools, and businesses. These families produced teachers, plumbers, electricians, ministers, policemen, nurses, caregivers, town councilmen, librarians, school administrators, lawyers, mothers, fathers, and other contributors to society.

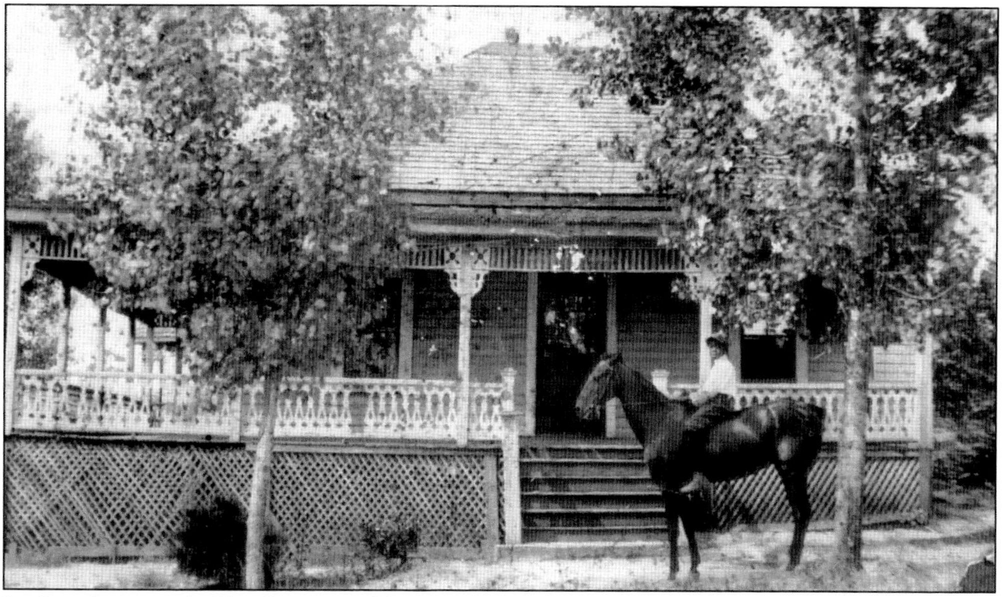

In this photograph, Floyd McDonald sits on a horse at his house on Stephens Street and New Hampshire Avenue where he grew up. This picture was taken around 1937. Floyd learned the art of plastering from his father, Thomas G. McDonald, who plastered many homes in West Southern Pines over the years. Quite a few of these homes are still standing today, including his home on West Pennsylvania Avenue.

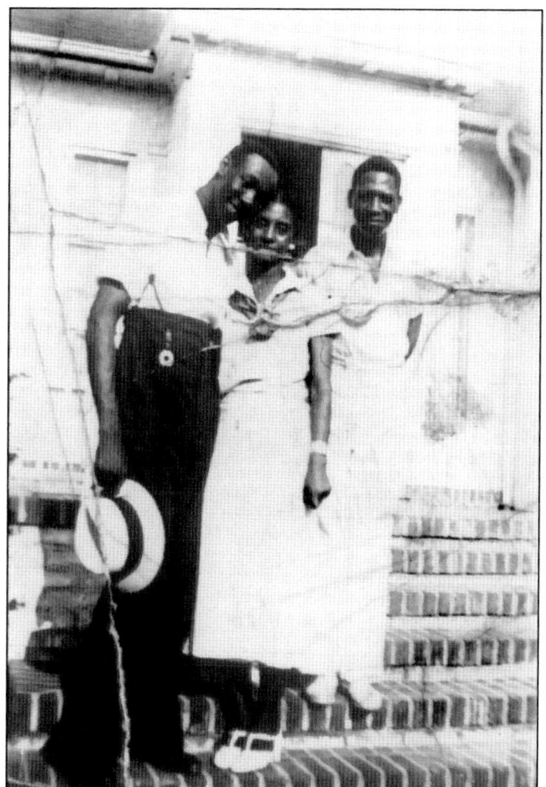

This is a photo of Floyd McDonald on the left, Clyde Drayton on the right, and an unidentified woman between them at a house on the corner of Saylor Street and West Pennsylvania Avenue.

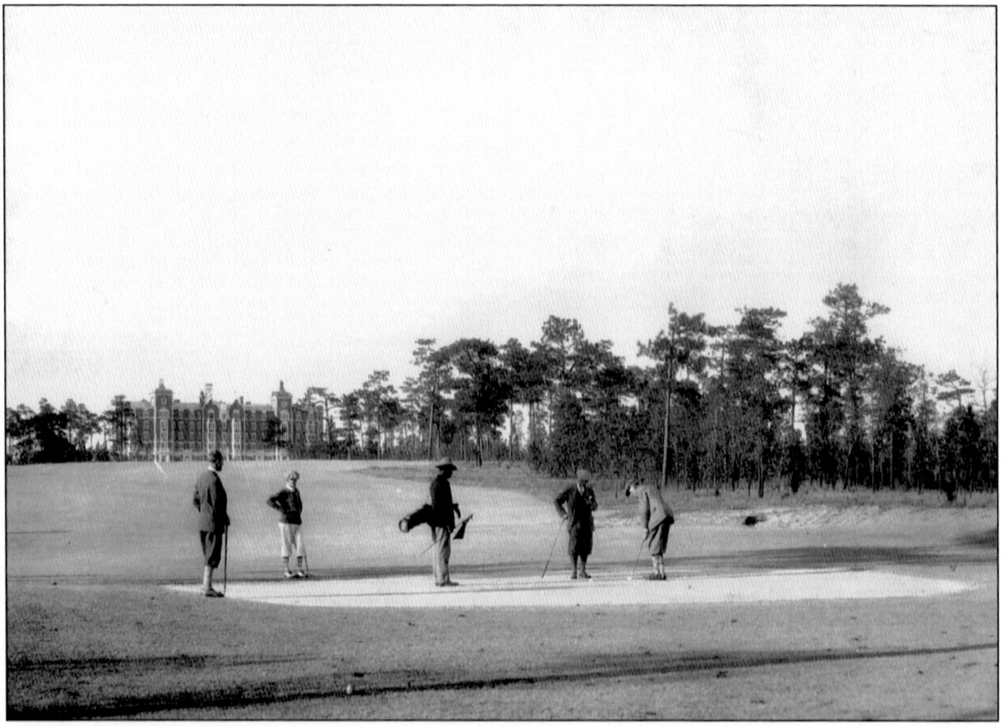

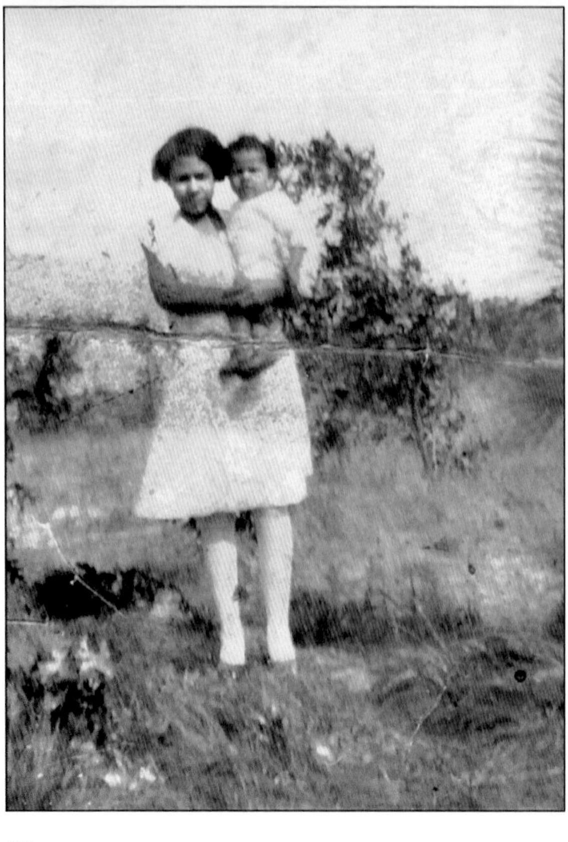

This photograph shows Donald Ross and caddies on the sand green at Pine Needles. Donald Ross designed this course and several others in the area. He began designing courses in the early 1900s, and many consider them a work of art. It is said that during the last 10 to 15 years of his life, Ross played most of his golf at Pine Needles. In the background is the Pine Needles Inn.

Juanita Blue holds her nephew, Edward Blue. In an extended family, there is usually an aunt to look after the newest baby in the family. This picture was taken by an unknown photographer in the late 1920s.

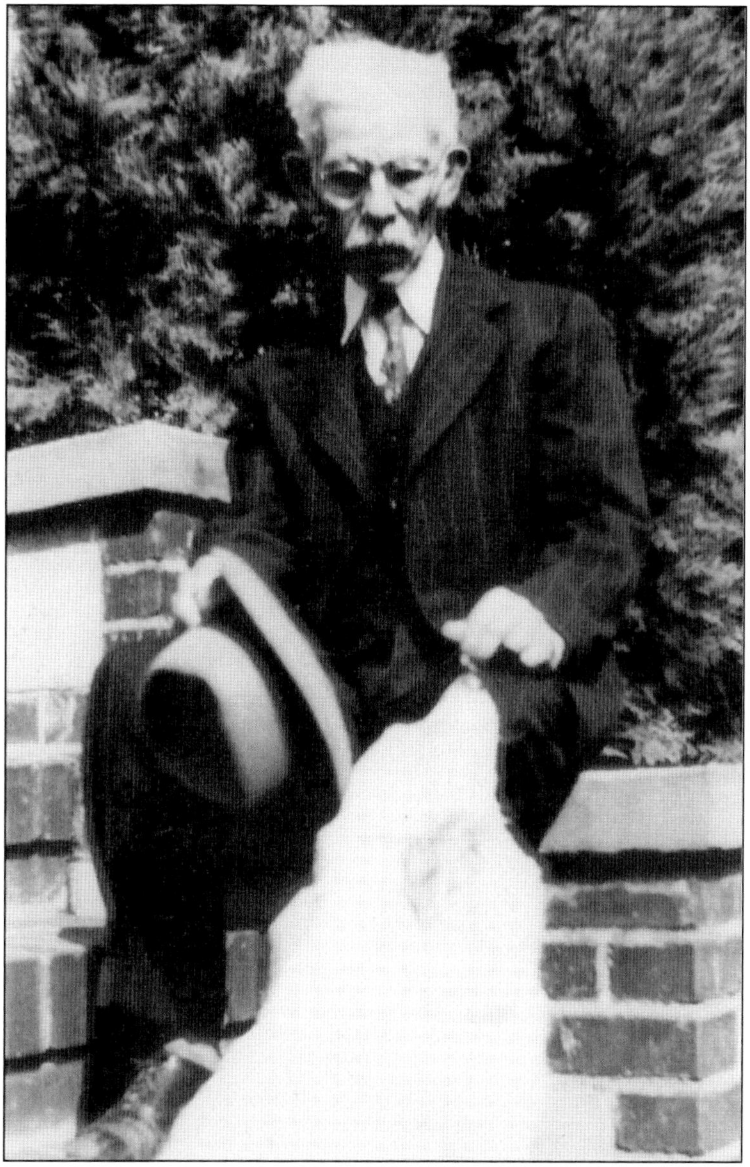

On June 7, 1927, West Southern Pines elected James Ellis Hasty, pictured here, as the second mayor of West Southern Pines with 43 votes. His opponent, Walter C. Mitchell, received 34. Five commissioners were also elected, and they were sworn in at a public meeting held at "the A.M.E. Zion Church, by lawyer, P.P. Pelton of Southern Pines, N.C." Minutes from West Southern Pines Town Council show that they sought to make street improvements, buy land for a town hall, and adopt more ordinances. However, in 1931, West Southern Pines's charter was revoked, with East Southern Pines saying it was a haven for criminals, unable to govern itself, and a health risk that could endanger the resort community. Because no reports suggest such concerns and neither towns' minutes reflect discussion between the them about the alleged problems, it appears that there were no less drastic attempts to correct the problems. Interestingly, in 1925, East Southern Pines had built a new water plant, and with an increasing population, the water system needed more water. Since the majority of McDeeds Creek was in West Southern Pines, the creek seems to have been the real reason for the annexation.

Southern Pines, N. C. 1
Feb. 10, 1931

Regular Meeting:

The regular semi-monthly meeting of the Board of Town Commissioners of the Town of Southern Pines was held at the office of the City Clerk on Tuesday, Feb. 10, 1931, rather than Wednesday Feb. 11th. Present: D. G. Stutz, Mayor, Commissioners Chas. S. Patch, E. C. Stevens, Geo. W. Case and A. B. Yeomans. A number of citizens of the town were present at the meeting to discuss the matter in reference to the Town asking the General Assembly to cancel the charter of the Town of West Southern Pines and make that section a part of the city limits of Southern Pines.

An informal discussion followed and Mr. John Powell asked for what reason it was necessary for the Board of Town Commissioners of Southern Pines to take over West Southern Pines. Mr. Stutz stated that in order to protect the interests of tax payers of this town, the Town Board felt that it was necessary to have control over West Southern Pines. First, for the reason that many criminals of North Carolina are drifting into West Southern Pines where they are protected from being apprehended by officers and to be in a community where they are protected by a negro form of government. Second, that there is considerable danger from a health standpoint of an epedemic breaking out in the negro section that would cause serious danger to Southern Pines as a resort community and a town that is dependent upon the negroes as servants. Mr. Stutz gave as his third reason that the negroes were not capable of governing themselves and that they did not have sufficient funds to build streets and to look after the other civic needs of the negroes.

James Boyd, Albert Vittum, Ralph Chandler and others stated that they thought it was wise that the Board of Town Commissioners of Southern Pines take over the negroes even though it was considered a liability, due to the fact that as the community continues to grow it is necessary that Southern Pines be able to control that section west of McDeed's Creek from a health standpoint as well as from a police standpoint.

The Clerk brought to the attention of the Board a letter from Mrs. L. S. Johnson in reference to her account for water for the quarter ending January 1st, amounting to $31.29. She stated in her letter that during the cold weather in December she sent a colored boy over to cut the valve off in the yard and that later children went into the yard and turned the valve on again, and there were a number of spigots open at the time as the plumbing had been drained. Mrs. Johnson further stated that as long as the cottage was vacant and the accident happened without her knowledge, the Board should made an adjustment. A motion was then made by Chas. S. Patch, seconded by E. C. Stevens, that the Clerk be authorized to reduce Mrs. Johnson's bill to the five dollar minimum.
Ayes: Chas. S. Patch, E. C. Stevens, Geo. W. Case, A. B. Yeomans.
Nays: None.

The Southern Pines Board of Town Commissioners Minutes dated February 10, 1931, document the cancellation of West Southern Pines's charter. Mayor Stutz gave as one reason that West Southern Pines did not "have sufficient funds to build streets and to look after the other civic needs of the Negroes."

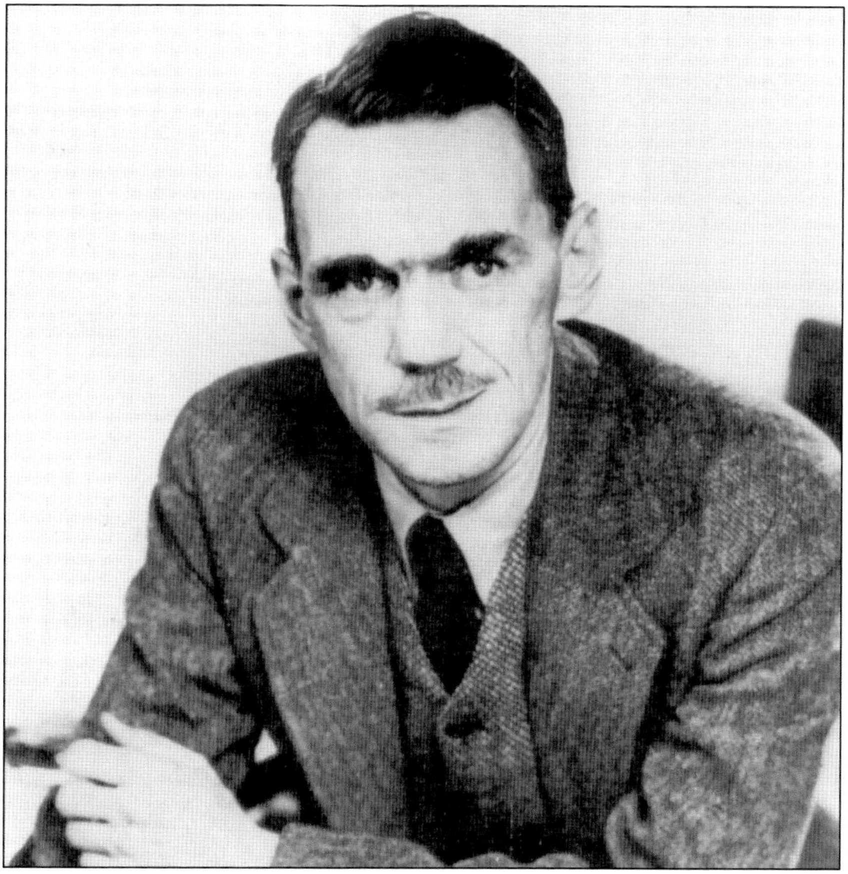

East Southern Pines residents James Boyd (shown above), Albert Vittum, Ralph Chandler, and others believed it was necessary to control the section of town west of McDeeds Creek from a health standpoint. However, no documentation was found to substantiate the reasons given by East Southern Pines to take over West Southern Pines. There was no evidence of an outbreak of a contagious illness, nothing about the need to quarantine the area, and nothing about concerns from the resort community. But, the lack of enough water for the wastewater treatment plant would be a health concern for East Southern Pines because their community was growing. West Southern Pines did not have much taxable property, so it would not have been an asset to East Southern Pines; however, West Southern Pines did have McDeeds Creek, and water rights are an important asset. Indeed, it was easier to claim that West Southern Pines was unable to govern itself and annex it than to negotiate the water rights. The original court documents filed opposing the annexation of West Southern Pines were missing from the courthouse in Carthage; however, the North Carolina Archives had the appellate court documents, which included the documents prior to the appeal. According to those documents, J.E. Hasty and the citizens of West Southern Pines filed a written complaint against Mayor D.G. Stutz and the Town of Southern Pines stating that West Southern Pines had been annexed unconstitutionally; that the Senate Bill No. 218 and the act revoking the charter should be declared void; and that the status of the town should be returned along with any property seized. Southern Pines responded that the General Assembly of North Carolina was authorized and empowered to enact the legislation annexing West Southern Pines under the provisions of the constitution of North Carolina. The hearing was held in Wadesboro, North Carolina, on September 30, 1931. Judge T.B. Finley found that there were not enough facts presented to stop the annexation of West Southern Pines.

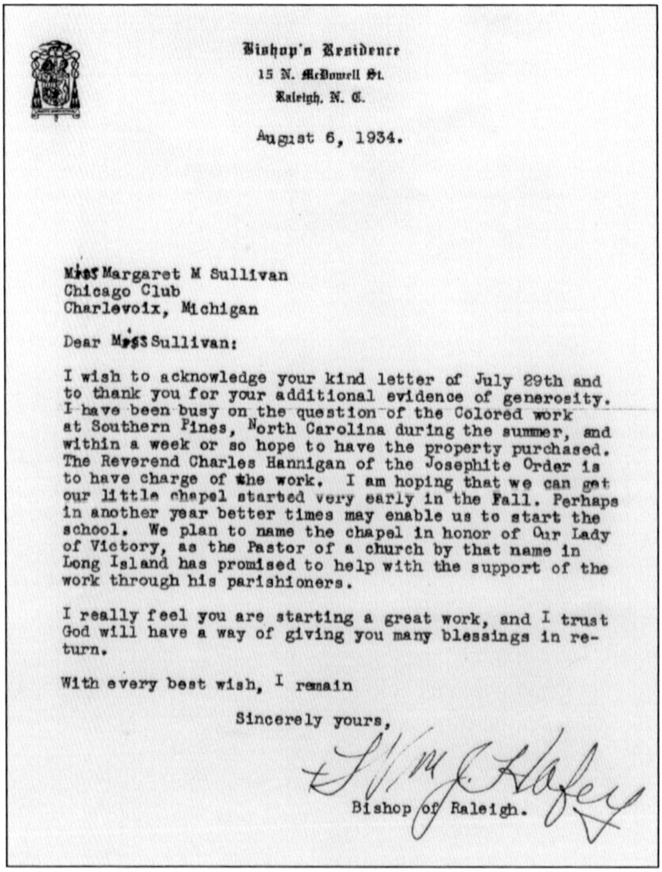

Bishop's Residence
15 N. McDowell St.
Raleigh, N. C.

August 6, 1934.

Miss Margaret M Sullivan
Chicago Club
Charlevoix, Michigan

Dear Miss Sullivan:

I wish to acknowledge your kind letter of July 29th and to thank you for your additional evidence of generosity. I have been busy on the question of the Colored work at Southern Pines, North Carolina during the summer, and within a week or so hope to have the property purchased. The Reverend Charles Hannigan of the Josephite Order is to have charge of the work. I am hoping that we can get our little chapel started very early in the Fall. Perhaps in another year better times may enable us to start the school. We plan to name the chapel in honor of Our Lady of Victory, as the Pastor of a church by that name in Long Island has promised to help with the support of the work through his parishioners.

I really feel you are starting a great work, and I trust God will have a way of giving you many blessings in return.

With every best wish, I remain

Sincerely yours,

+ Wm J. Hafey
Bishop of Raleigh.

This letter was written by the Catholic Bishop of Raleigh, William Hafey, addressing the construction of a Catholic church in West Southern Pines. In this letter, he explains that the chapel will be named in honor of a church in Long Island, because the parishioners there had promised to help finance its construction.

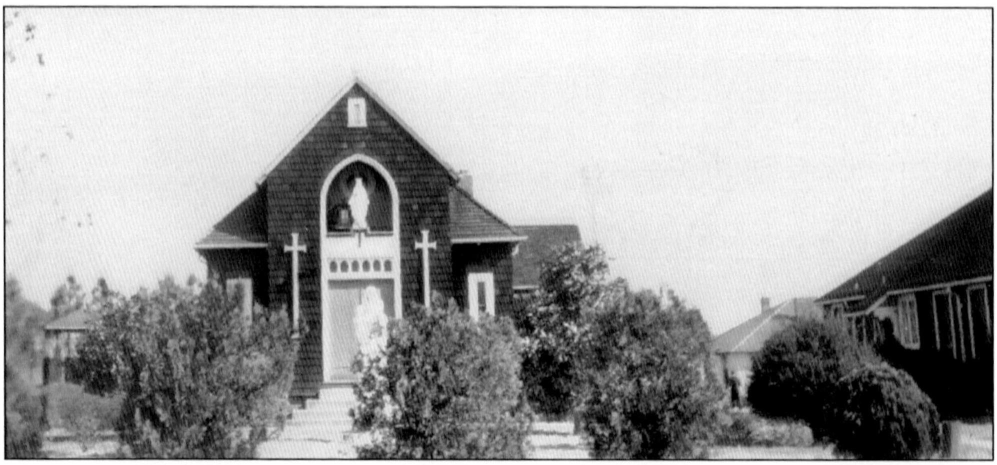

This picture shows Our Lady of Victory Church, the Catholic church that was built in West Southern Pines. Margaret Sullivan wrote to Bishop Hafey on June 14, 1933, expressing her desire to assist financially in the construction of a Catholic church for "the colored people." In another of her letters, written to a nun, Sullivan said that she "want[ed] the colored people to have a church." Margaret Sullivan was an Irish housekeeper for the Meehan family, owners of Quaker Oats Company in Chicago, Illinois. The Meehan family and their servants lived in Pinehurst during "the season," November through April.

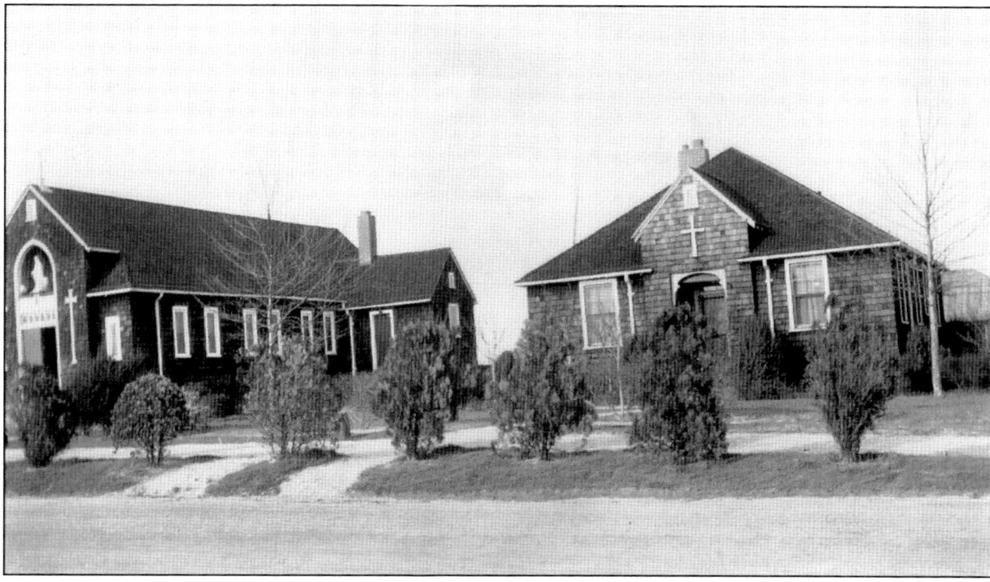

Pictured on the right is the rectory where the priests stayed while they were at Our Lady of Victory Church. Rev. Charles Hannigan of the Josephite Order was the first priest to serve in West Southern Pines.

Bishop's Residence
15 N. McDowell St.
Raleigh, N. C.

December 7, 1934.

Miss Margaret M Sullivan
4850 Woodlawn Avenue
Chicago, Illinois

Dear Miss Sullivan:

Only yesterday I was in Southern Pines and concluded all arrangements to begin the building of the Chapel and a little home for the priest. It was a coincidence that on my return to Raleigh your letter was awaiting me, and certainly we again must say, "thank you" for your very deep interest in this new beginning.

We hope to have the dedication sometime early in March and I know it will be a very happy day for you. I trust you will be in Pinehurst at that time.

Certainly we will arrange to have the altar erected in memory of your departed father and mother. We use a very simple but attractive altar, with the large crucifixion scene immediately above it.

Again thanking you and asking you to continue your prayers that God will bless this effort, and with every best wish, I remain

Sincerely yours,

+ Wm J. Hafey
Bishop of Raleigh.

This letter discusses the building of the church and the rectory and the dedication of the buildings in early March 1935. The total cost of the church and furnishings totaled $5,000. It was not until 1944 that the final payment was made for the construction of the church.

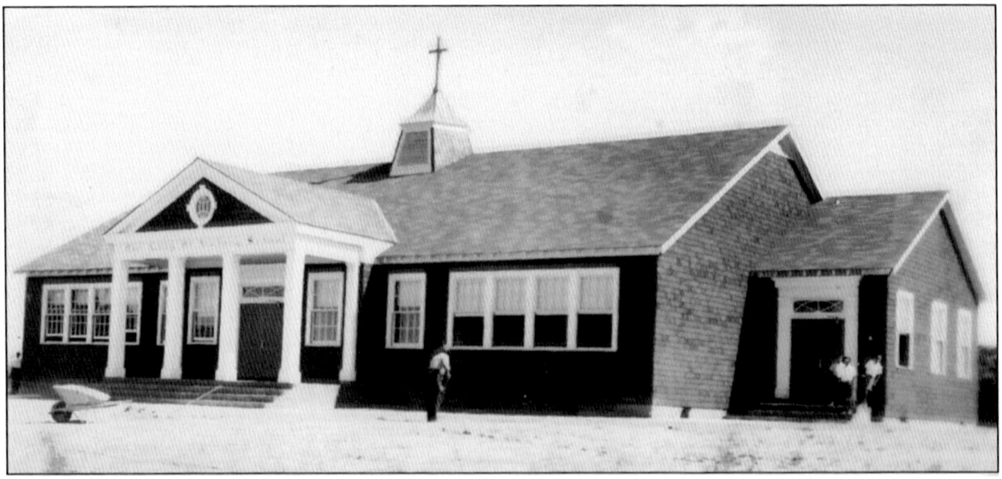

The success of the Our Lady of Victory vacation school during June 1941 brought about the desire to build a school for the children of West Southern Pines. When an orphan asylum in Rochester, New York, was closed, the proceeds from the sale of the buildings were distributed to several institutions to be used for educational purposes. The amount given to the Southern Pines area was used to build Our Lady of Victory School. On October 7, 1942, Rev. Eugene J. McGuinness blessed the building. On opening day, 28 children arrived, and 14 were Catholic. During the first six months, there was some open hostility demonstrated against the Sisters Notre Dame at the church that included literal mud-slinging. This did not last long and did not threaten the continuance of the school.

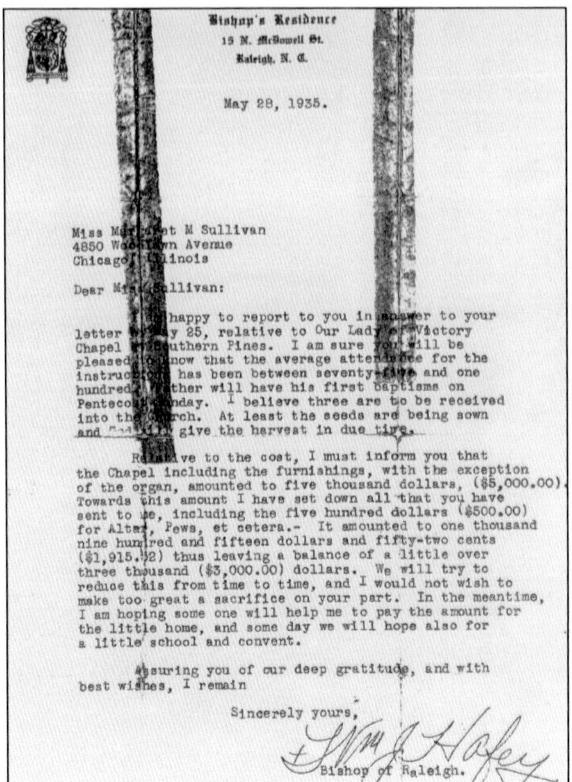

Bishop's Residence
15 N. McDowell St.
Raleigh, N. C.

May 28, 1935.

Miss M[illegible]t M Sullivan
4850 W[illegible]n Avenue
Chicago, [illegible]inois

Dear M[illegible]llivan:

[illegible] happy to report to you in [illegible]er to your letter [illegible]y 25, relative to Our Lady [illegible] Victory Chapel [illegible]uthern Pines. I am sure [illegible] will be pleased [illegible]now that the average atte[illegible]e for the instruc[illegible] has been between seventy-[illegible] and one hundred. [illegible]ther will have his first baptisms on Penteco[illegible]nday. I believe three are to be received into th[illegible]rch. At least the seeds are being sown and [illegible] give the harvest in due time.

R[illegible]ve to the cost, I must inform you that the Chapel including the furnishings, with the exception of the organ, amounted to five thousand dollars, ($5,000.00). Towards this amount I have set down all that you have sent to me, including the five hundred dollars ($500.00) for Altar, Pews, et cetera.- It amounted to one thousand nine hundred and fifteen dollars and fifty-two cents ($1,915.52) thus leaving a balance of a little over three thousand ($3,000.00) dollars. We will try to reduce this from time to time, and I would not wish to make too great a sacrifice on your part. In the meantime, I am hoping some one will help me to pay the amount for the little home, and some day we will hope also for a little school and convent.

Assuring you of our deep gratitude, and with best wishes, I remain

Sincerely yours,

+ Wm J. Hafey
Bishop of Raleigh.

Bishop William Hafey wrote this letter to Margaret Sullivan in 1935, regarding the building of a school and convent in West Southern Pines. He also informed her that there were almost 100 people attending the convert classes held by Father Hannigan.

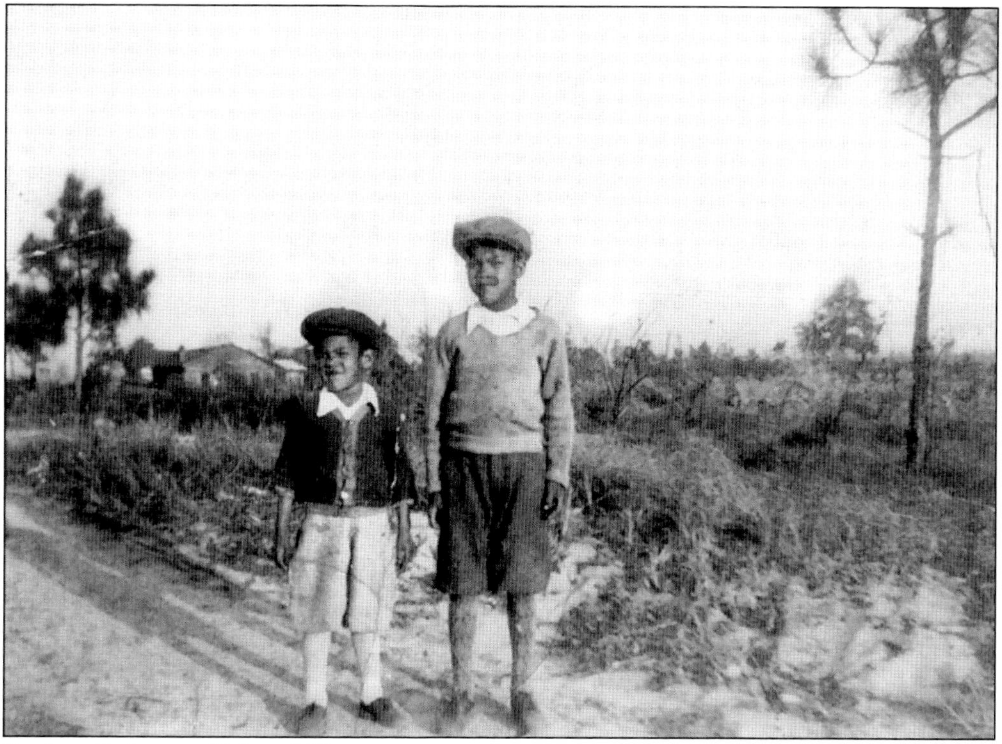

Brothers Robert and Edward Blue pose near their home on a hot summer afternoon, c. 1940s. The children thought it was a special treat to have their pictures taken, because most families could not afford a camera of their own.

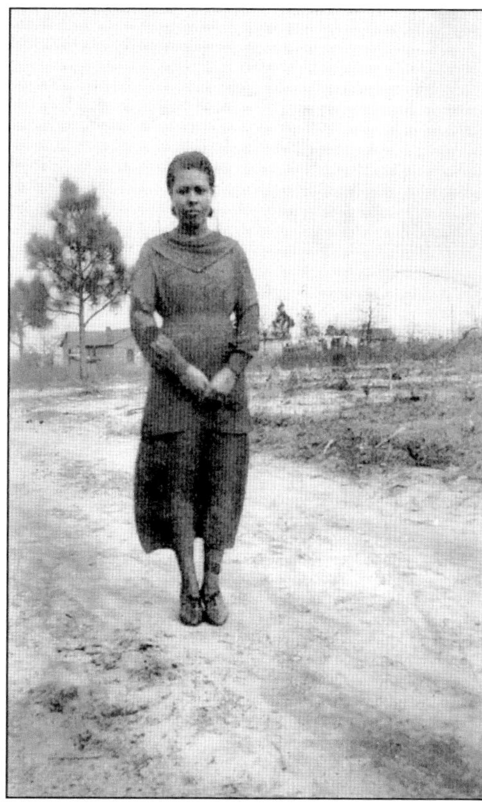

Juanita Blue stands on a sandy dirt road in the middle of West Southern Pines in the 1940s. It would be at least two decades before the roads were paved, despite the concerns of East Southern Pines when the charter was revoked.

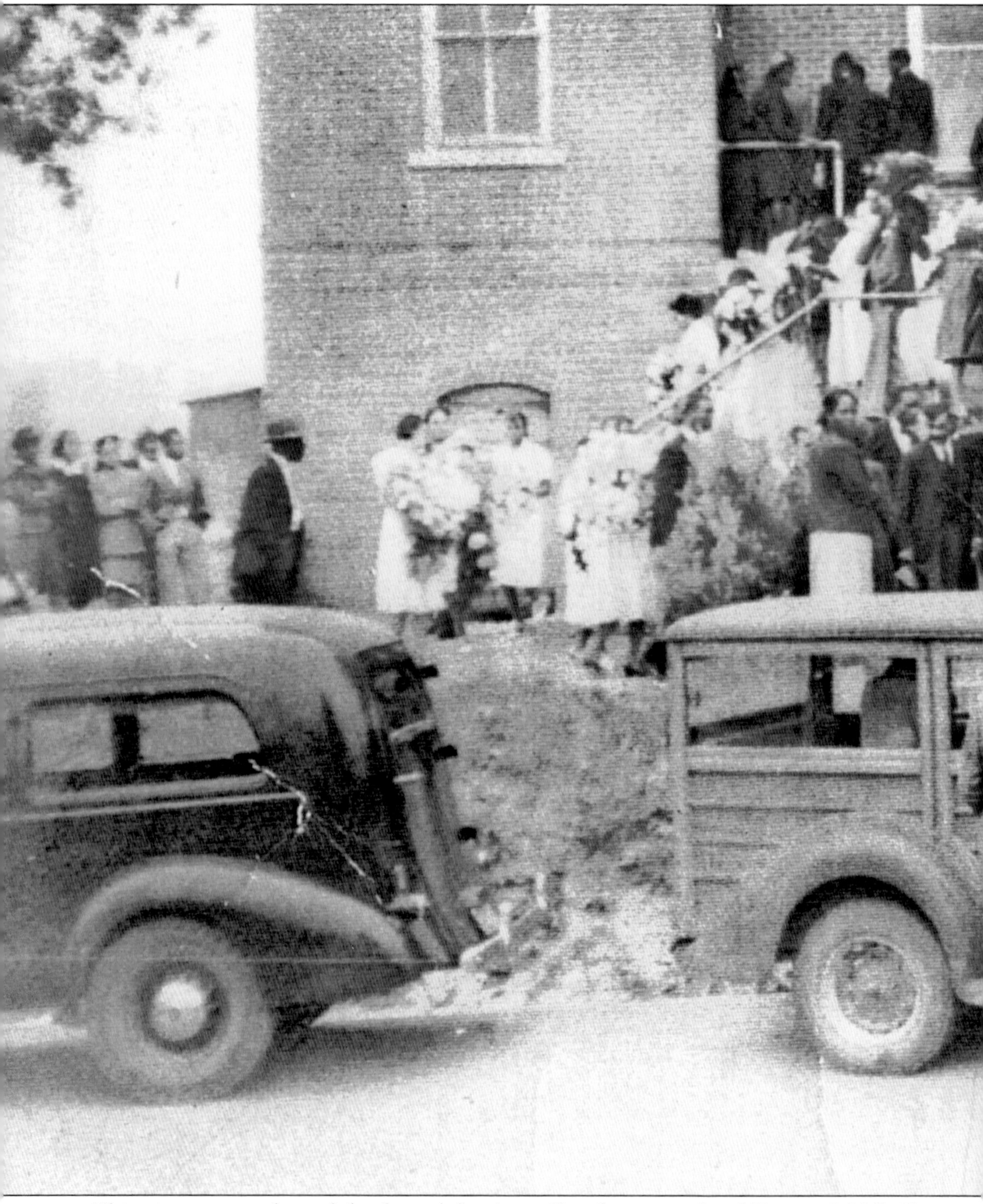

This picture was taken of the funeral for Amos Broadway outside of Trinity A.M.E. Zion Church with Southern Pines Police Chief Newton in the foreground. Amos Broadway owned and operated a cafe, movie theater, and pool hall. He was said to be one of the best bricklayers in the area. Amos sponsored dances, and although they were only advertised by word of mouth, people came to them from miles around. There was the some gambling and drinking at his

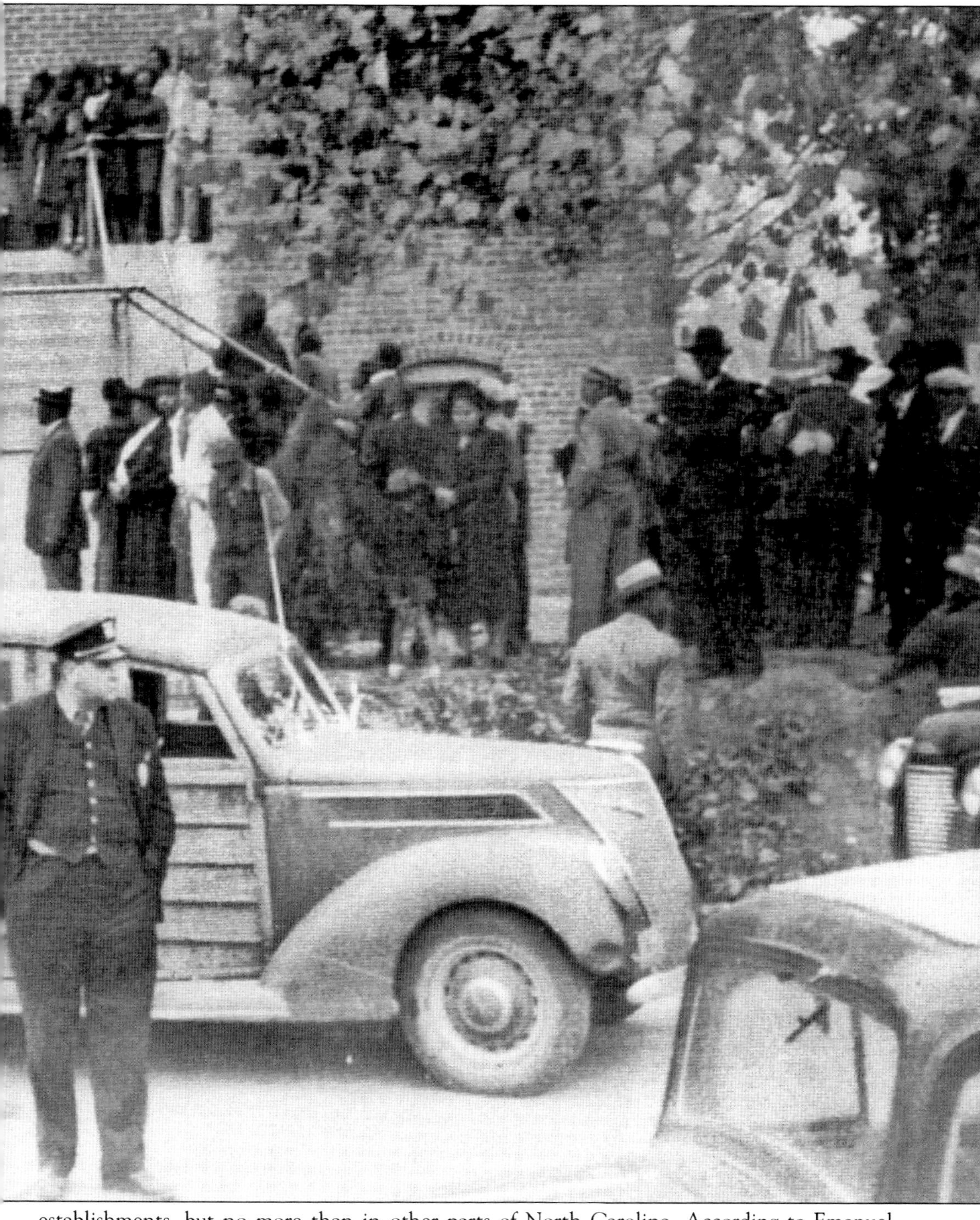

establishments, but no more than in other parts of North Carolina. According to Emanuel Douglass, Amos would call his uncle, Paul R. Brown, the principal at West Southern Pines High School, if a child was cutting class to hang around his place. Sadly, Amos Broadway was ambushed and killed as he closed up for the night. Police Chief Newton was later killed in the line of duty.

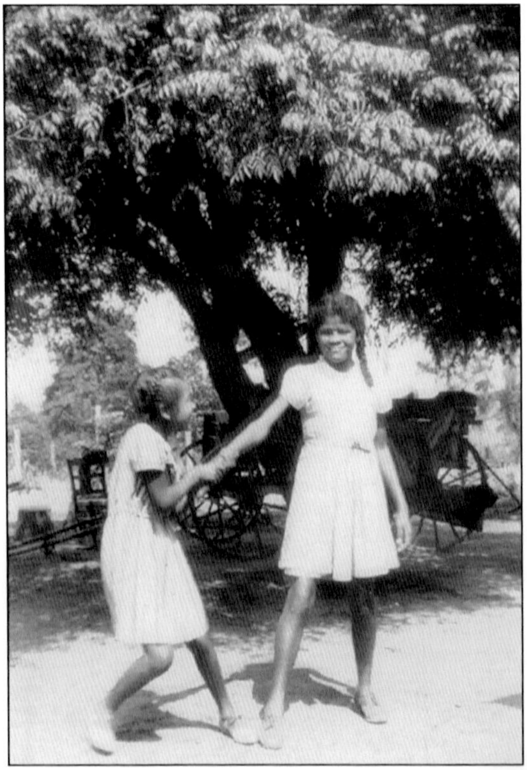

This photograph shows two sisters, Martha and Delores Blue, enjoying one another while playing beneath a chinaberry tree at their grandmother's house. The children of this period had certain chores they must do, but they still found time to play outside.

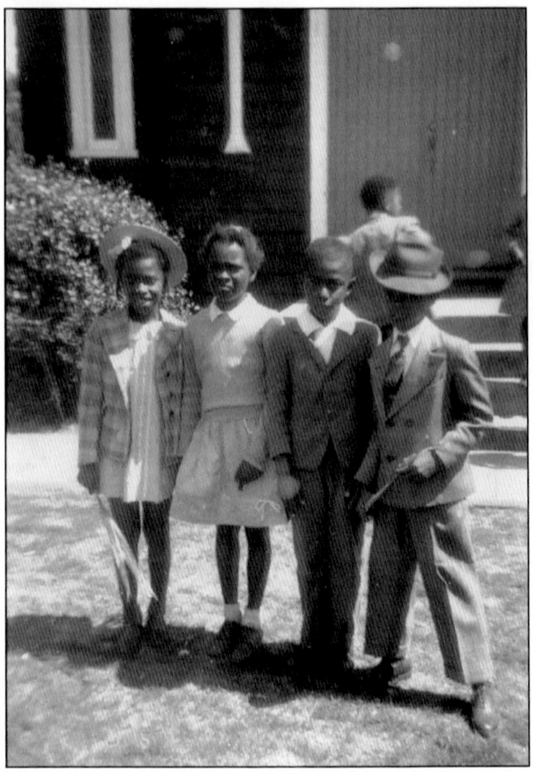

It was always a special occasion for children to have their pictures taken. This photograph was taken outside of the Catholic school on West Pennsylvania Avenue in West Southern Pines.

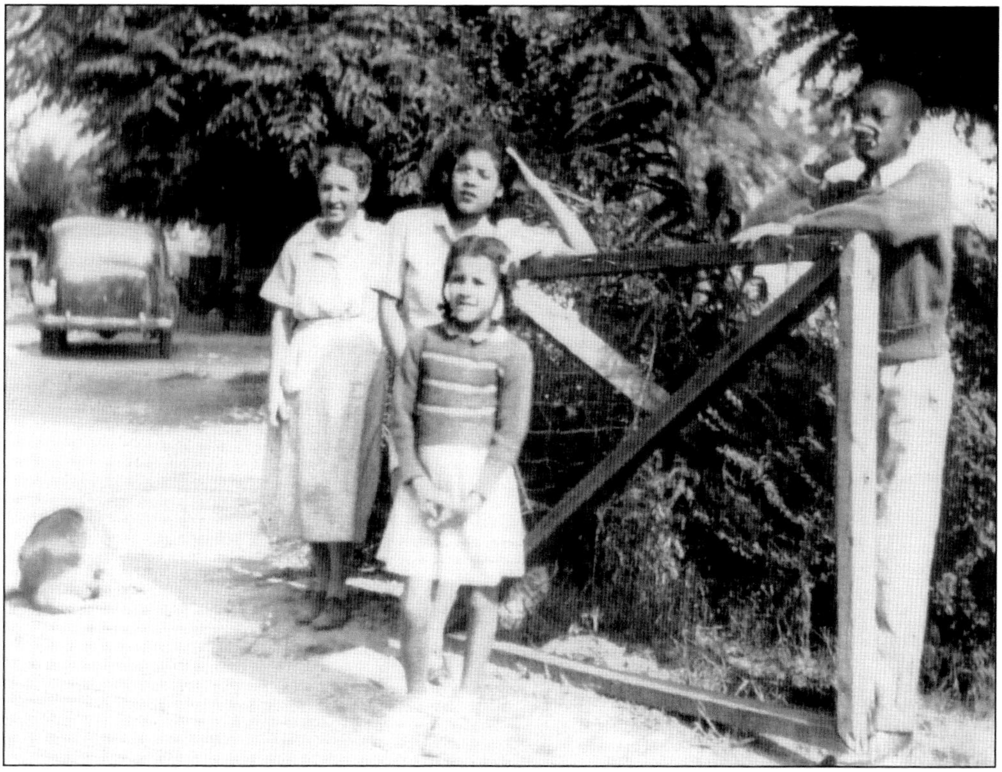

Pictured from left to right are Martha Evans Blue; her daughter, Gertie Blue; her granddaughter, Delores Blue; and her husband John Blue. They are standing outside their home on Carlisle Street. West Southern Pines was a close knit community with many extended families living near one another.

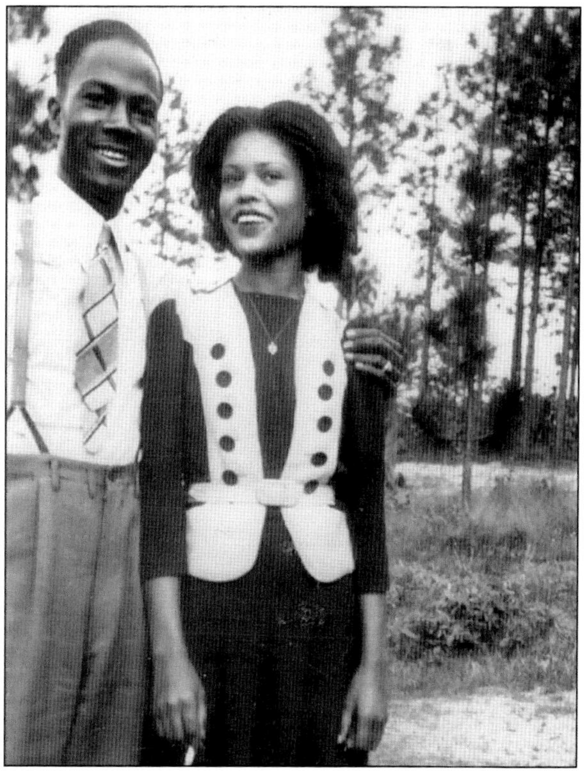

Ann Blue is pictured with her fiancé, Leroy McLaurin. Ann worked as a domestic in the Weymouth area of East Southern Pines and also at Mid Pines. She and her fiancé often went to the Sunrise Theater, even though they were required to sit in the balcony. Many African Americans joked that they had the best seats in the house. Many years later, the theater was desegregated by Felton Capel and his friend, former state senator Voit Gilmore.

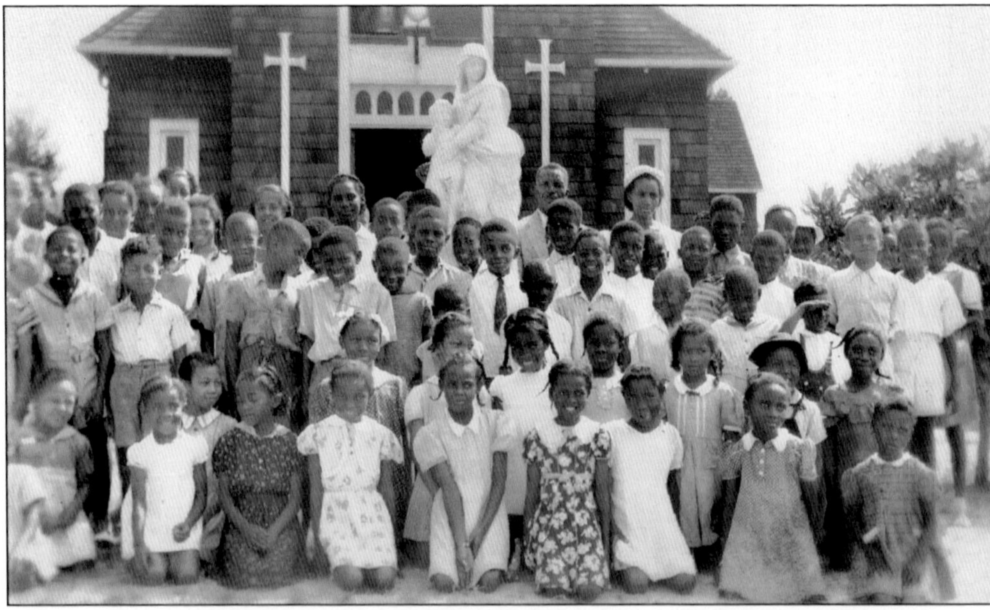

This is a group picture of the 1942 vacation school at Our Lady of Victory. The man in the back row and his family were converted the Christmas before and were at that time the only Catholic family in the parish.

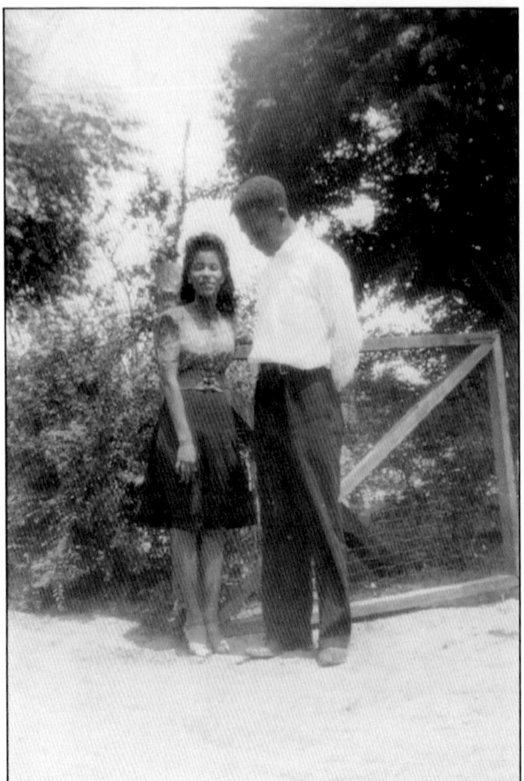

This picture shows a young man and his girlfriend standing hear his parents' home on a Sunday afternoon. He was to leave after Sunday dinner to chauffeur a Northern couple back to Massachusetts.

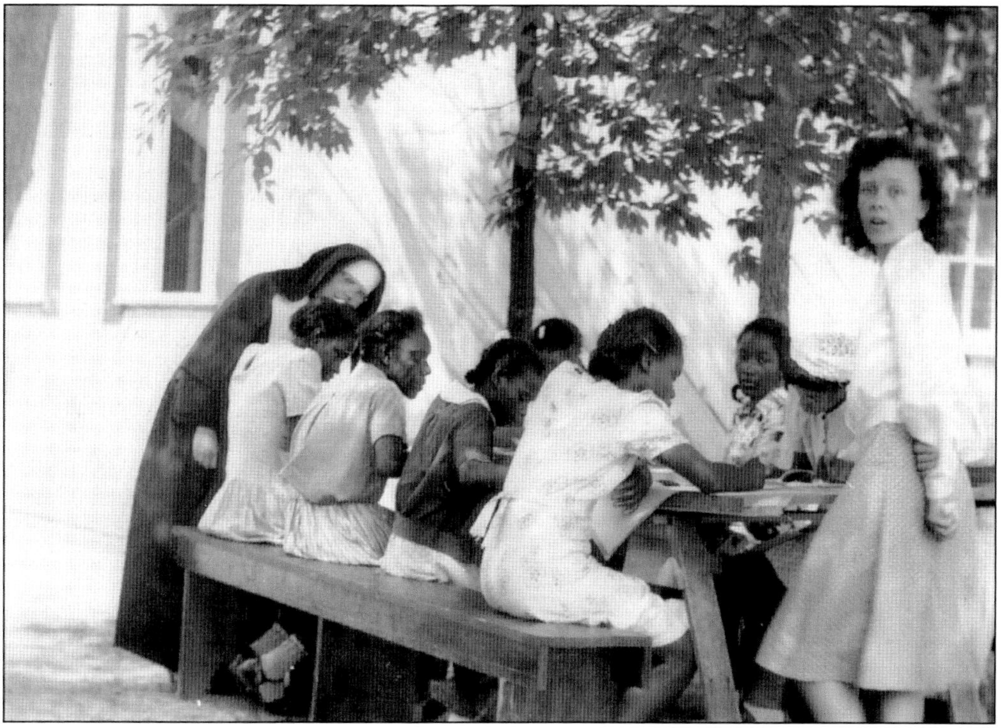

The vacation school was held outside in a grove adjoining the church of Our Lady of Victory. The faculty consisted of four Sisters of Notre Dame and five students from Trinity College, Washington, D.C. School began each day at 9 a.m., after which classes were held in a pine grove beside the church. Each morning, the priests made and handed out sandwiches and lemonade.

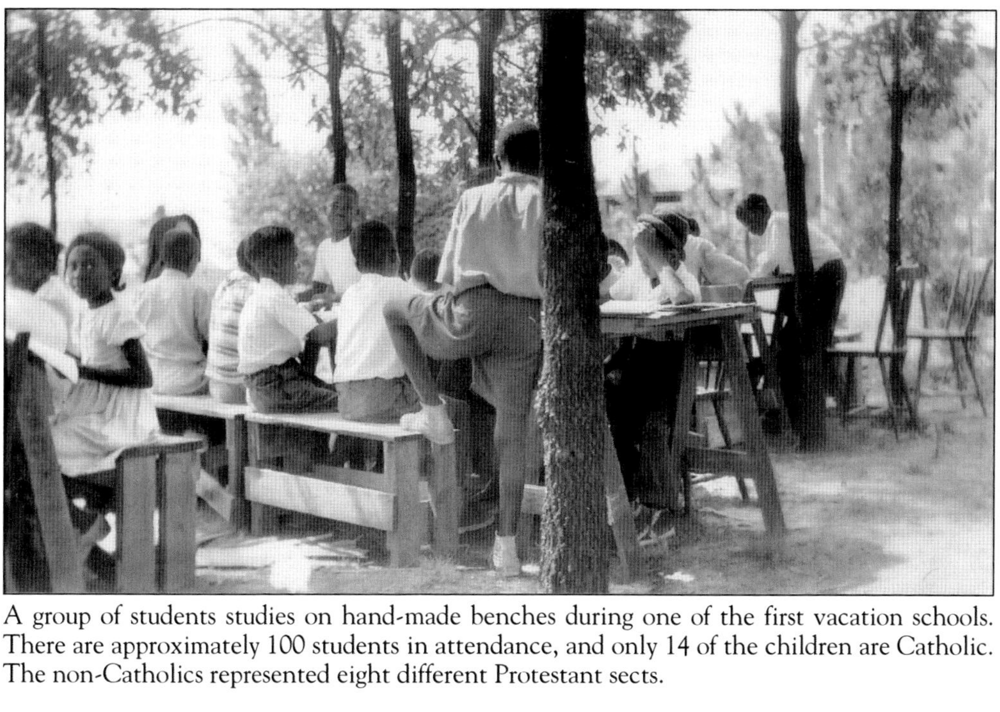

A group of students studies on hand-made benches during one of the first vacation schools. There are approximately 100 students in attendance, and only 14 of the children are Catholic. The non-Catholics represented eight different Protestant sects.

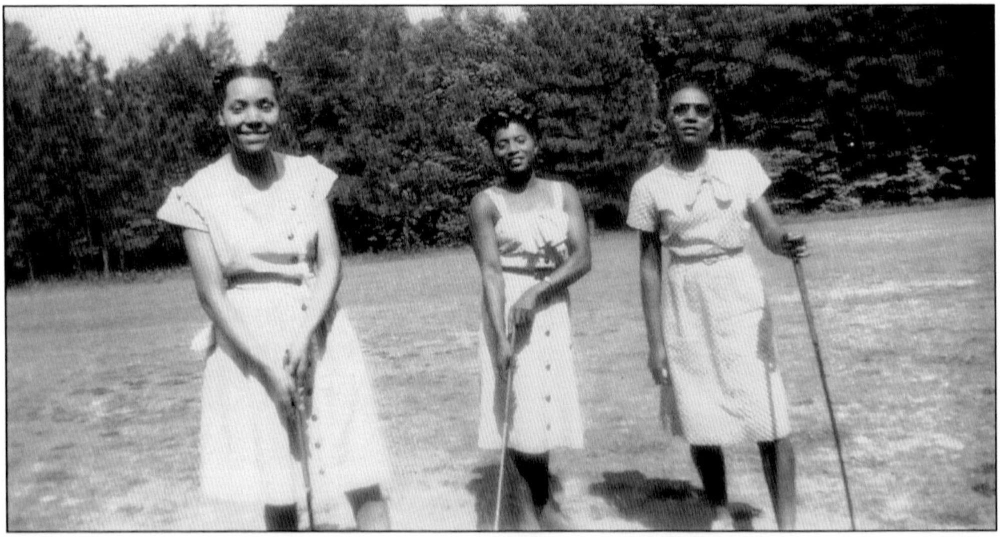

This photo shows the May Day Party that took place a few weeks before vacation school closed. Parents of the children were also in attendance, and the party took place on the grounds of the Mid Pines Inn, which was closed for the summer. These ladies are holding their golf clubs, but African Americans were not allowed on the golf course, except to caddy. Many African Americans would sneak on the course when it was closed, sometimes with only one or two clubs. Some of the caddies played better golf than the golfers they caddied for. For example, Harold Williams, known as "Mr. Pines Needles," worked at Pine Needles for more than 40 years and performed almost every duty at the resort. At least once, he drove the fringe of the green of the long par-four, 18th hole at Pine Needles. To the family's knowledge, no one has matched that feat.

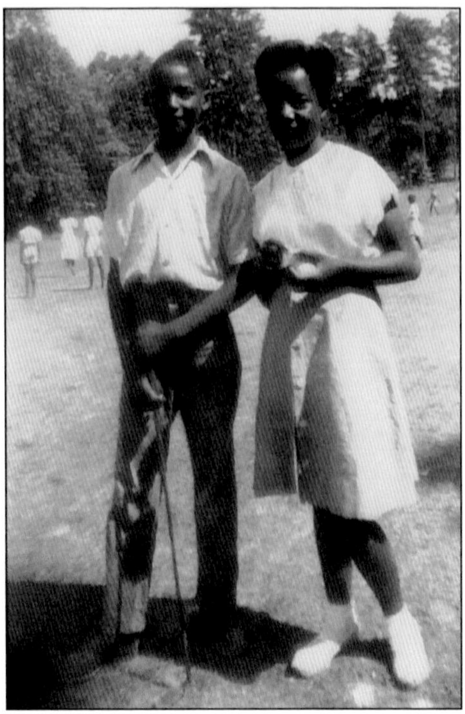

This photograph shows an unidentified couple getting ready to play a round of golf during the May Day Party. During the 1960s, a course in Rockingham, North Carolina, was one of the only golf courses in the state that allowed African Americans to play golf; the other was in Greensboro, North Carolina.

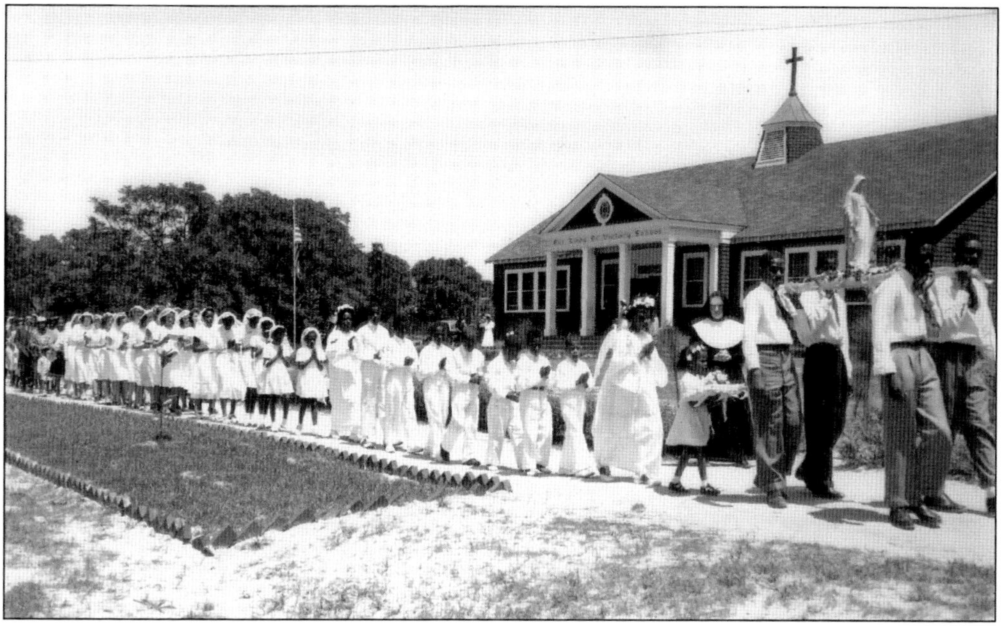

Pictured here are the first communion class members and the boarders from Notre Dame Academy who came to help with the singing. This was the May procession in 1948.

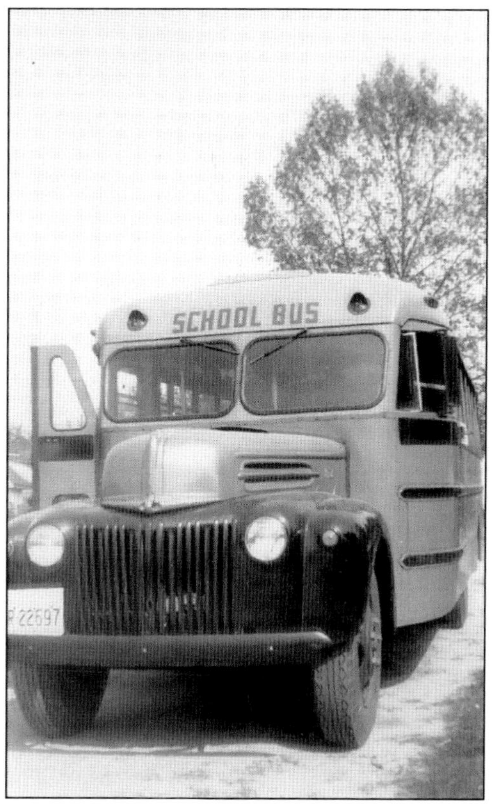

Children from neighboring towns such as Pinehurst, Taylortown, Jackson Hamlet, and Aberdeen would be picked up by the school bus to attend school at Our Lady of Victory, even though there was a public school. With the bus service, the number of pupils increased to 128 in 1947. James Dockery was the first school bus driver, and he also assisted in teaching the boys about metal craft and carpentry.

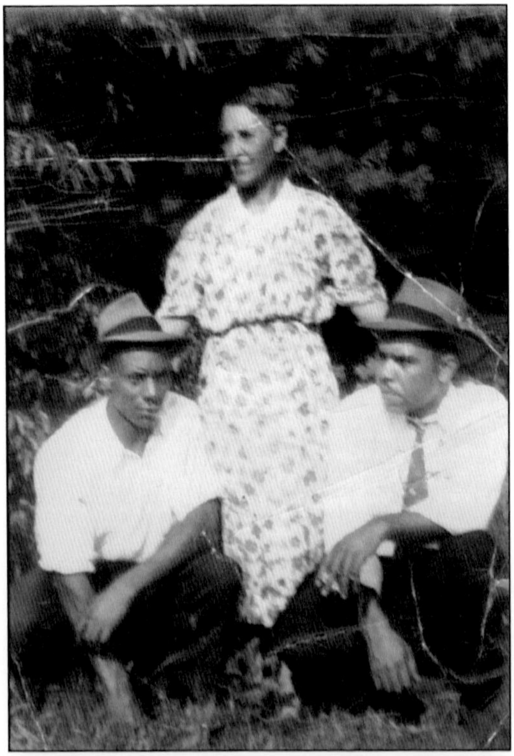

Martha Blue poses for a picture outside her home with her son-in-law, Doug Alexander, and her son, Chester Blue.

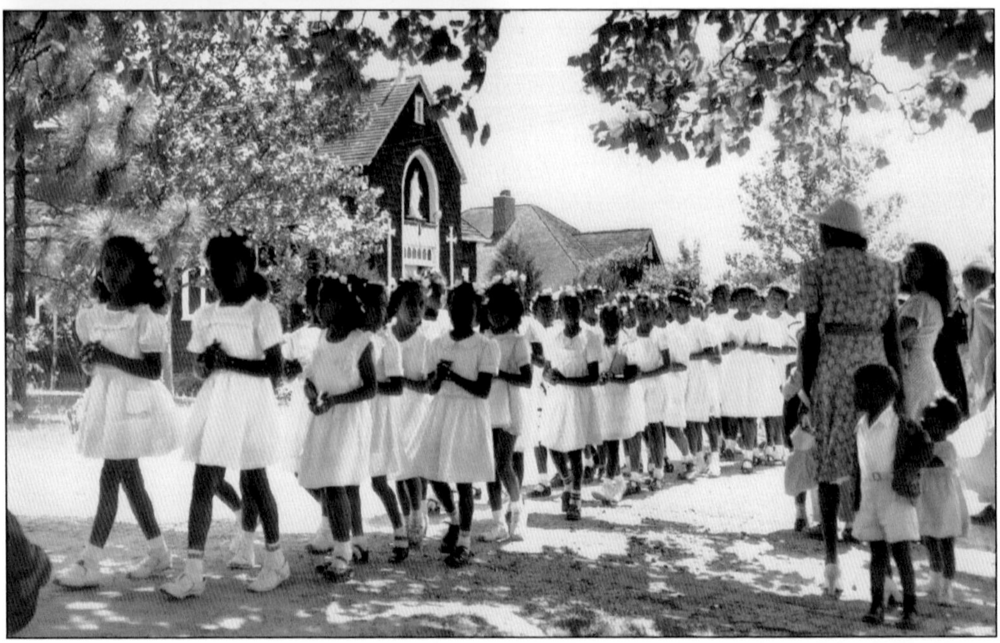

Outside Our Lady of Victory Church, a procession heads to the school for refreshments after a special celebration. Family and friends watch the procession and will join the students inside. Many parents sent their children to this school because they believed the education was better; others chose it for the discipline that Catholic schools typically provide. The tuition began at 50¢ and increased over the years, and many families made sacrifices to pay this tuition.

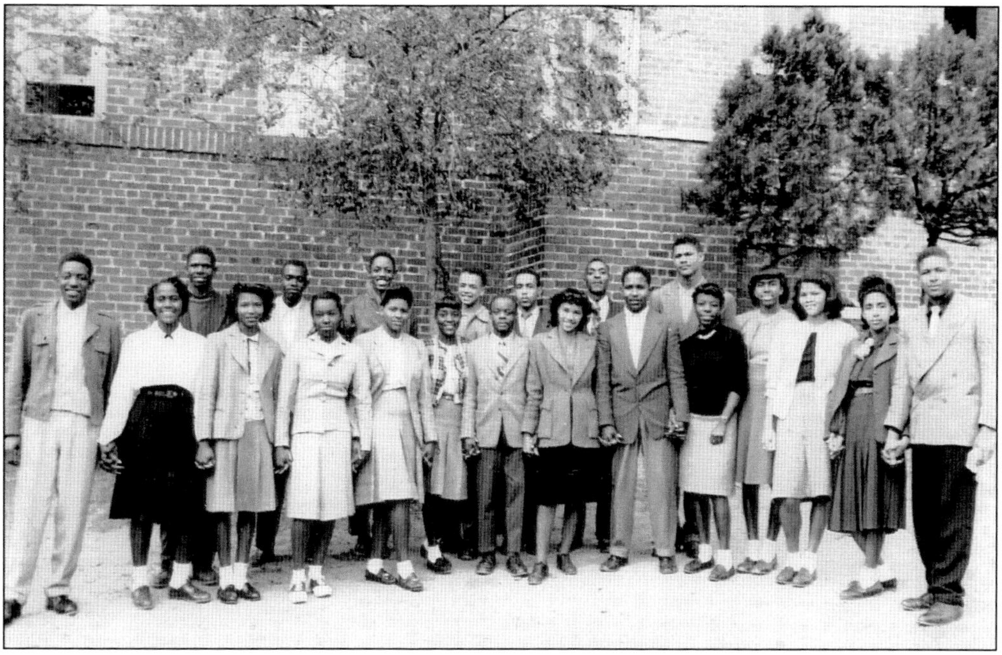

Here, the graduating class of 1948 poses outside of West Southern Pines High School for the class picture. Today, this is the site of Southern Pines Primary School.

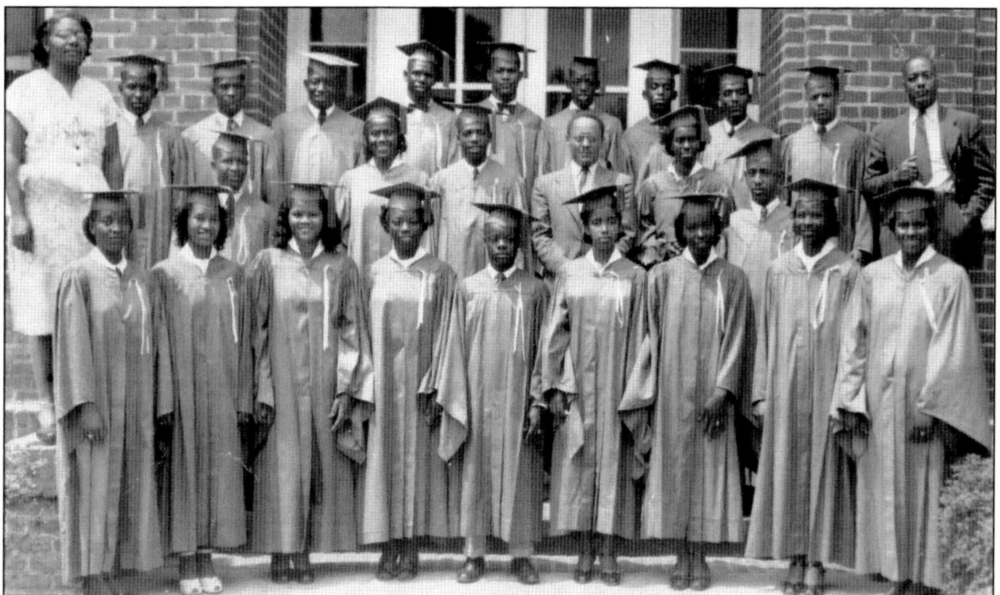

Here is the West Southern Pines High School Class of 1948. From left to right are (front row) Waltsie Cotton, Ruth Baldwin, Martha Blue, Middie Kirkland, Floyd Goode, Jeanette McNeil, Mildred Waddell, Helen Hainsworth, and Margarita Caldwell; (middle row) Lynwood Flowers, Lillian Dockery, unknown, Mr. Ward (band leader), Lorraine McNeil, and John Robinson; (back row) Mrs. Clark, James McFadden, James Gillis, Babe Stephenson, William King, Edward Blue, Charles Hill, John Stubbs, Tommy Lewis, Mitchell McClain, and Mr. Moore (principal.)

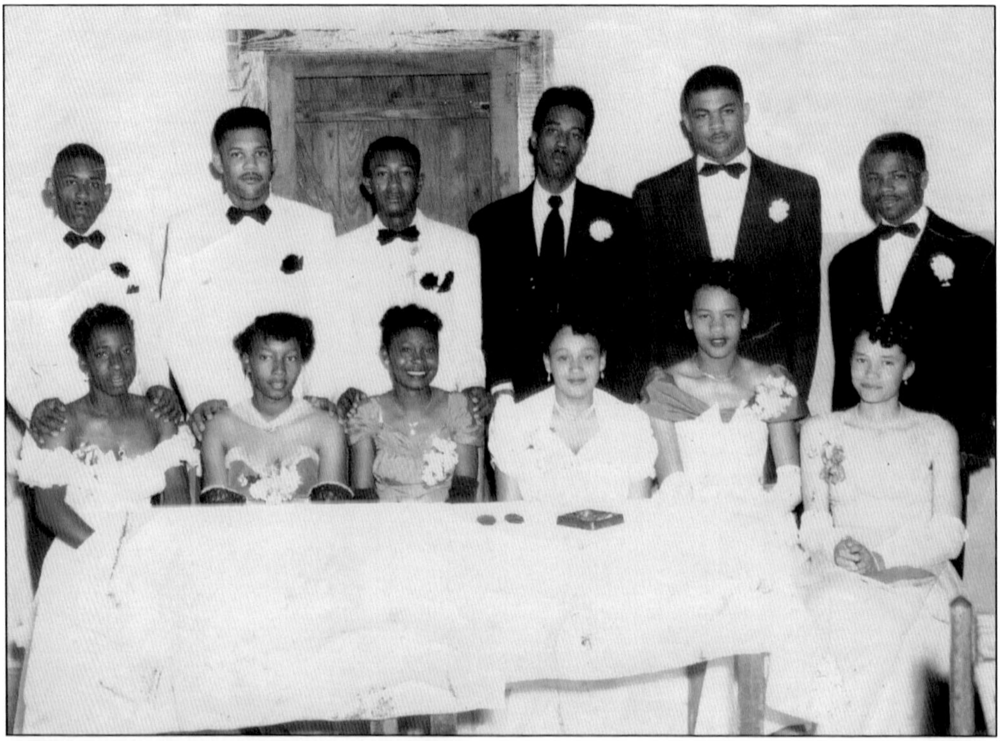

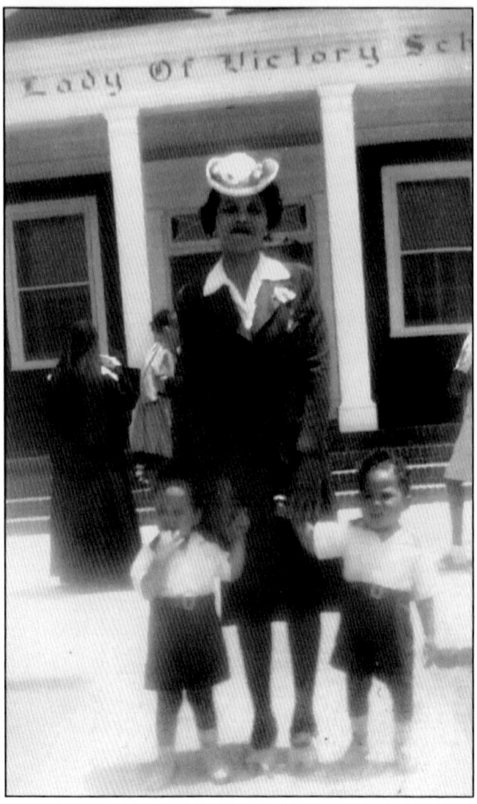

It's prom time in West Southern Pines. Some students pose for a picture taken in the late 1940s. From left to right are (seated) three unidentified women, Alice McDougal, Grace France, and Betty Baldwin; (standing) Victor Headen, Robert Blue, Henry Holland, Frank Nelson, Edward Blue, and Haywood Jones.

Franklin and Oliver Goode are future students of Our Lady of Victory School and West Southern Pines High School. They are pictured with their mother, Mrs. Bella Goode.

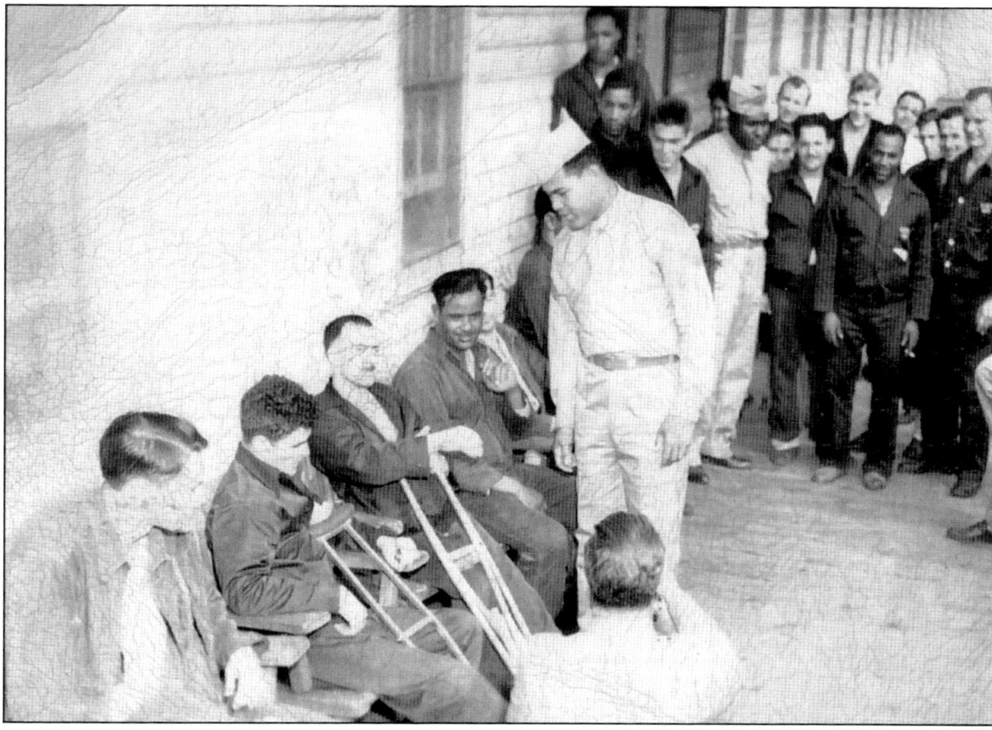

Heavy-weight boxing champion Joe Louis visits one of the local hospitals during wartime.

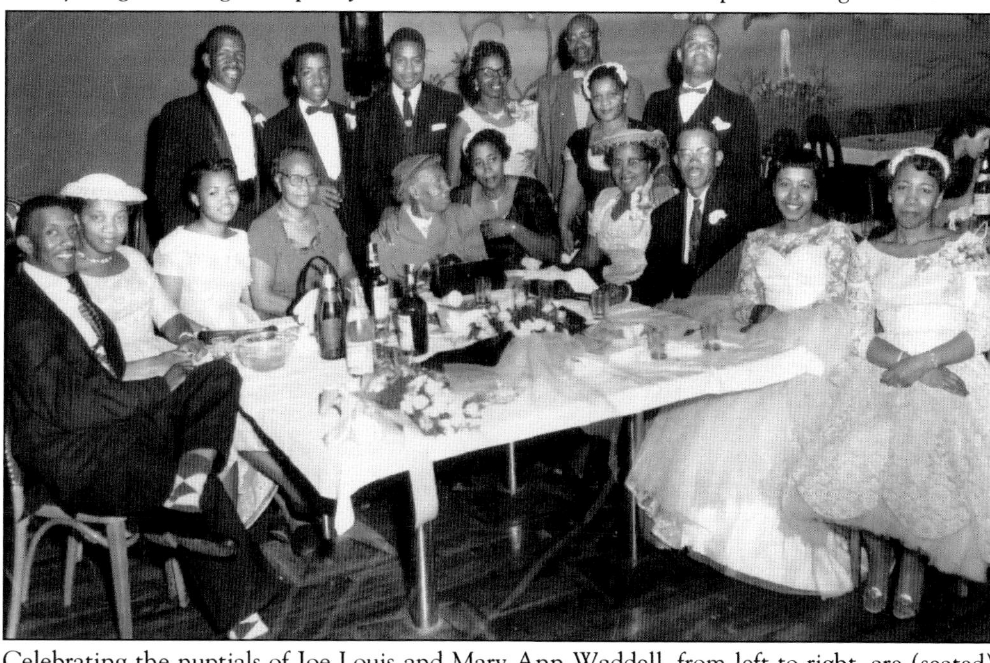

Celebrating the nuptials of Joe Louis and Mary Ann Waddell, from left to right, are (seated) Ernest and Evelyn Waddell, Alice Dockery, Odessa Dockery, Betsy Covington, Betty Covington, Julia and Joe Waddell, Mary Ann Wadell, and Mrs. Santos; (standing) Joe Louis Waddell, Milton "Super" Waddell, Joe Wells, Mildred Waddell Wells, Lacey Fairley, and Mr. and Mrs. Stedwell.

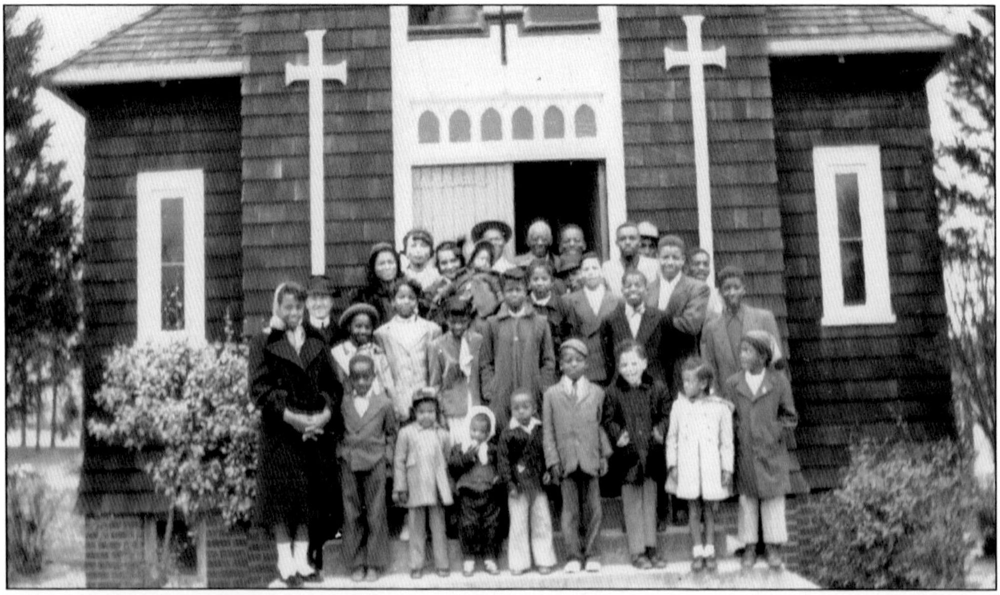

Our Lady of Victory Church members stand in front of the church. Included in this picture are Dorothy, Charlie, and Vic Headen; Teddy Holland; Michael Gooch; Elaine Goode; Mrs. Bella Goode; Oliver Goode; and Father Kuhn.

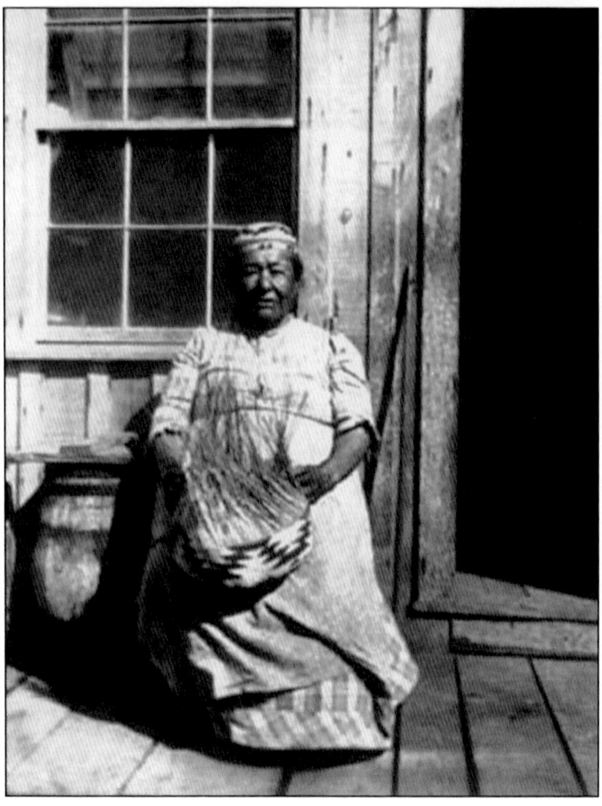

Pictured here is a woman in West Southern Pines making a basket with sweetgrass and pine needles.

Priests stayed at this rectory during their tenure at Our Lady of Victory School. One priest who was a resident there was Father Joseph L. Howze, the only African-American priest to come to Our Lady of Victory. Father Howze was ordained for the priesthood on May 7, 1959, for the Diocese of Raleigh, North Carolina. Then, on November 8, 1972, he was appointed by Pope Paul VI as the auxiliary bishop of the Diocese of Natchez-Jackson, Mississippi. In March 1996, Bishop Howze became Bishop Promoter of the Apostleship of the Sea. In that post, he worked with local bishops to oversee the chaplaincies of seaports throughout the United States. Bishop Howze is now retired and living in Biloxi, Mississippi.

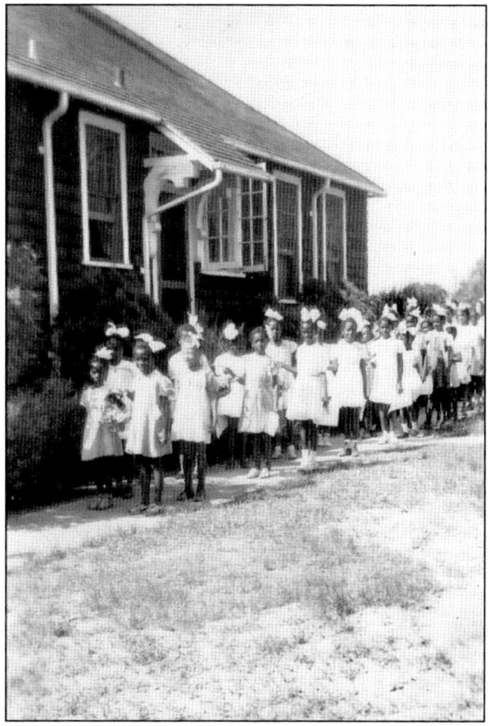

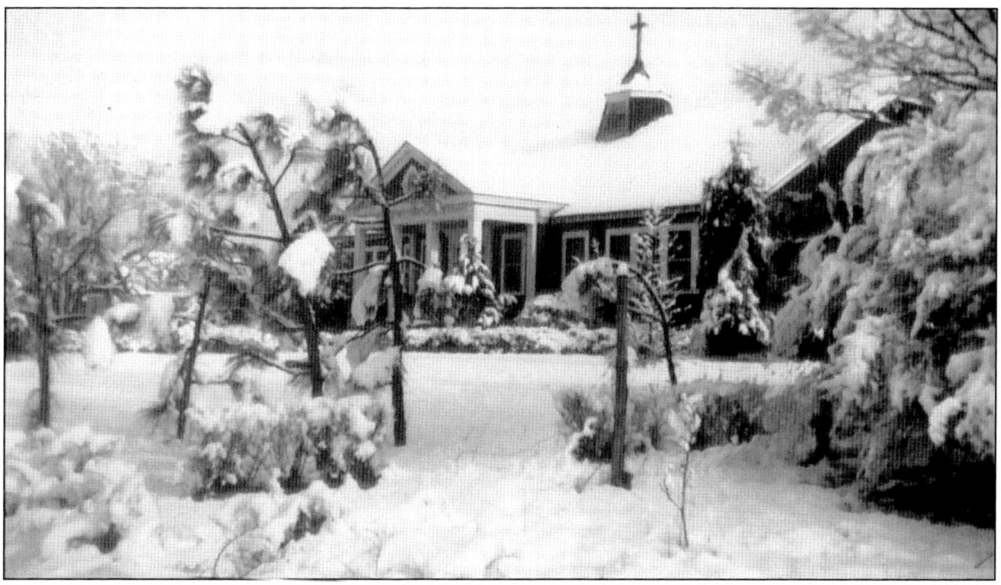

Many Northerners traveled numerous hours to winter in "the Mid-South Resort" of Southern Pines. On occasion, Mother Nature teased them with a Southern snowstorm, but fortunately it usually did not last very long. Due to the sandy soil of the Southern Pines area, there are frequent severe storms, but usually not in the winter months. In 1923, it was reported in the *Sandhill Citizen* that West Southern Pines was "hit by a wind storm" causing severe damage: "The Baptist church, which was a small frame structure, and three dwelling houses in the vicinity of the church were completely demolished, as were also the Broadway Theatre and the West Side Garage adjoining it."

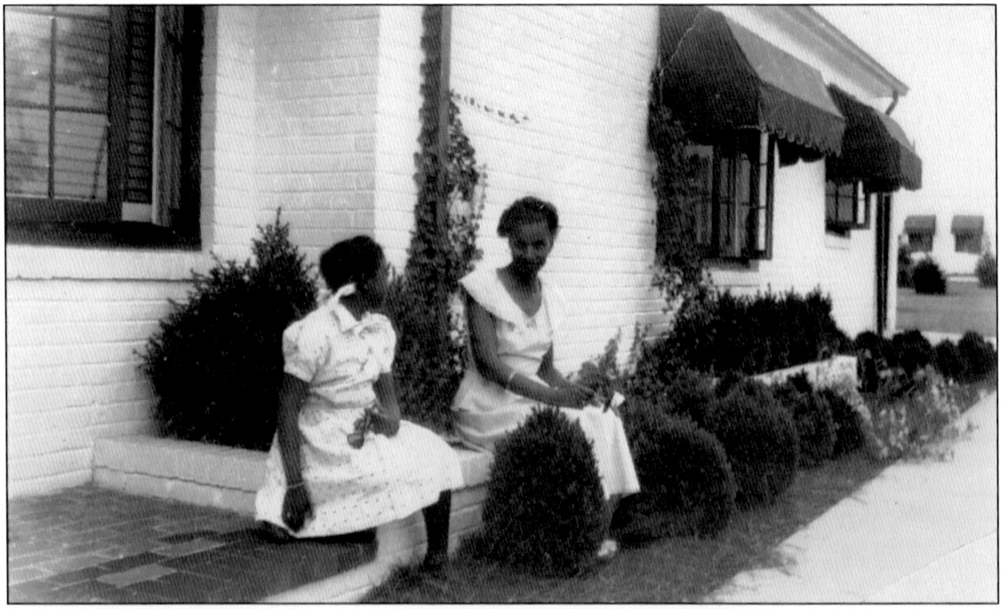

Two young women sit outside of Dr. Ross's office on Pennsylvania Avenue, *c.* 1940s. Dr. Ross was the first black doctor to both practice and live in the community of West Southern Pines.

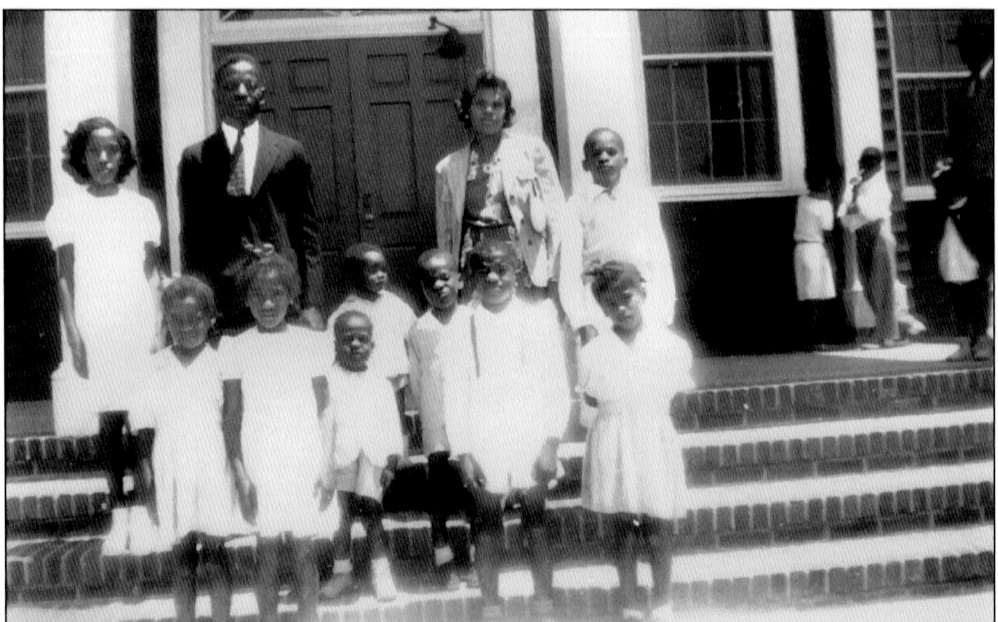

Pictured here are Mr. and Mrs. Kelley Young with their nine children; they were the first family to join Our Lady of Victory Church. June Young was the oldest, and she graduated from Our Lady of Victory School in 1948 with honors. She received a partial scholarship to attend St. Francis Academy in Baltimore, Maryland.

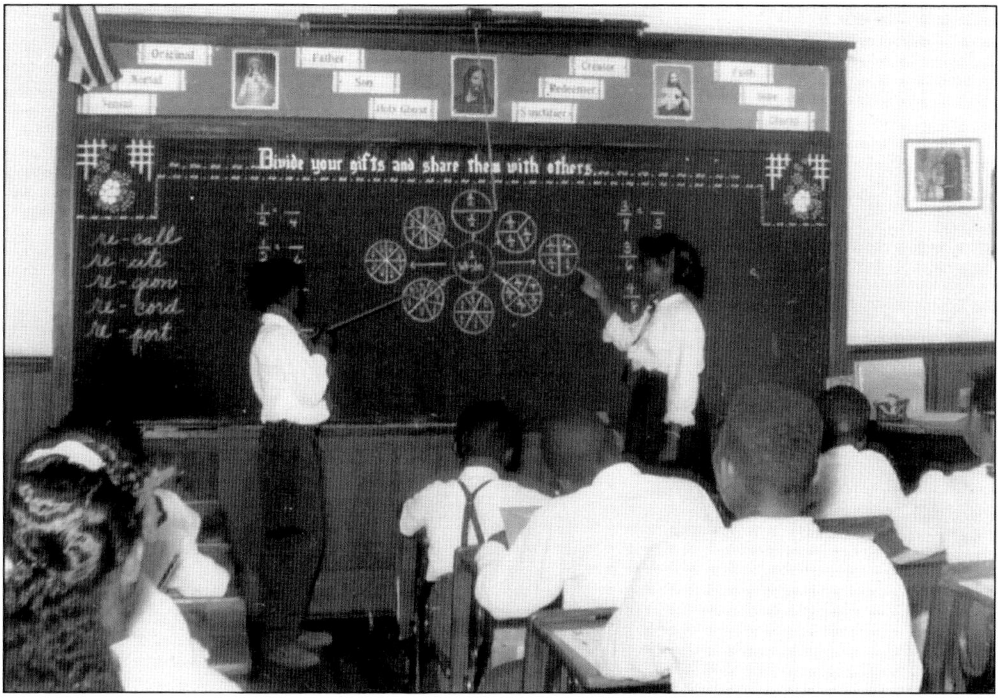

This is a picture of the children studying math in one of the classrooms at Our Lady of Victory School in 1953. During the first years of the school, children could not afford to purchase their school books, so the school would loan the books to them. Other schools taught by the Sisters of Notre Dame in Philadelphia, Baltimore, and Washington, D.C., sometimes sent used textbooks to Our Lady of Victory.

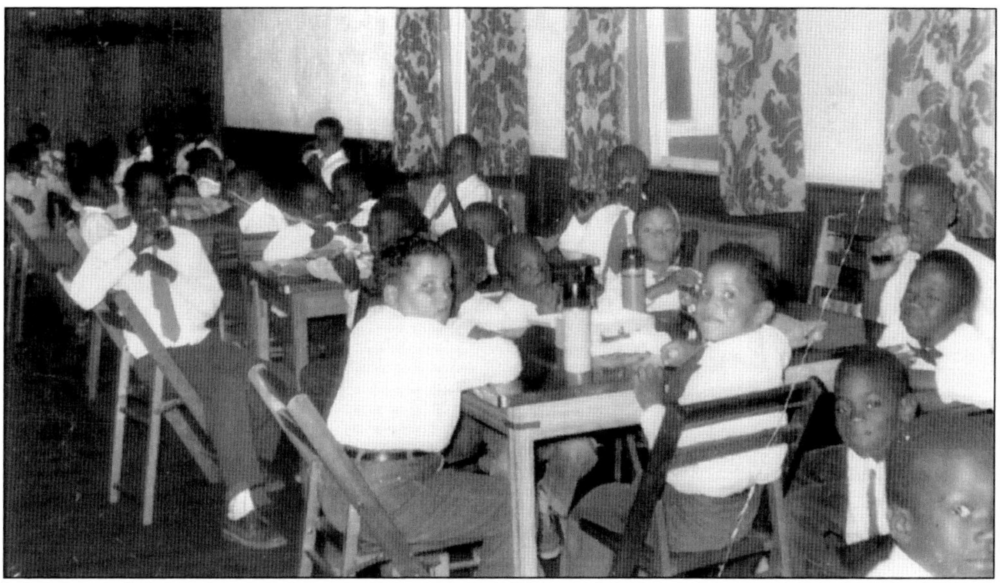

The children at Our Lady of Victory enjoy their lunches in the school cafeteria. The school uniform consisted of a navy blue skirt and white blouse for the girls, and blue jeans and a white shirt with a tie for the boys. However, during hot days at recess, the boys would often hang their shirts and ties on tree branches while they played baseball.

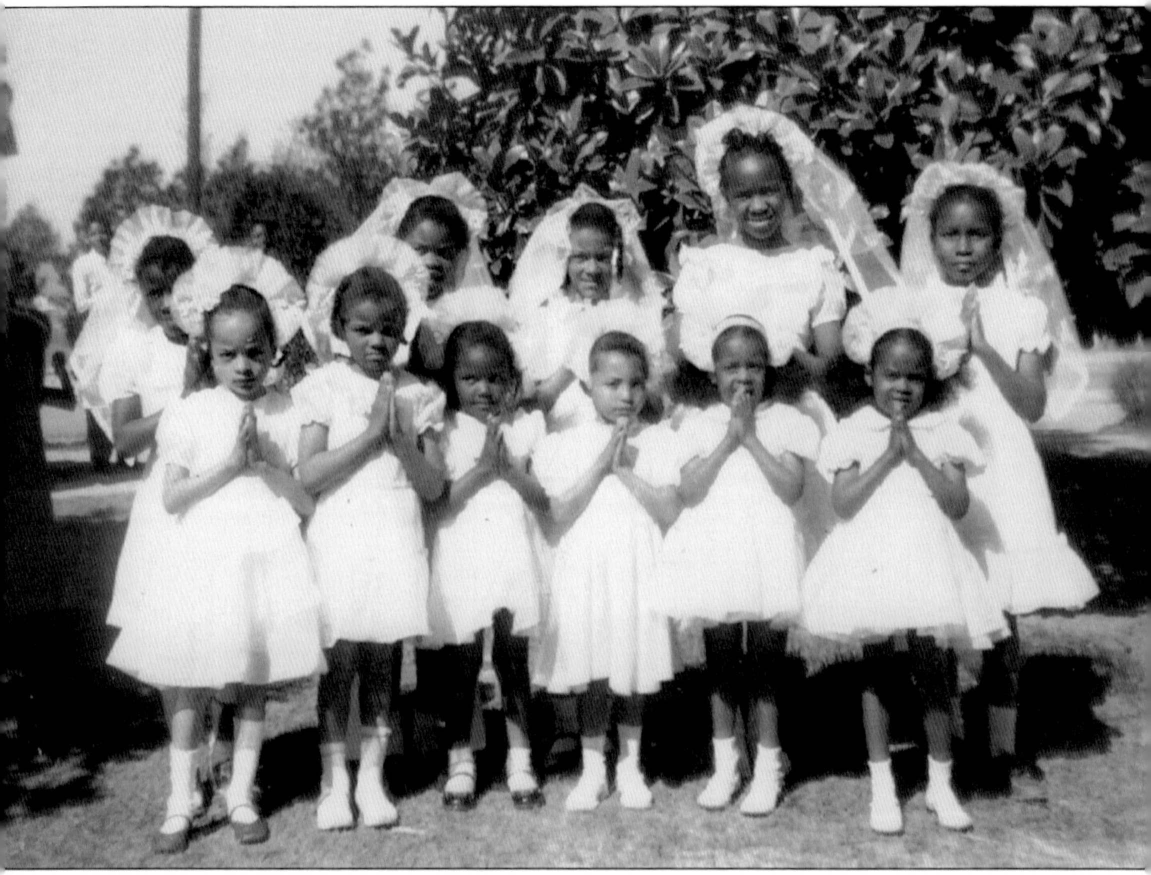

This picture is of the girls first communion in 1955. The girls received approximately two years of religious education before they were able to receive their first communion. They are dressed in the traditional white dresses with white veils, because they are not allowed to enter the church without their heads being covered. First communion usually occurs in the second grade.

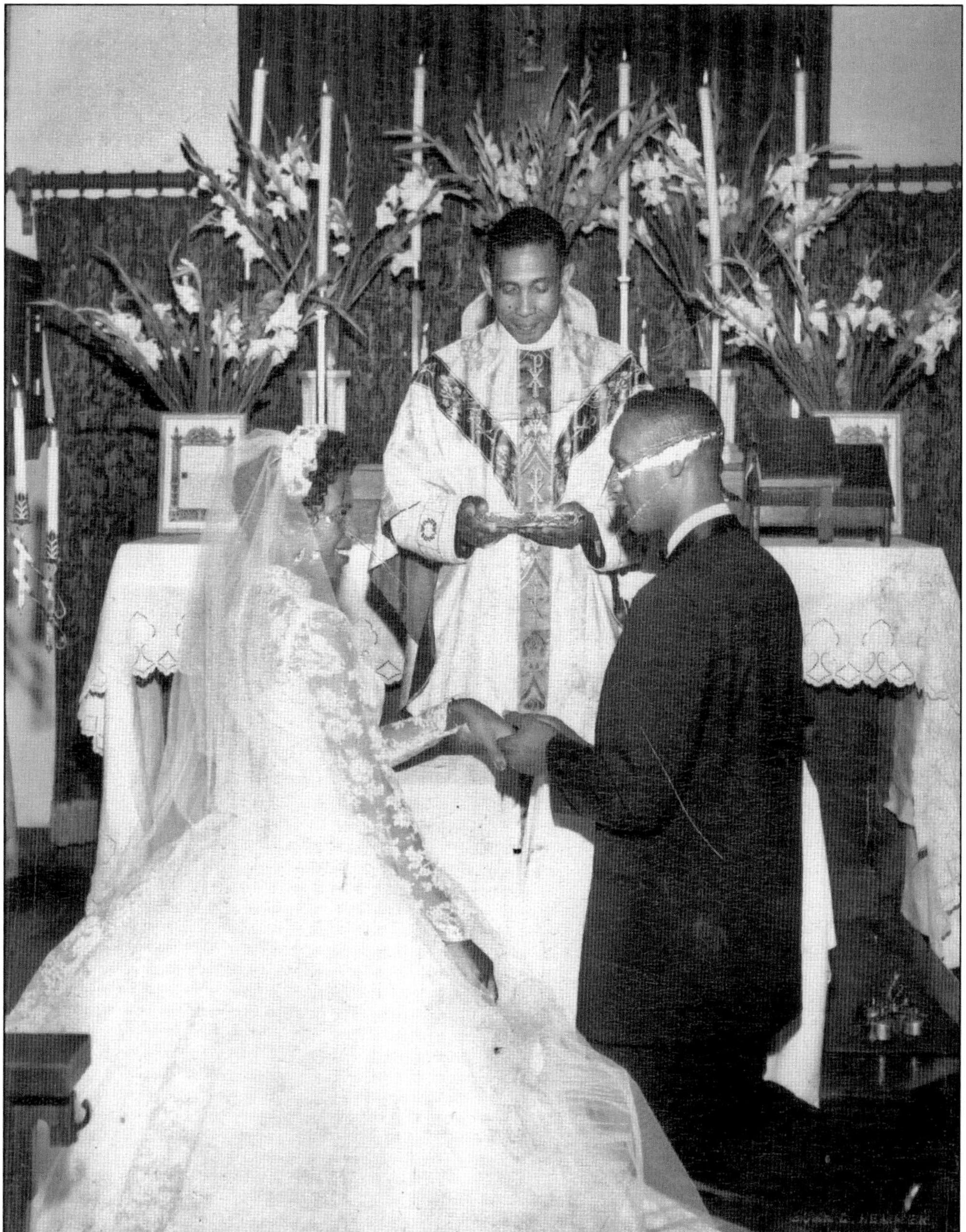

Dorothy Headen married Donald Thomas Lutz on May 7, 1960, in Our Lady of Victory Church. Father Howze officiated. Dorothy graduated from Johnson C. Smith University in Charlotte, North Carolina, and taught in West Southern Pines until she married. She then moved to Virginia. Several years later she returned to Southern Pines and resumed teaching in the school system.

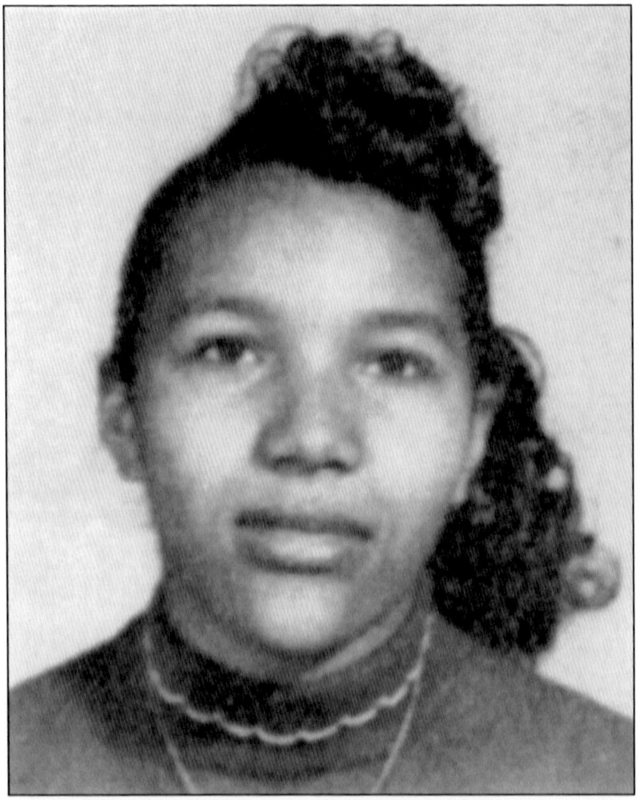

This is a photograph of Neutrice Quick. Her father, Ed Quick, had a boarding house for people of color on Saylor Street. Because African Americans could not stay in or use white facilities, traveling could be difficult for them. When winter residents came down from the Northern states, they often brought with them their servants and/or chauffeurs. Those who could not stay in servant's quarters lodged instead in rooming houses like Mr. Quick's.

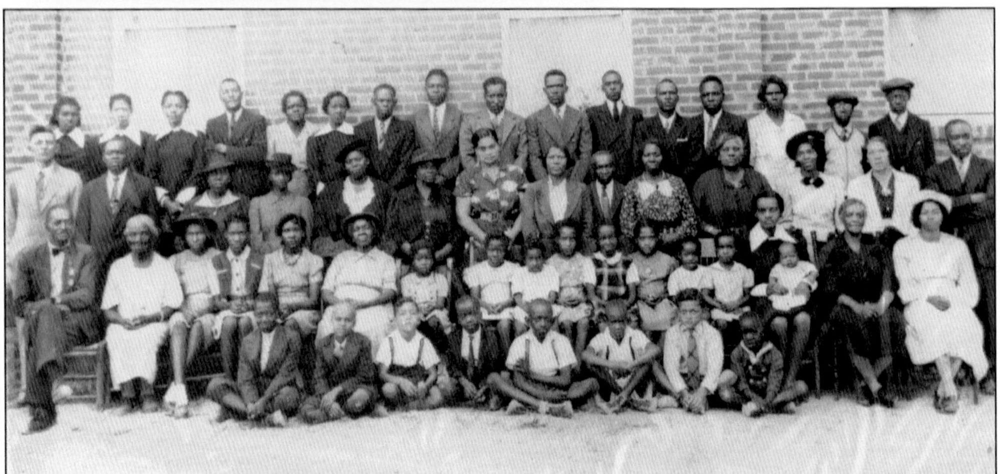

This is a picture of the members of First Missionary Baptist Church. From left to right in the first row are Ernest Waddell, Allan Goins, unidentified, Milton Waddell, three unidentified boys, and Joe Louis Waddell. The only person identified in the second row is Mrs. Porter Vine, second from the left. Identified in the third row are Mr. Goins at the far left; Marie Goins, seventh from left; and Rev. Works at the far right. Identified in the fourth row are Julia Waddell, sixth from the left; Joe Wadell, seventh from the right; and Lucius Ross, sixth from the right. Mildred Waddell Wells's father, Joe Waddell, helped to build this church. For many years Mr. Waddell had a barber shop in West Southern Pines.

Three

Southern Pines

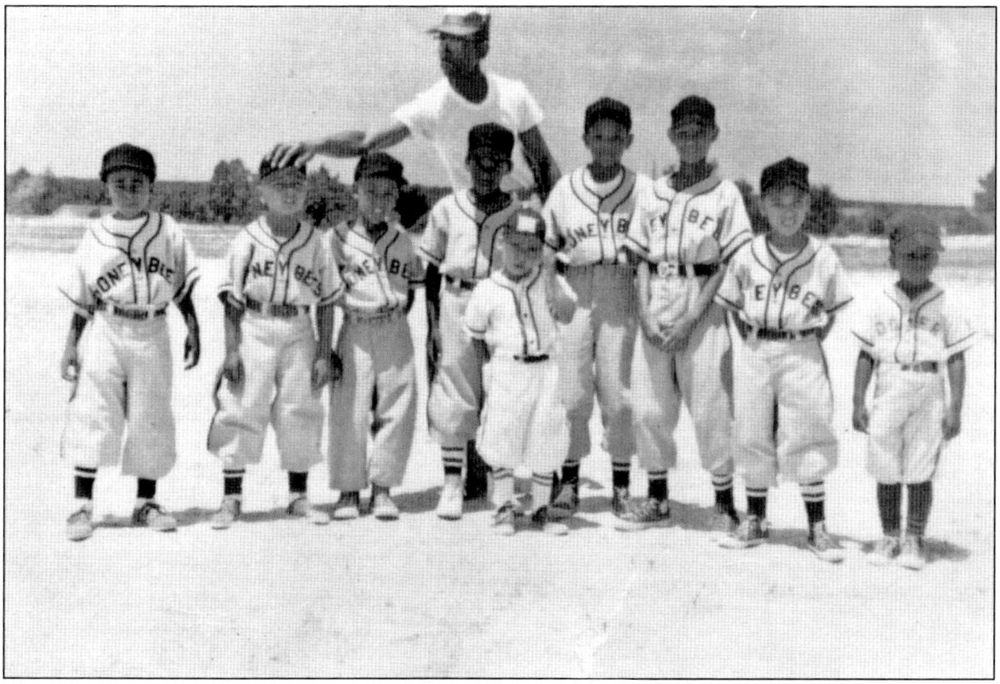

This photograph shows the West Southern Pines Little League team, the Honey Bees, with the team's coach Willie Harrington in the spring, *c.* 1960. The team played its games at the "Clay Hole," what is now named the Pool Park in West Southern Pines. The future leaders on the team, from left to right, are Greg Gordon, Jeff Capel, Ernest Clark, Charles Waddell, Mitch Capel, Thaddeus Jones Jr., Maurice Waddell, and Skipper Waddell.

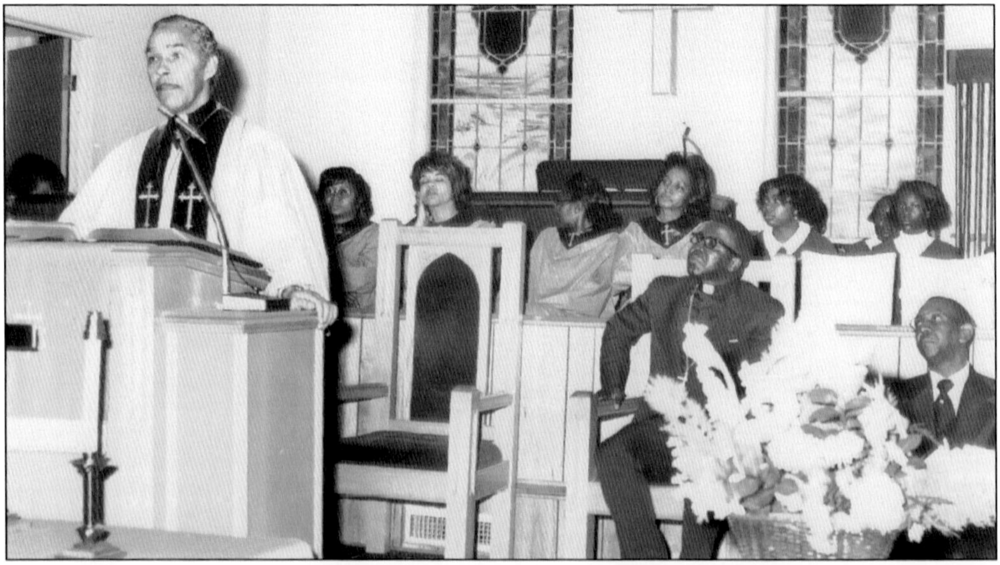

In 1920, Rev. J.W. Marsh and the members of the congregation raised $2,500 to build the Trinity A.M.E. Zion Church in West Southern Pines, and the same brick structure is used today. The church, whose interior is shown here, was organized in 1894, but earlier Sunday school and prayer meetings had been held in the homes of Lydia Shaw, Amy McIver, Laura Powell, and others. Behind the lectern is Pastor Johnson; sitting to his left is Rev. Chalmers. In the back, at the far left is JoAnn Marks, and beside her is Janet Gaines. All others are unidentified.

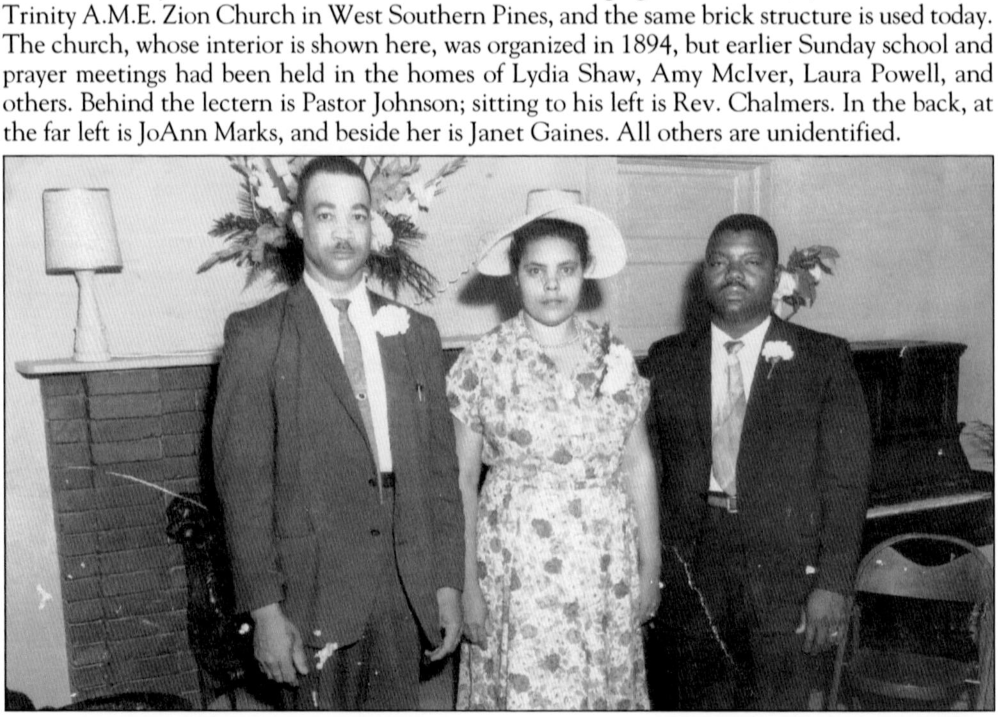

James E. Pugh and his business partner, Henry Brower, are pictured at the opening of their first funeral home in West Southern Pines, just one of many successful business projects that "Pygie" Pugh handled after coming to the area in 1941 from rural Ellerbe at age 15. His first job was with Dr. Mudgett as a handyman. Later, he worked at Clark Funeral Home where Mrs. Clark trained him as an embalmer. Several years later he received his state license as a funeral director. In 1968, he became the sole owner of the funeral home, which had been leased from H.L. Lewis. The West Southern Pines Civic Club awarded him the Generous Spirit Award for his service and many outstanding contributions to the community.

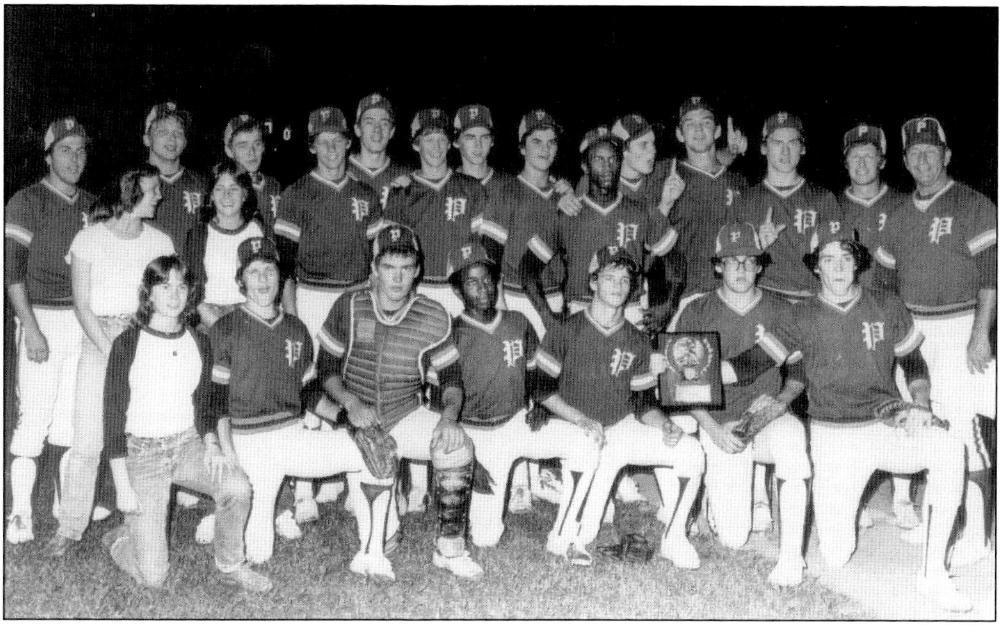

The Pinecrest High School baseball team made it to the state championship a decade after the new consolidated, integrated high school opened in 1969. The team members and their cheerleaders grin victoriously after the big win. John Williams (far right) coached an integrated team at Pinecrest after a successful career doing the same thing at the former Southern Pines High School.

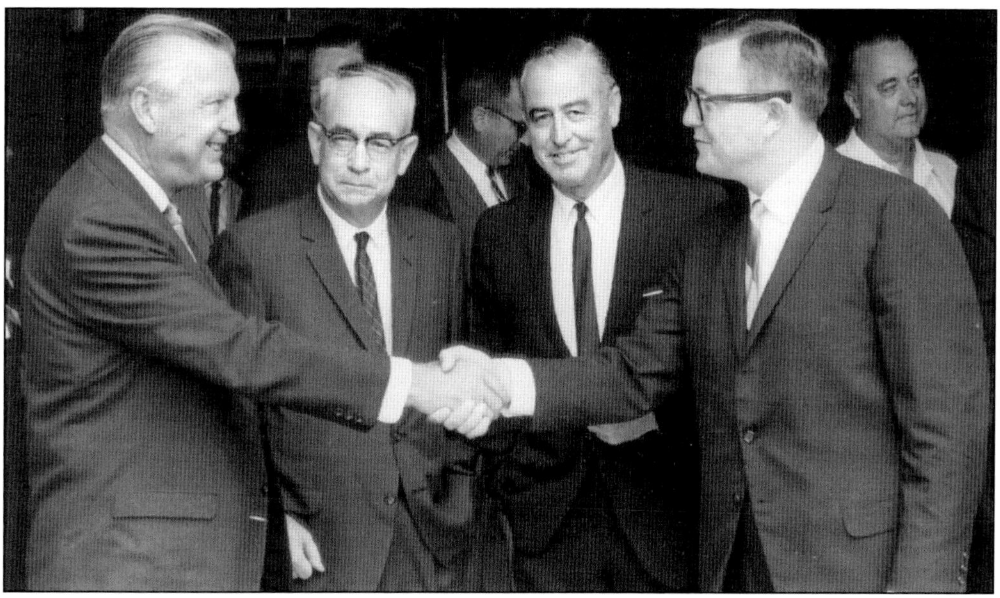

Sandhills Community College opened in 1963, the first of 60 community colleges designed to teach non-college bound North Carolina youth skills to earn a living. Here, Gov. Dan K. Moore (left) shakes hands with Raymond Stone, SCC's first president. North Carolina speaker of the house H. Clifton Blue stands next to the governor. Blue was a prominent businessman and civic leader in Aberdeen, a neighboring town to Southern Pines. Also pictured is a state senator at the time, Tom White.

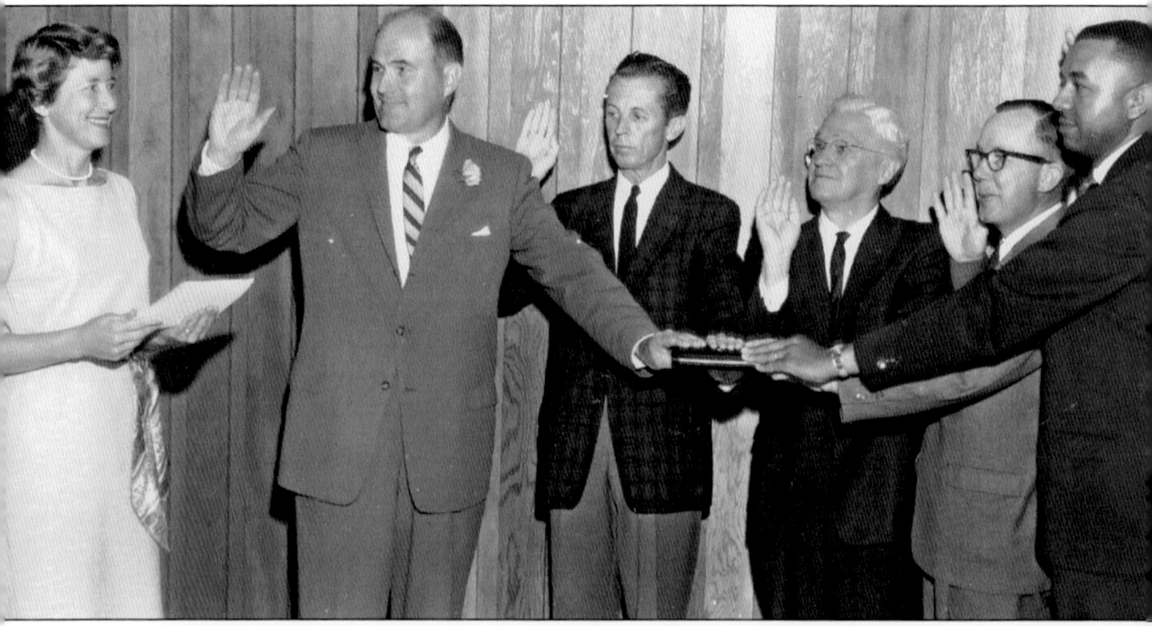

In 1959, Felton Capel became the second elected African-American man to serve on the Southern Pines Town Council. Here, he is sworn in with Mayor Bob Ewing and others. Capel first served on the council to finish the term of T.T. Morse, who had been elected in 1957. The West Southern Pines Civic Club endorsed Capel, who ran and was elected to five terms on the council. The civic club was formed in 1943 by T.R. Goins Sr., Rev. J.R. Funderburk, T.T. Morse, and several others. The club's objective was to increase public interest in all areas related to good citizenship. Attendance was high at meetings, which were held in the African-American churches. The club acted as a group to promote and bring to the Southern Pines Town Council the issues and interests of the community. Capel was president of the club from 1959 to 1961 and from 1976 to 1977. His campaign to pave the dirt roads in West Southern Pines resulted in paving 97 percent of the streets. During Capel's second term as councilman, Our Lady of Victory School merged with St. Anthony's Catholic School to become the first integrated school in Moore County. In 1971, Felton Capel was appointed by Gov. Bob Scott to the North Carolina Board of Conservation and Development.

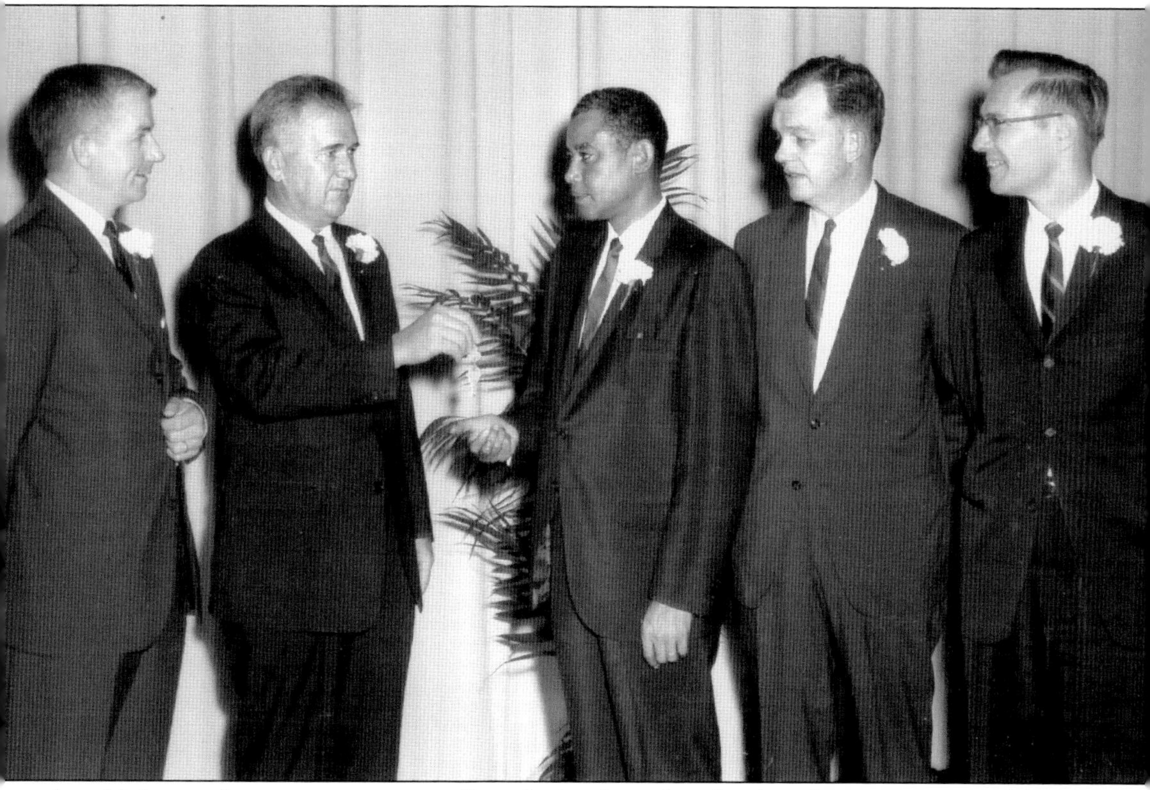

In addition to the new community college for local youth, other big changes came to public education in Southern Pines. In the 1960s the segregated East and West Southern Pines schools merged and integrated into a county-wide public system that became the Moore County Schools. The formerly all-black West Southern Pines School became Southern Pines Primary School. Here, a dedication ceremony is performed by, from left to right, the following: Jim Jenkins, superintendent of the Southern Pines schools; Dr. Cliff McLean, chairman of the Southern Pines school board; H.A. Wilson, principal of West Southern Pines School; Philip J. Weaver, former Southern Pines city school superintendent; and Kirby Watson, an administrator with the Moore County schools. Wilson's name is on a plaque honoring him as the last West Southern Pines principal. The still-used school auditorium is named for Wilson.

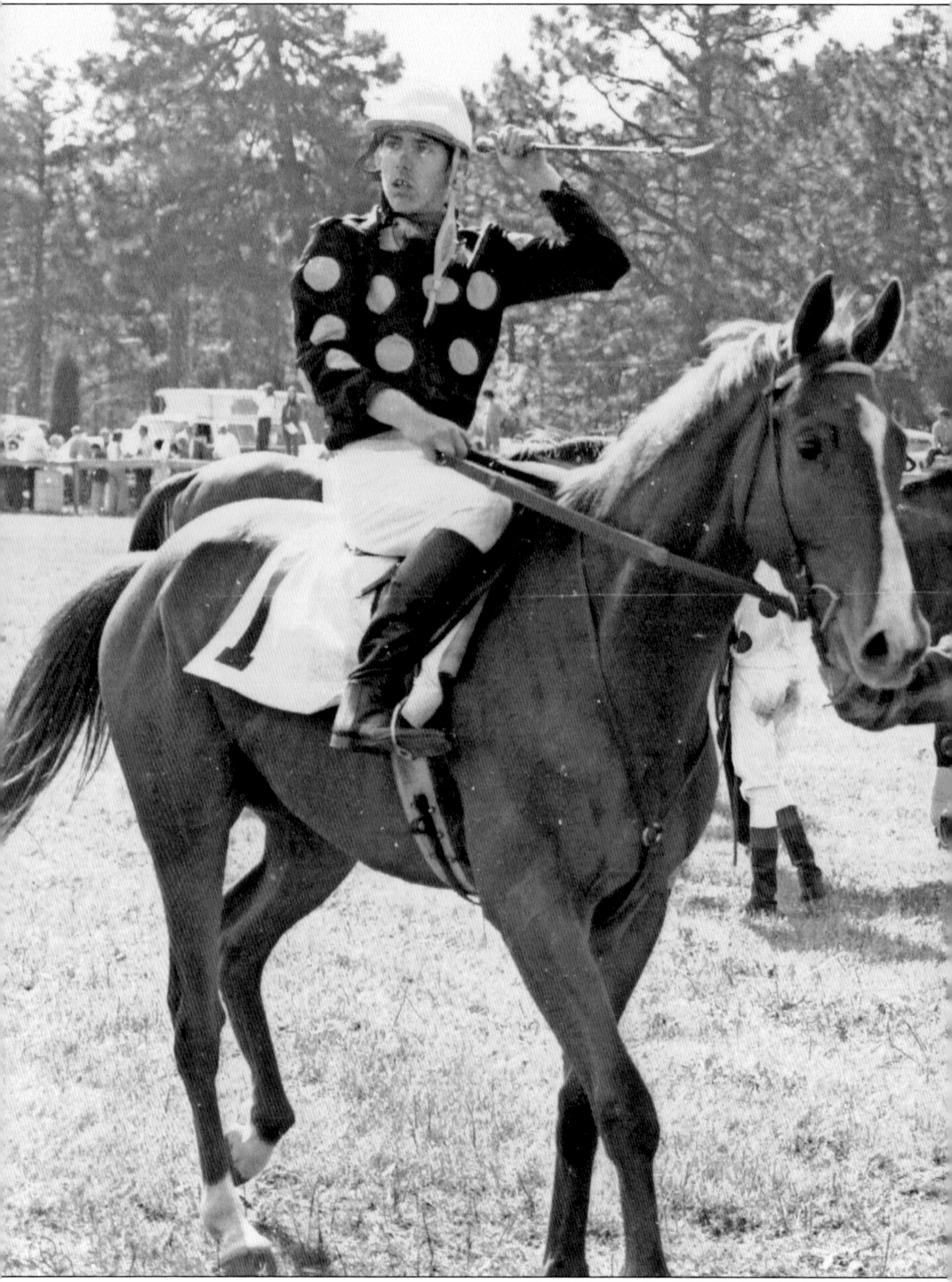

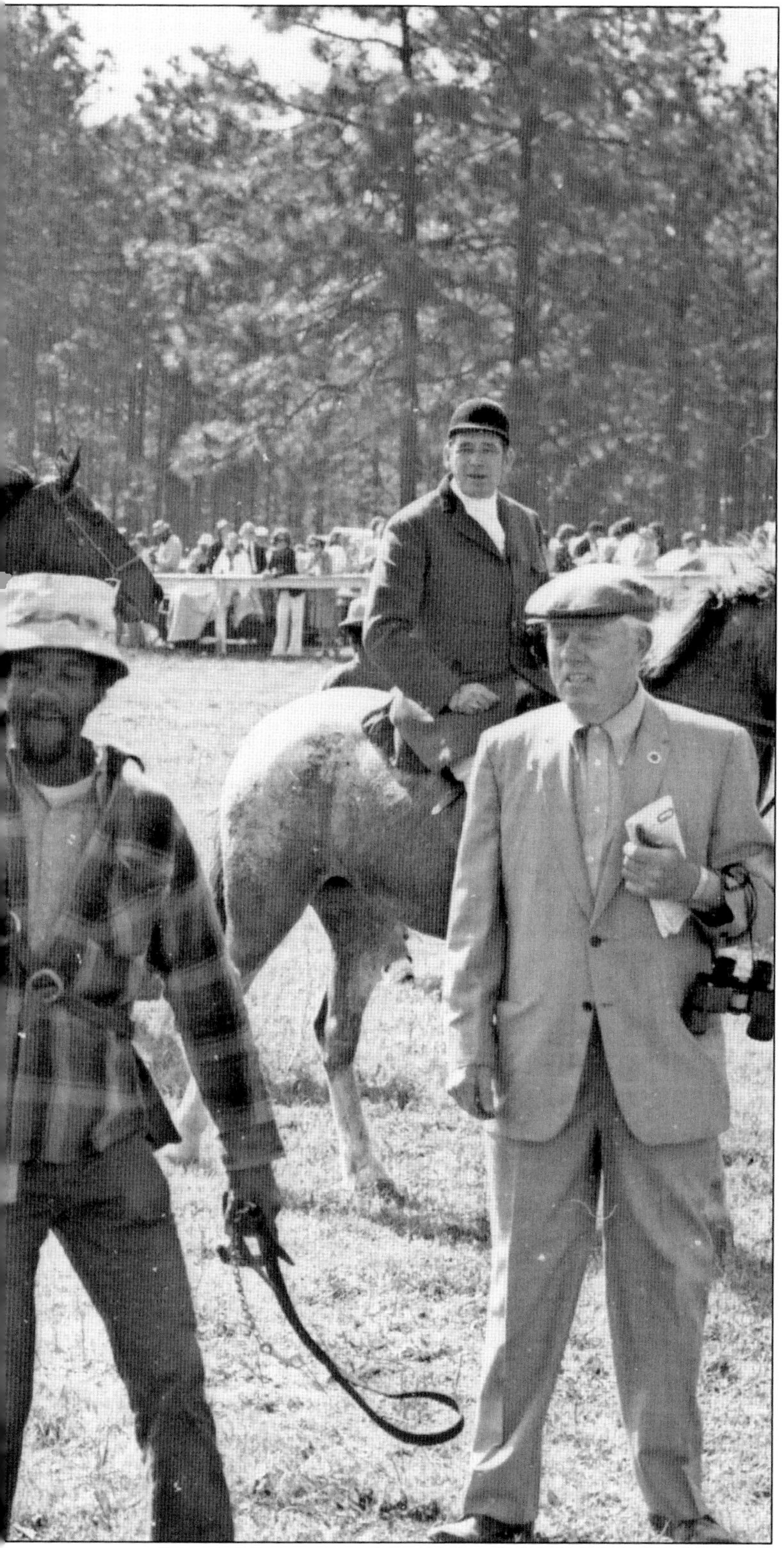

Pictured here are the four key players in a Stoneybrook Steeplechase: a spectator, a horse, a jockey, and a trainer. This photograph must have been taken during one of the 49 races since 1949 held at the Southern Pines farm in Horse Country. The man on the right, who resembles Mickey Walsh, founding father of Stoneybrook, is a spectator whose binoculars and racing guide came in handy. The horse, the mounted jockey, and the trainer in a plaid shirt are probably headed back to the stables after the race, as the jockey's helmet strap is undone and he looks a little winded. The thoroughbred, though, looks as cool as a cucumber.

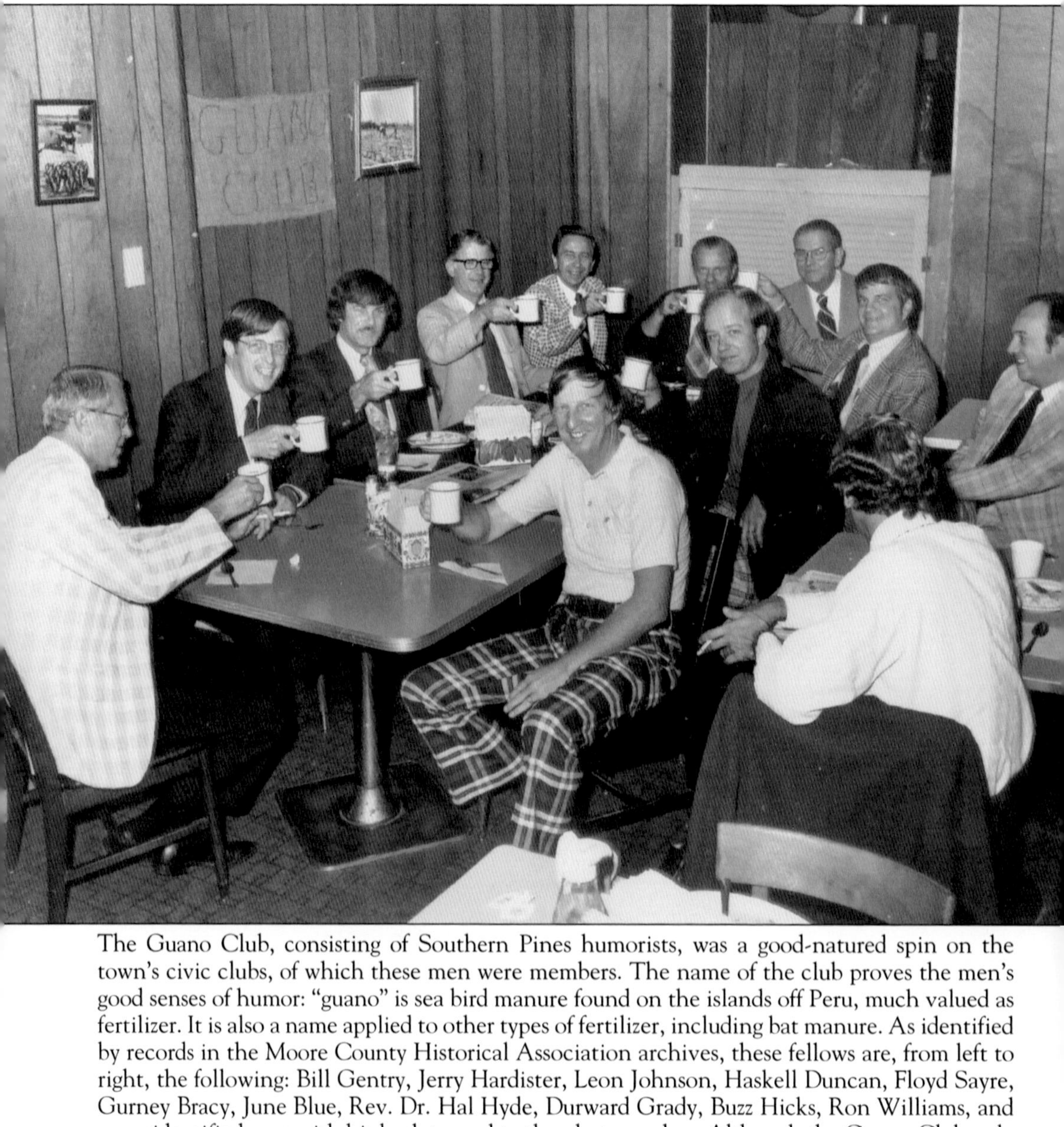

The Guano Club, consisting of Southern Pines humorists, was a good-natured spin on the town's civic clubs, of which these men were members. The name of the club proves the men's good senses of humor: "guano" is sea bird manure found on the islands off Peru, much valued as fertilizer. It is also a name applied to other types of fertilizer, including bat manure. As identified by records in the Moore County Historical Association archives, these fellows are, from left to right, the following: Bill Gentry, Jerry Hardister, Leon Johnson, Haskell Duncan, Floyd Sayre, Gurney Bracy, June Blue, Rev. Dr. Hal Hyde, Durward Grady, Buzz Hicks, Ron Williams, and an unidentified man with his back turned to the photographer. Although the Guano Club only lasted for a short while, these members had fun while it lasted.

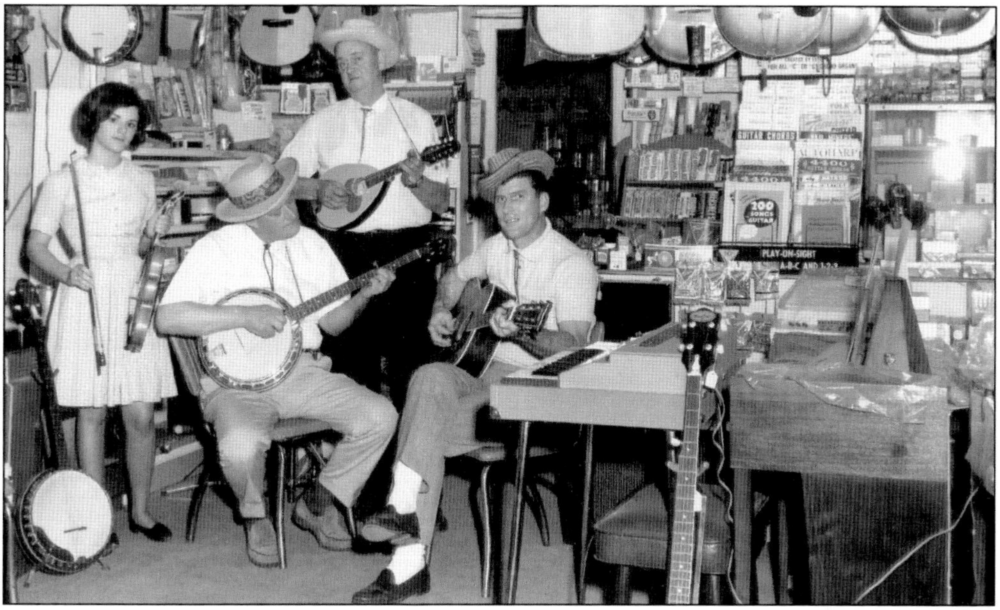

The Pinedene Jazz Center was home to a group of musicians who enjoyed homespun wisdom and shooting the breeze. The head musician was Russell Powell, standing with the hat and the mandolin. Powell was a Southern Pines character treated with affection and respect. He loved politics but had a gentle humor: he ran a spoof election campaign for president in a non-election year, among other jokes. From left to right are Casey McDonald, Bill Benson, Russell Powell, and Jack Stancil.

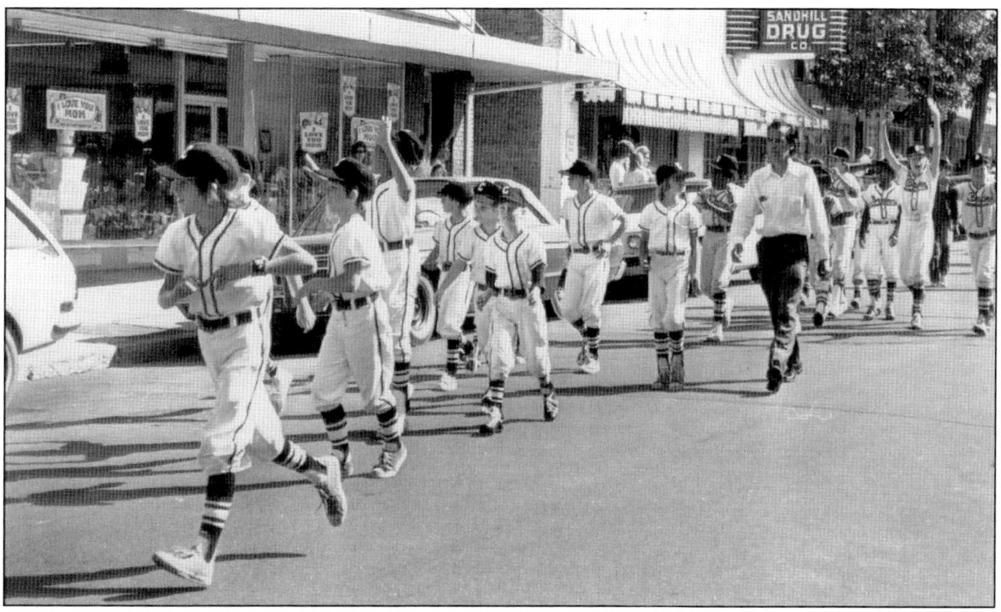

By 1964, the little league teams were integrated. In those days, Southern Pines downtown streets were quiet enough for a team of excited, baseball-uniformed boys to trot down the main street, accompanied by their coach, without stopping traffic. Southern Pines's Broad Street, which runs the length of the town's shopping district, is a good place for a parade, as these kids learned for themselves one sunny spring day.

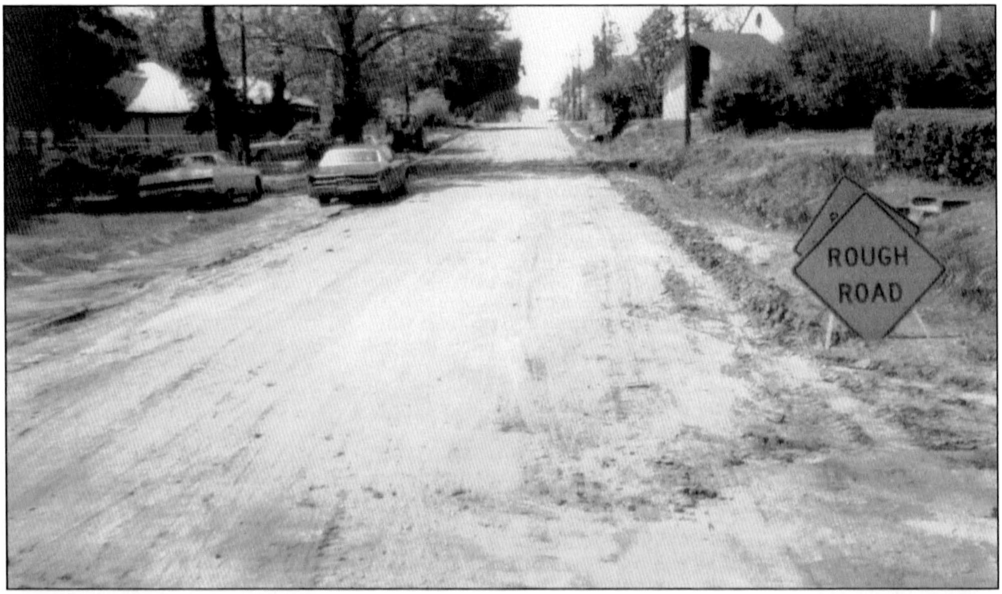

The dirt roads like this one were a common sight all over West Southern Pines for 40 years after the community was annexed into Southern Pines. Councilman and president of the West Southern Pines Civic Club, Felton Capel, campaigned successfully for the paving of these streets. The project was supposed to have been completed after East Southern Pines annexed West Southern Pines in 1931.

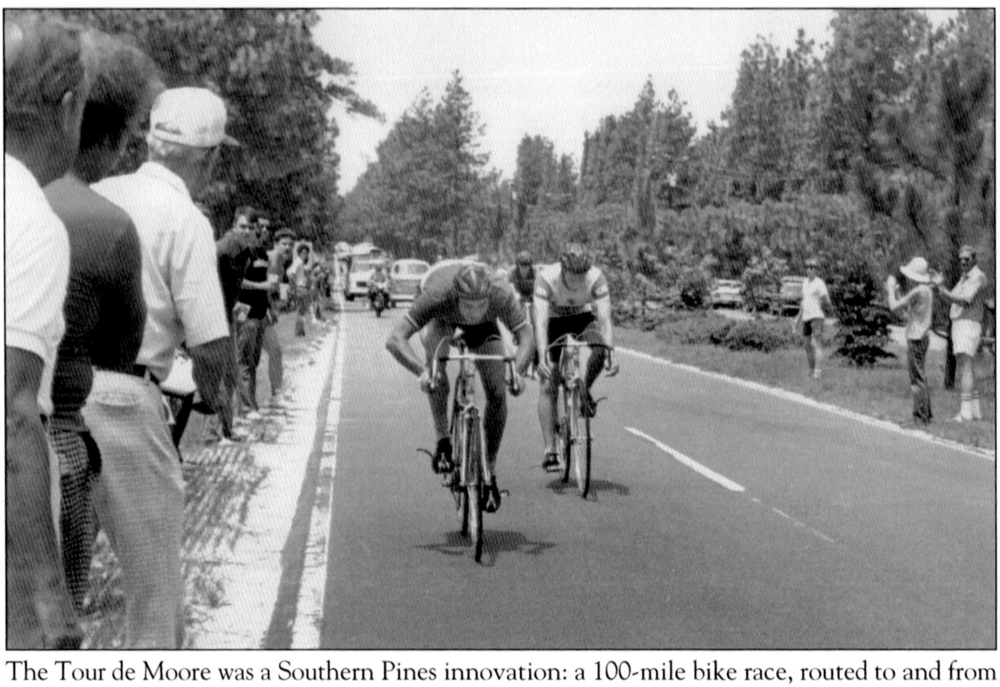

The Tour de Moore was a Southern Pines innovation: a 100-mile bike race, routed to and from downtown Southern Pines along two-lane blacktops through rural areas north of town and back again. Resident Bruce Cunningham initiated the race in the 1970s, and it is still held in a shortened form on the last Saturday in April, along with a street fair called Springfest. Here, riders from Canada and Europe join those from North Carolina and other states.

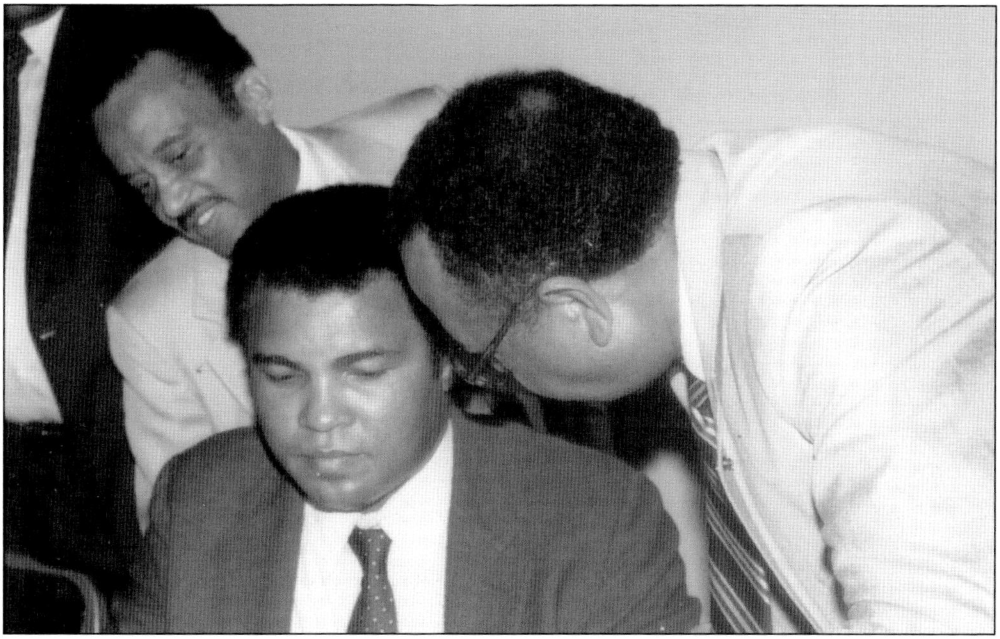

Heavyweight boxing champion Muhammad Ali talks with West Southern Pines businessman Felton Capel at a sports conference in Fayetteville, North Carolina. Capel still has the photograph hanging in his office with many other pictures of sports and television personalities.

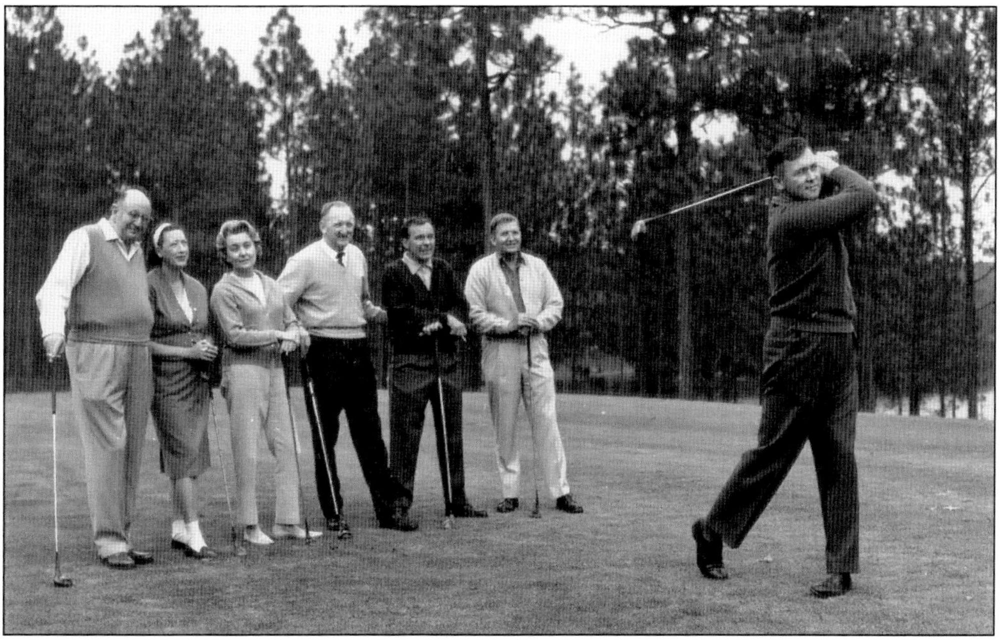

Distinguished golfers have come frequently to Southern Pines and area golf resorts as the game has grown in popularity. The first gated community in Southern Pines's outskirts was the Country Club of North Carolina, a private place attractive to many prestigious golf tournaments and events. Vermont's Gov. Phil Hoff tees off in the early 1970s with CCNC president Dick Urquhart, CCNC pro Buck Adams, North Carolina governor Terry Sanford, and Mr. and Mrs. Ed Richards.

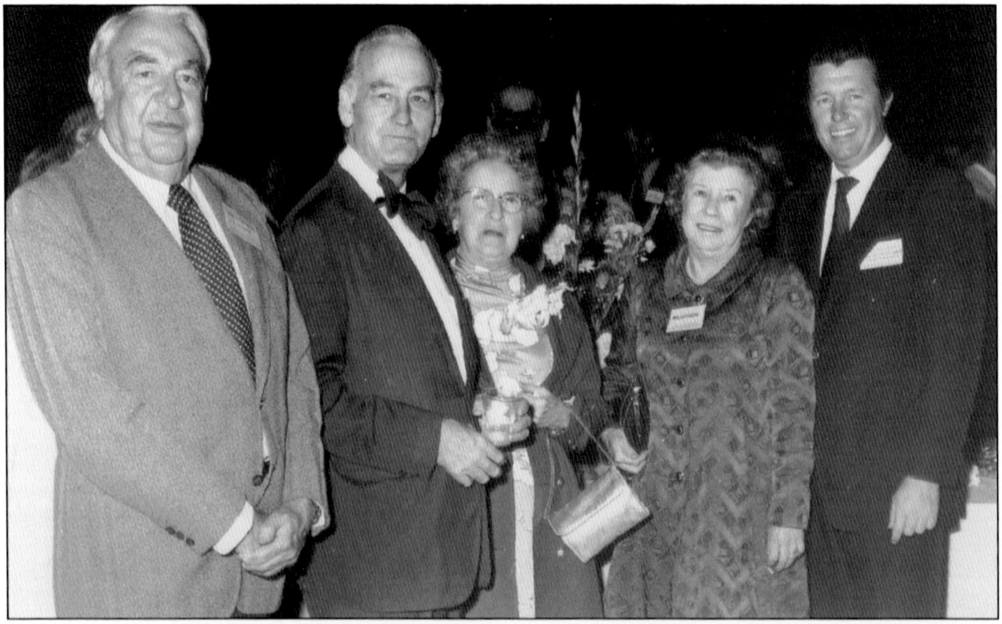

U.S. senator Sam Ervin, the famous Watergate figure who called himself "just a country lawyer from North Carolina," is pictured on a visit to Southern Pines in the 1970s. Also pictured are his hosts, Sam Ragan (second from left) and wife Marjorie (second from right), owners and proprietors of *The Pilot* weekly, which had been owned and operated by the James Boyds before Ragan purchased it. Ragan was also North Carolina's poet laureate and a retired editor from the *Raleigh News and Observer*.

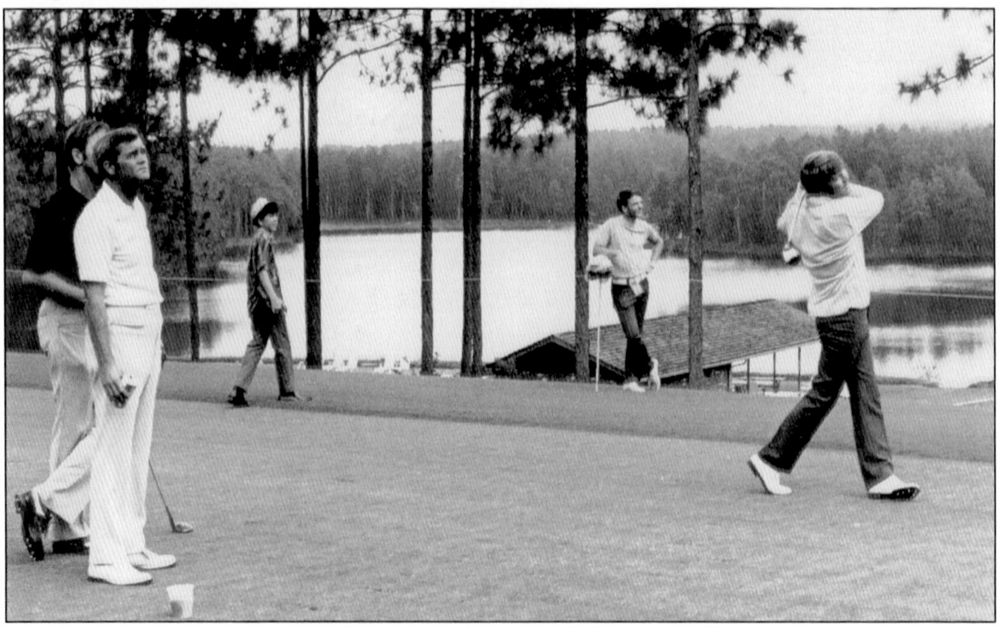

Popular singer Glenn Campbell (far right) takes a swing during a golf game at the Country Club of North Carolina. Also pictured are Gary Brewer and Bobby Nichols, equally celebrated in the field of golf. The occasion was a match play championship at the gated country club course on the outskirts of Southern Pines.

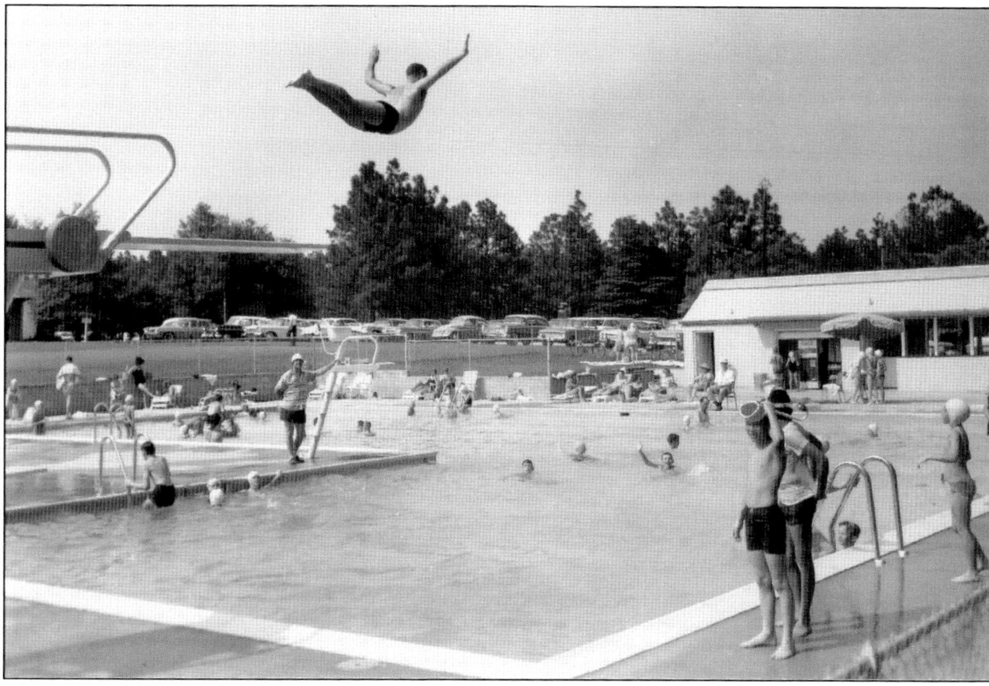

The private swimming pool at the Southern Pines Elks Club is the place to cool off in 1970, when the new, modern clubhouse replaced one destroyed by fire. For a landlocked area, Southern Pines abounds in private pools at clubhouses and even a few backyards. The general public can still swim at the town-owned Pool Park in West Southern Pines .

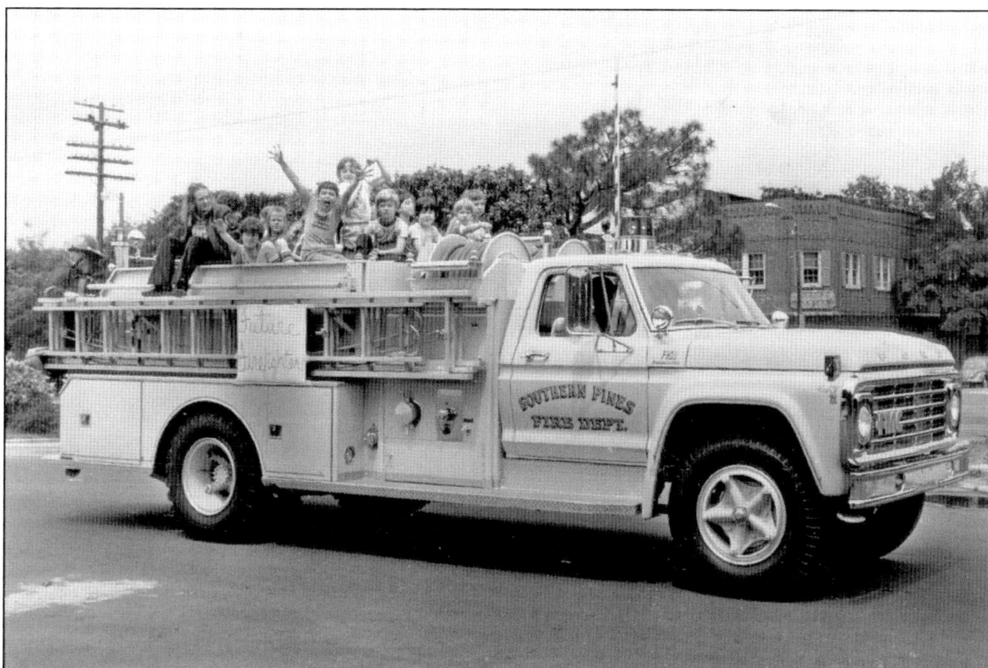

The celebration of Independence Day inspires joy rides on the noisy town fire trucks. Although these kids may not grow up to be firefighters, they certainly enjoy riding the truck this summer.

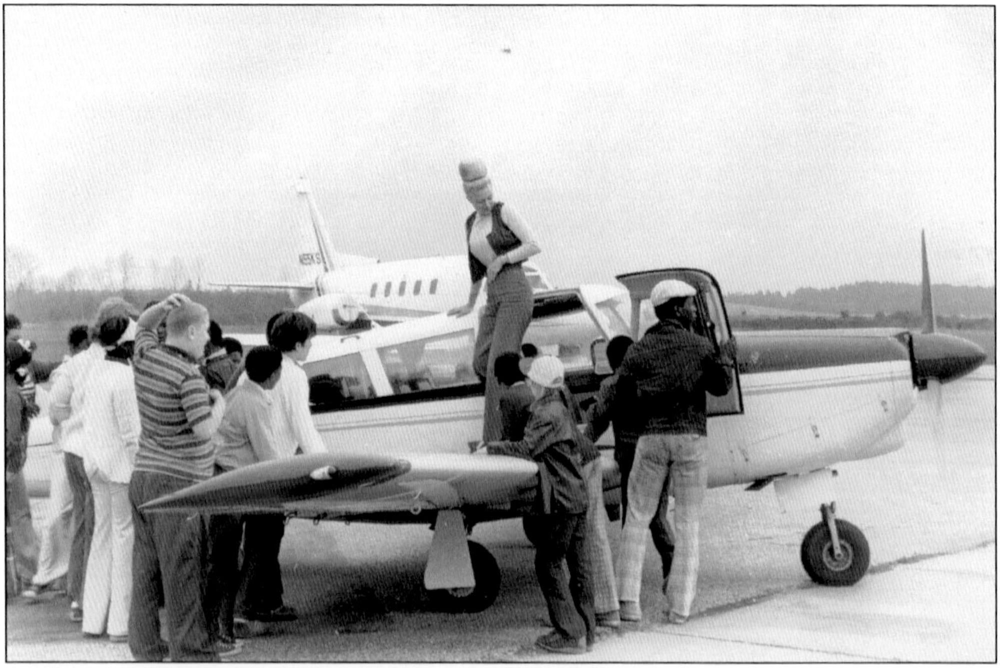

Cheryl Monroe, pilot, gives plane rides to this class of school children at the Southern Pines–Pinehurst Airport.

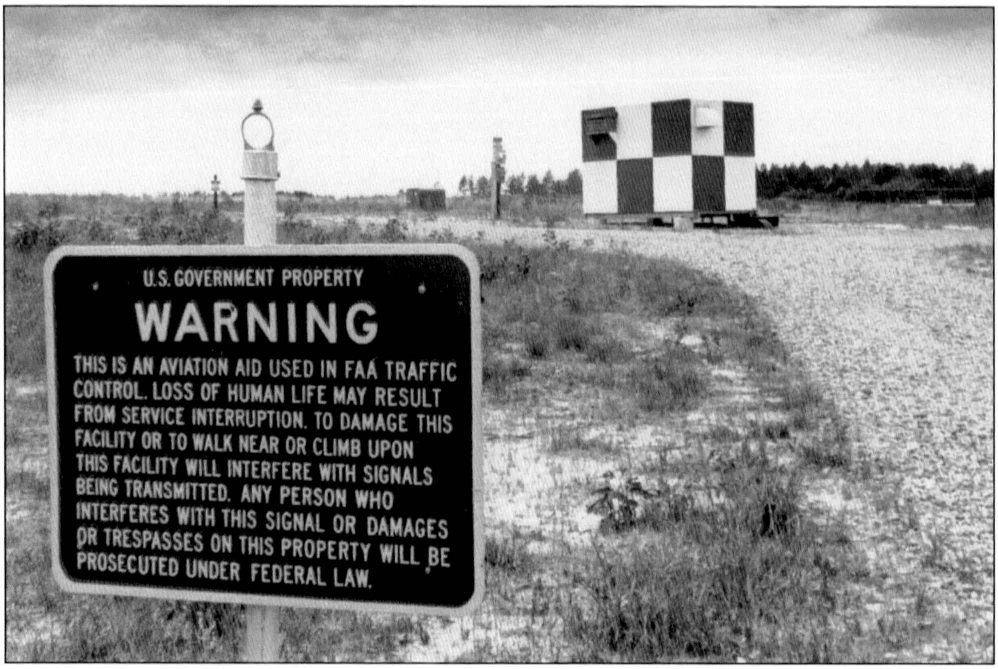

An air traffic control aid from the Federal Aviation Administration was installed at the Moore County Airport to provide all-weather landing and takeoff guidance. This was one of the first devices of its kind to be used by a small airport. The airport has existed for many years and most consistently has served private charter planes or piloting golfers back and forth on vacation in Southern Pines and Pinehurst.

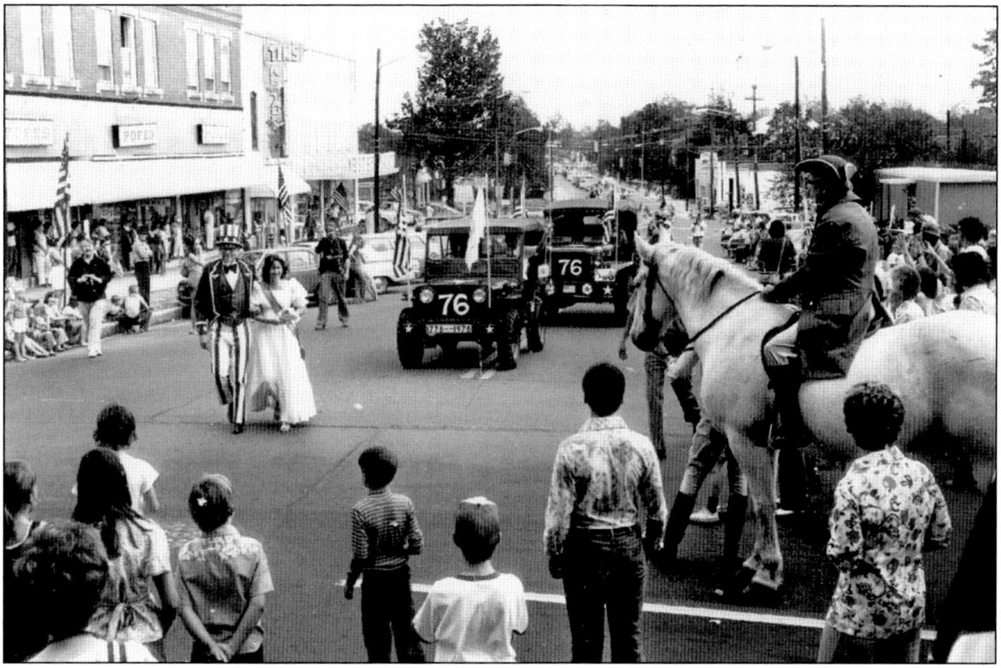

The Independence Day Bicentennial Parade in 1976 commemorates the heroes of the American Revolution. H. Clifton Blue, state legislator, is seated on the white horse, costumed as a patriot, watching Uncle Sam and possibly a Betsy Ross character march ahead of a platoon of jeeps. This celebration is to remember the revolutionists who fought British Loyalists in what would be the Moore County area.

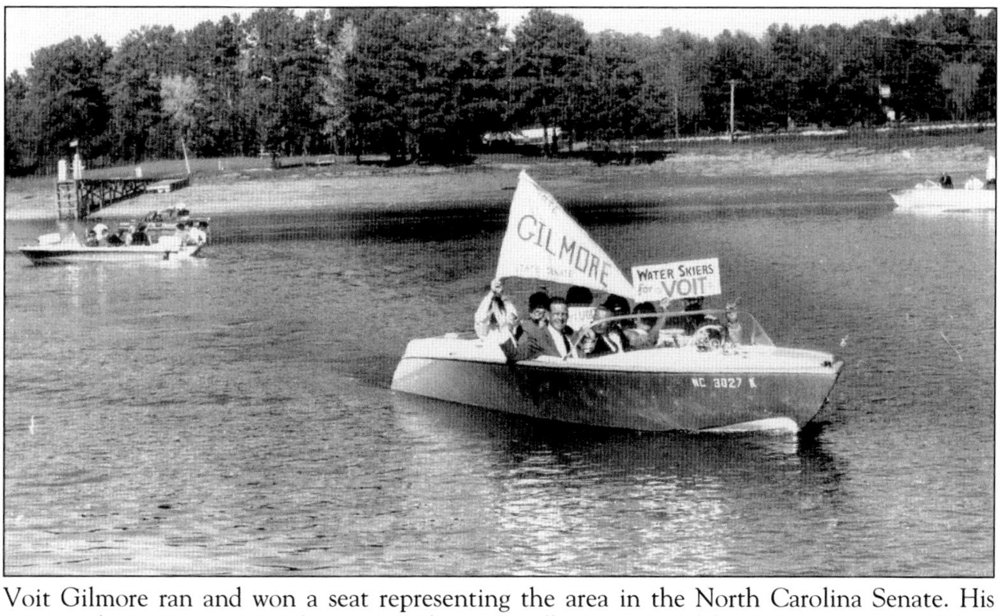

Voit Gilmore ran and won a seat representing the area in the North Carolina Senate. His noteworthy campaigning technique involves a speedboat on one of the area's recreational lakes. "Water skiers for Voit" demonstrate their political affiliations by waving signs from the boat carrying Gilmore. Gilmore peacefully integrated a movie theater and restaurant in Southern Pines with fellow businessman, Felton Capel.

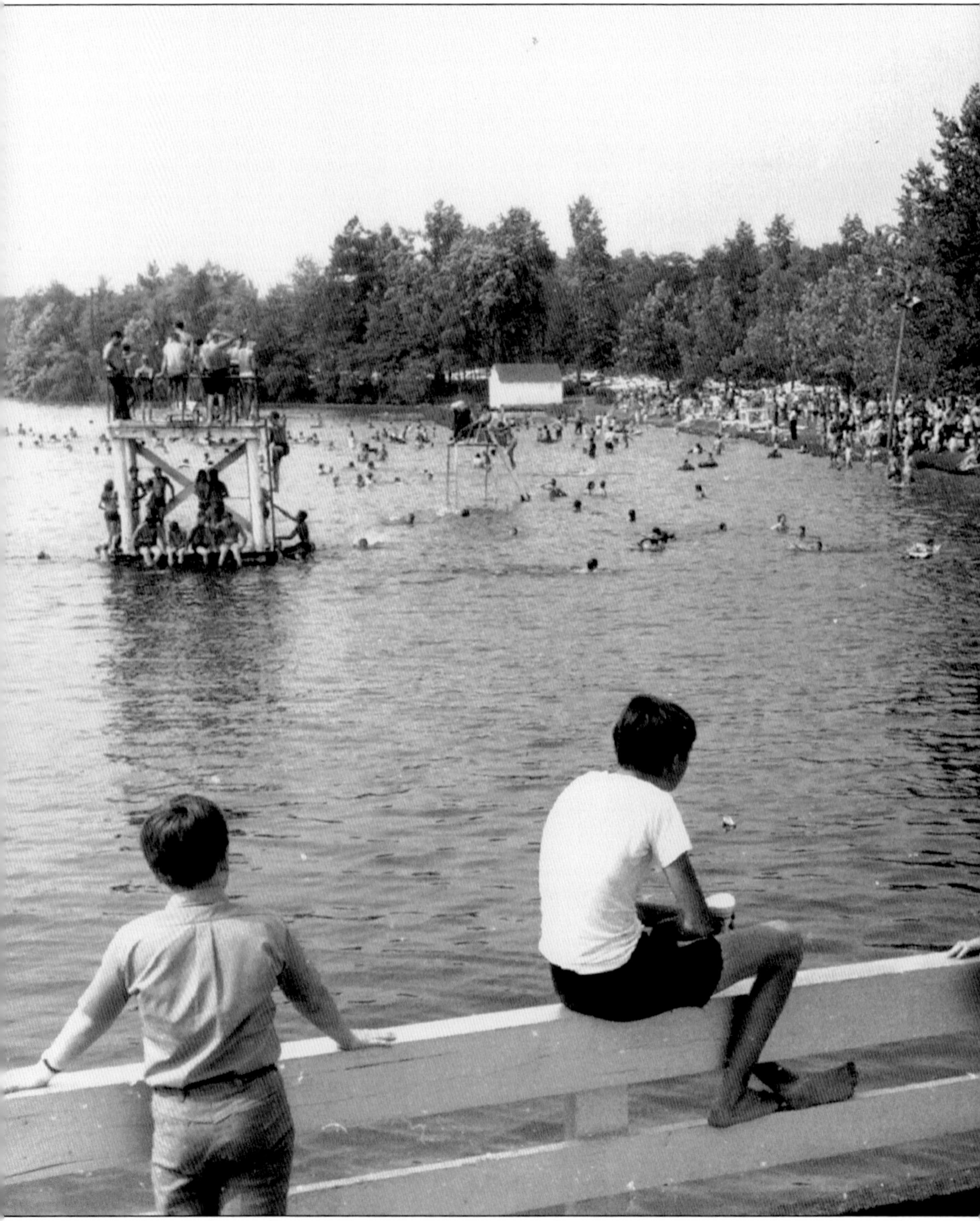

Aberdeen Lake, or Page's Lake as it was first named, is a major recreational spot for Southern Pines residents as well as those in the much smaller neighboring town. For many years, until the 1970s and early 1980s, the townspeople swam, fished, sunned themselves, picnicked, and generally had a good time at the town lake. Teenagers parked and necked on the opposite side of

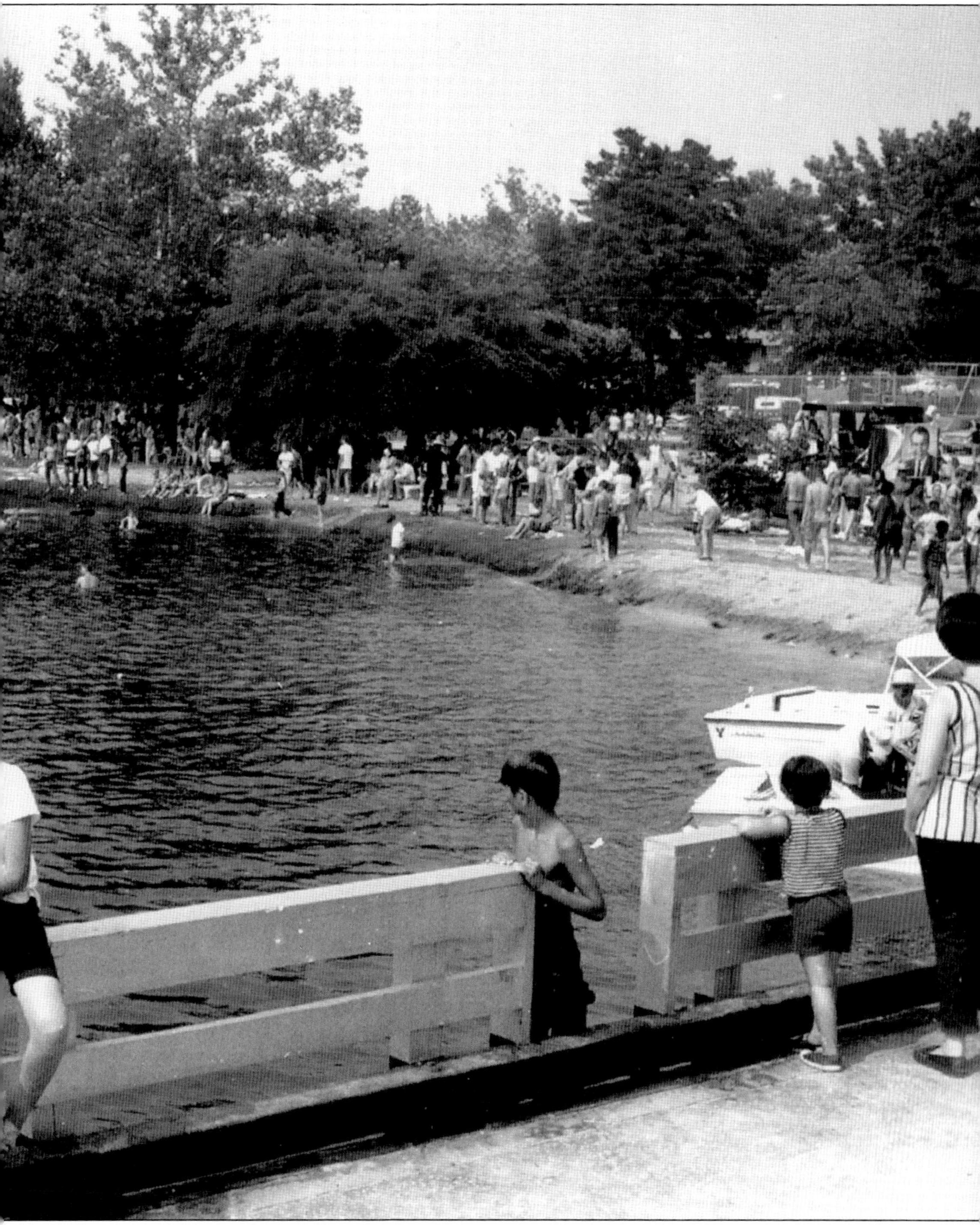

the beach, and families had a place for their kids to go. In later years, Aberdeen Lake was closed to swimming. Although mercury was discovered in fish from the lake, people still fish from the shore and bridge over the dam. Tennis courts, playground equipment, and picnic tables still attract crowds, particularly on Independence Day when fireworks are shot after dark.

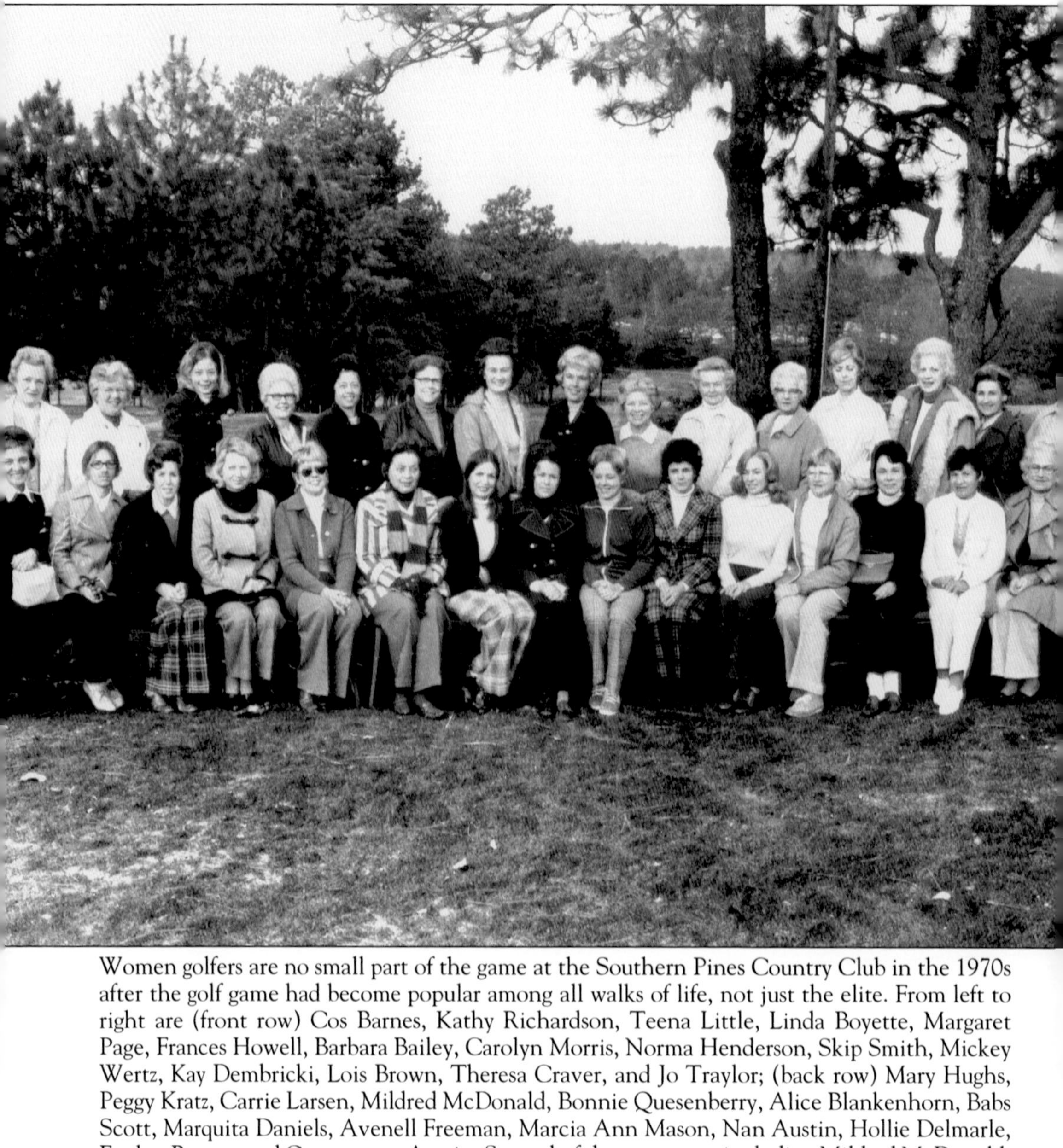

Women golfers are no small part of the game at the Southern Pines Country Club in the 1970s after the golf game had become popular among all walks of life, not just the elite. From left to right are (front row) Cos Barnes, Kathy Richardson, Teena Little, Linda Boyette, Margaret Page, Frances Howell, Barbara Bailey, Carolyn Morris, Norma Henderson, Skip Smith, Mickey Wertz, Kay Dembricki, Lois Brown, Theresa Craver, and Jo Traylor; (back row) Mary Hughs, Peggy Kratz, Carrie Larsen, Mildred McDonald, Bonnie Quesenberry, Alice Blankenhorn, Babs Scott, Marquita Daniels, Avenell Freeman, Marcia Ann Mason, Nan Austin, Hollie Delmarle, Evelyn Barnes, and Georgeanne Austin. Several of these women, including Mildred McDonald, Marquita Daniels, and Teena Little, ran for and held elective offices. McDonald was Southern Pines town clerk and manager, and Marquita Daniels later won the election and served 14 years on the town council. Teena Little was a member of the Moore County Board of Education in the 1980s, served on the State Board of Education, and held a seat in the North Carolina Senate for a term.

Douglass Center was named for Southern Pines's first African-American mayor, Emanuel "Jug" Douglass. Town attorney Lamont Brown is pictured at the unveiling of a plaque honoring Douglass at the Southern Pines Senior Center on West Pennsylvania Avenue. In 1971, Douglass was nominated by the West Southern Pines Civic Club and appointed by the Southern Pines Town Council to finish the term of Felton Capel, who had resigned his council seat upon being appointed to the North Carolina Board of Conservation and Development.

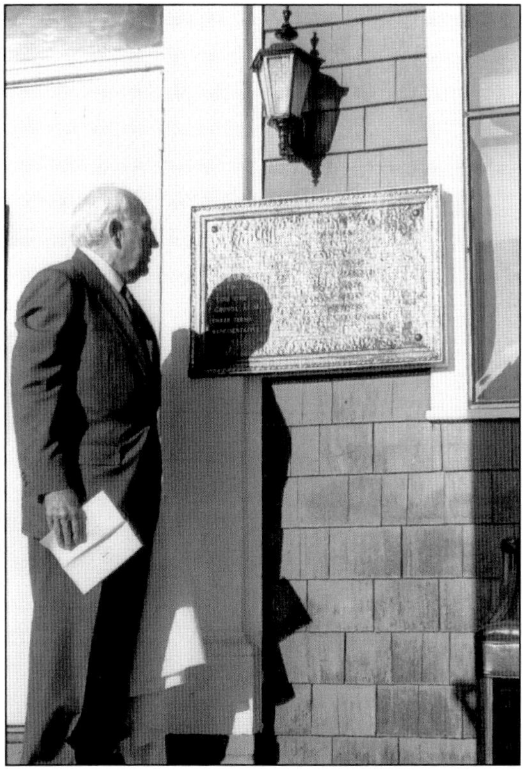

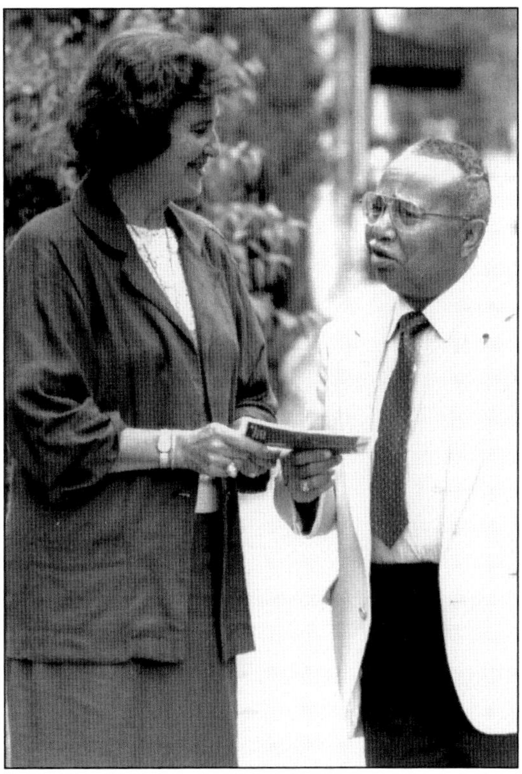

The Southern Pines Centennial Celebration in 1987 included the publication of a book, *Southern Pines: The First 100 Years*, published by the town council. Centennial Committee chairwoman Sara Hodgkins sells Mayor "Jug" Douglass the first copy of the book. The book is still for sale in the Country Bookshop downtown.

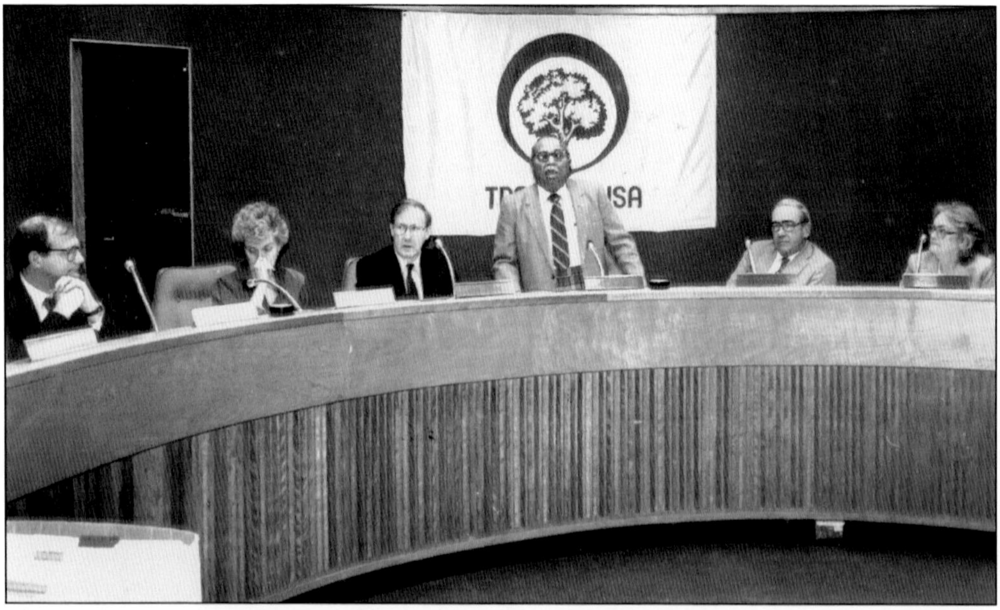

The newly-elected mayor of Southern Pines, Emanuel "Jug" Douglass, stands to speak. The first African-American mayor in the town's history and one of the first in the South, Douglass was first elected mayor in 1977 by the four white council members. From left to right are town manager Bill Coleman, Jane Clark, Jerry Daeke, Mayor Douglass, Luther Adams, and Anita Lillard. In those days, the council customarily chose the candidate with the most votes as the mayor. Douglass continued to be re-elected to council and mayor every two years until 1987.

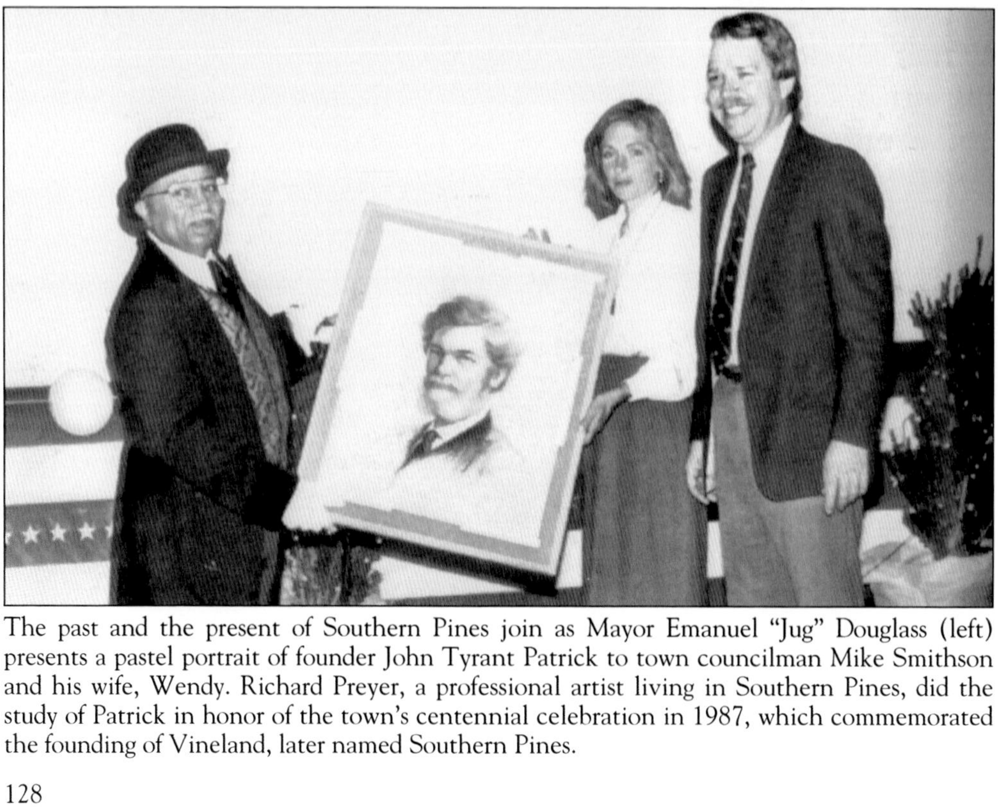

The past and the present of Southern Pines join as Mayor Emanuel "Jug" Douglass (left) presents a pastel portrait of founder John Tyrant Patrick to town councilman Mike Smithson and his wife, Wendy. Richard Preyer, a professional artist living in Southern Pines, did the study of Patrick in honor of the town's centennial celebration in 1987, which commemorated the founding of Vineland, later named Southern Pines.